A NEW BOOK OF
SOUTH AFRICAN VERSE IN ENGLISH

A New Book of South African Verse in English

Selected and edited by

GUY BUTLER & CHRIS MANN

1979

OXFORD UNIVERSITY PRESS

Cape Town

Oxford University Press

OXFORD   LONDON   GLASGOW
NEW YORK   TORONTO   MELBOURNE   WELLINGTON
NAIROBI   DAR ES SALAAM   CAPE TOWN
KUALA LUMPUR   SINGAPORE   JAKARTA   HONG KONG   TOKYO
DELHI   BOMBAY   CALCUTTA   MADRAS   KARACHI

Copyright © 1979 Oxford University Press Southern Africa

ISBN 0 19 570141 0

Printed in South Africa by Citadel Press, Lansdowne, Cape.
Published by Oxford University Press, Harrington House,
Barrack Street, Cape Town 8001, South Africa.

CONTENTS

PREFACE

Many languages are spoken in South Africa. This book is a selection from the poetry of one of these languages only, and can no more claim to be representative of South African poetry as a whole than can a collection in Afrikaans or Zulu.

This volume's predecessor, *A Book of South African Verse*, was published in 1959. Despite the appearance of several other anthologies, demand for it remained steady, and it was decided in June 1977 that the original editor, together with a younger writer, would revise and update it. In the event, we have produced something closer to an entirely new book. Not only have less than half the poems of the original volume survived, but the size of the book has increased by a third, and the number of poets has nearly trebled.

We have continued to interpret the term 'South African poetry in English' broadly, and have considered not only poems composed in English by South Africans, but poems about South Africa by non-South Africans as well. We have also considered poems that were originally written in other South African languages, and which were rendered into English by their authors.

The original selection was made 'on the principle of representing each poet by more than one piece'. It was felt at that time, when the existence of indigenous English literature was barely accepted, 'that it was better to give a few people as reasonable a hearing as an anthology would allow, than to include so many that none had the chance of making an impression'. This meant in many cases including 'at least one difficult or longer poem which might better suggest the poet's depth or range'. This policy has been abandoned. While we have not hesitated to give a poet's work the space we think it deserves, there is no longer any need to build presences, and we have been content to present poems.

This confidence is due to the surge of English writing that has gathered momentum during the nearly twenty years that have passed since the first appearance of the original volume. Numerous little magazines[1] have brought a large number of poets into contact with a larger readership than before; several publishing houses[2] have boldly and regularly published new verse; conferences of English-language poets, in Grahamstown in 1969, and Cape Town in 1974, gave the movement impetus and some definition; and the banning and/or exile of numerous prominent writers, both Black and White[3], has drawn attention to the political importance of the writing community. Although at the time of writing, there appears to be a decrease in this activity, we are still too close to the start of the surge to know the sources of the currents which fed it. The most we can be certain about is that, as in other parts of Africa, it has taken place. The more recent poems of this anthology give some indication of its local directions.

This selection also reflects our expanded knowledge of South African poets, and poetry concerning South Africa, prior to 1959. The poetic output of the first century of English writing (1820–1920) is surprisingly large, but from the hands of local poets it seldom achieves a level much above competence – many of the liveliest items are the work of visitors. Its interest lies in its materials and its comments on the times, and it will come into its own once more historical and critical studies have been made.[4]

While many of the themes described in the 1959 introduction could be traced through this volume as well, and while new preoccupations could be indicated, we have refrained from doing so here. Space is limited, and there is no longer so acute a lack of critical awareness as there used to be. Several university English Departments, for example, have begun to teach some South African writing in English, and some of the little magazines regularly review new work.

Anthologists who have to select from the work of their contemporaries, particularly if they are members of a complex multi-lingual society in the midst of turbulent transition, cannot pretend that their task is easy. As the title suggests, we make no claim to Olympian judgements, or infallible criteria. We have included only poems which have survived many readings by each of us. It is not, however, in the nature of taste that both editors could have liked every item to the same extent. Nevertheless, all poems in this volume have our joint approval.

In a total population of over twenty million, fewer than two million South Africans have English as a home language; but by virtue of the fact that it is one of the official languages, and, perhaps more importantly, because it is our only international language, it is becoming a lingua franca for the whole society. From the beginning of South African English literature, its writers were aware of the pressures of the other languages, and in poems such as 'Kaatje Kekkelbek', 'A Kafir's Lament', 'Jong Koekemoer', 'Ag Pleez Deddy', 'Hotknife', 'Lena's Song', 'Da Same, Da Same' and 'Kobus le Grange Marais', there is evidence of the general tendency to accept and enjoy this fact. More significant, however, is the adoption of English by writers for whom it is a second language. Several contributors to this volume have Afrikaans as their mother-tongue (Leipoldt, Marais, Jensma, Nortje, Small) while others (Jolobe, Dhlomo, Mtshali, Serote, Nthodi) employ one of the Nguni or Sotho languages. Such writers will to some extent bring to their English poems rhythms, metaphors and perceptions influenced by their own languages. Their use of English can result in a welcome enrichment and diversification. Those who believe that there is an immutable standard of correct English might think that these poems are smudged with unacceptable variations. We make no apology for including them. A genuine poem, so long as it is adequately expressive and comprehensible, has a way of vindicating itself with the passage of time. Students of the English language know that one of the sources of its strength is its hospitality.

With very few exceptions, we have adhered to the spelling and orthography of the originals, although this has meant reproducing words, such as 'Caffre' and 'Hottentot', which have over the years gathered more pejorative connotations than they once had. Clearly, editors are not at liberty to substitute words in an old text to cater for changed sensibilities, even though they may wish to do so. Where we have been obliged to shorten a text, we have indicated the omission in the usual way (. . .). Finally, we should like to thank:

Miss Ruth Harnett, whose work on a proposed earlier anthology was most useful in preparing this one, and who kindly assisted us with our penultimate choices; Professor André de Villiers of the Institute for the Study of English in Africa; Miss Leonie Prozesky of the S.A. Documentation Centre for

English, for providing the biographical appendix; and Miss
Patricia Kelly, for kindly assisting in the proof-reading.

Grahamstown,   G. B.
Easter 1979.   C. M.

We deeply regret that in spite of repeated requests
the Minister of Justice has refused permission to print
four poems by Dennis Brutus.

[1]Contrast 1960–   New Coin 1965–   Purple Renoster 1956–72
Classic 1963–71   Ophir 1967–76   Izwi 1971–74
Bolt 1970–   New Classic 1974–   Donga 1976–78 (banned)
                      Standpunte 1945–

[2]Most notably A. A. Balkema, David Philip, Ad. Donker, Bateleur Poets, the
Ravan Press. Since 1959 more than 230 volumes of verse have been published
locally.

[3]Amongst those who have had volumes banned are Dennis Brutus, Wopko
Jensma, James Matthews, Mark Swift, Sipho Sepamla, Mazisi Kunene and
Ezekiel Mphahlele.

[4]e.g. G. M. Miller and Howard Sergeant *A Critical Survey of South African Poetry
in English* Cape Town: Balkema 1957, and M van Wyk Smith, *Drummer Hodge:
The Poetry of the Anglo-Boer War*, Oxford, 1978.

THOMAS PRINGLE

The Cape of Storms

O Cape of Storms! although thy front be dark,
And bleak thy naked cliffs and cheerless vales,
And perilous thy fierce and faithless gales
To staunchest mariner and stoutest bark;
And though along thy coasts with grief I mark
The servile and the slave, and him who wails
An exile's lot – and blush to hear thy tales
Of sin and sorrow and oppression stark: –
Yet, spite of physical and moral ill,
And after all I've seen and suffered here,
There are strong links that bind me to thee still,
And render even thy rocks and deserts dear;
Here dwell kind hearts which time nor place can chill –
Loved Kindred and congenial Friends sincere.

THOMAS PRINGLE

Evening Rambles

The sultry summer-noon is past;
And mellow Evening comes at last,
With a low and languid breeze
Fanning the mimosa trees,
That cluster o'er the yellow vale,
And oft perfume the panting gale
With fragrance faint: it seems to tell
Of primrose-tufts in Scottish dell,
Peeping forth in tender spring
When the blithe lark begins to sing.

But soon, amidst our Lybian vale,
Such soothing recollections fail;
Soon we raise the eye to range
O'er prospects wild, grotesque and strange;
Sterile mountains, rough and steep,

That bound abrupt the valley deep,
Heaving to the clear blue sky
Their ribs of granite, bare and dry
And ridges, by the torrents worn,
Thinly streaked with scraggy thorn,
Which fringes Nature's savage dress,
Yet scarce relieves her nakedness.

But where the Vale winds deep below,
The landscape hath a warmer glow:
There the spekboom spreads its bowers
Of light-green leaves and lilac flowers;
And the aloe rears her crimson crest,
Like stately queen for gala drest;
And the bright-blossomed bean-tree shakes
Its coral tufts above the brakes,
Brilliant as the glancing plumes
Of sugar-birds among its blooms,
With the deep-green verdure blending
In the stream of light descending.

And now, along the grassy meads,
Where the skipping reebok[1] feeds,
Let me through the mazes rove
Of the light acacia grove;
Now while yet the honey-bee
Hums around the blossomed tree;
And the turtles softly chide,
Wooingly, on every side;
And the clucking pheasant calls
To his mate at intervals;
And the duiker[2] at my tread
Sudden lifts his startled head,
Then dives affrighted in the brake,
Like wild-duck in the reedy lake.

My wonted seat receives me now –
This cliff with myrtle-tufted brow,
Towering high o'er grove and stream,
As if to greet the parting gleam.
With shattered rocks besprinkled o'er,
Behind ascends the mountain hoar,
Whose crest o'erhangs the Bushman's Cave,
(His fortress once, and now his grave),

Where the grim satyr-faced baboon
Sits gibbering to the rising moon,
Or chides with hoarse and angry cry
The herdsmen as he wanders by.

   Spread out below in sun and shade,
The shaggy Glen lies full displayed –
Its sheltered nooks, its sylvan bowers,
Its meadows flushed with purple flowers;
And through it like a dragon spread,
I trace the river's tortuous bed.

Lo there the Chaldee-willow weeps,
Drooping o'er the headlong steeps,
Where the torrent in his wrath
Hath rifted him a rugged path,
Like fissure cleft by earthquake's shock,
Through mead and jungle, mound and rock.
But the swoln water's wasteful sway,
Like tyrant's rage, hath passed away,
And left the ravage of its course
Memorial of its frantic force.
– Now o'er its shrunk and slimy bed
Rank weeds and withered wrack are spread,
With the faint rill just oozing through,
And vanishing again from view;
Save where the guana's glassy pool
Holds to some cliff its mirror cool,
Girt by the palmite's leafy screen,
Or graceful rock-ash, tall and green,
Whose slender sprays above the flood
Suspend the loxia's callow brood
In cradle-nests; with porch below,
Secure from winged or creeping foe –
Weasel or hawk or writhing snake;
Light swinging, as the breezes wake,
Like the ripe fruit we love to see
Upon the rich pomegranate-tree.

   But lo, the sun's descending car
Sinks o'er Mount-Dunion's peaks afar;
And now along the dusky vale
The homeward herds and flocks I hail,
Returning from their pastures dry

Amid the stony uplands high.
First, the brown Herder with his flock
Comes winding round my hermit-rock:
His mien and gait and vesture tell,
No shepherd he from Scottish fell;
For crook the guardian gun he bears,
For plaid the sheep-skin mantle wears;
Sauntering languidly along;
Nor flute has he, nor merry song,
Nor book, nor tale, nor rustic lay,
To cheer him through his listless day.
His look is dull, his soul is dark;
He feels not hope's electric spark;
But, born the White Man's servile thrall,
Knows that he cannot lower fall.

Next the stout Neat-herd passes by,
With bolder step and blither eye;
Humming low his tuneless song,
Or whistling to the hornèd throng.
From the destroying foeman fled,
He serves the Colonist for bread:
Yet this poor heathen Bechuan
Bears on his brow the port of man;
A naked, homeless exile he –
But not debased by Slavery.

Now, wizard-like, slow Twilight sails
With soundless wing adown the vales,
Waving with his shadowy rod
The owl and bat to come abroad,
With things that hate the garish sun,
To frolic now when day is done.
Now along the meadows damp
The enamoured fire-fly lights his lamp;
Link-boy he of woodland green
To light fair Avon's Elfin Queen;
Here, I ween, more wont to shine
To light the thievish porcupine,
Plundering my melon-bed, –
Or villain lynx, whose stealthy tread
Rouses not the wakeful hound
As he creeps the folds around.

But lo! the night-bird's boding scream
Breaks abrupt my twilight dream;
And warns me it is time to haste
My homeward walk across the waste,
Lest my rash tread provoke the wrath
Of adder coiled upon the path,
Or tempt the lion from the wood,
That soon will prowl athirst for blood.
– Thus, murmuring my thoughtful strain,
I seek our wattled cot again.

[1]buck
[2]small buck

THOMAS PRINGLE

The Emigrants

Sweet Teviot, fare thee well! Less gentle themes
Far distant call me from thy pastoral dale,
To climes where Amakosa's woods and streams
Invite, in the fair South, my venturous sail.
There roaming sad the solitary vale,
From native haunts and early friends exiled,
I tune no more the string for Scottish tale;
For to my aching heart, in accents wild,
Appeals the bitter cry of Afric's race reviled.

From Keissi's meads, from Chumi's hoary woods,
Bleak Tarka's dens, and Stormberg's rugged fells,
To where Gareep pours down his sounding floods
Through regions where the hunted Bushman dwells,
That bitter cry wide o'er the desert swells,
And, like a spirit's voice, demands the song
That of these savage haunts the story tells –
A tale of foul oppression, fraud, and wrong,
By Afric's sons endured from Christian Europe long.

Adieu, ye lays to youthful fancy dear!
Let darker scenes a sterner verse inspire,

While I attune to strains that tyrants fear
The deeper murmurs of the British lyre, –
And from a holier altar ask the fire
To point the indignant line with heavenly light,
(Though soon again in darkness to expire,)
That it oppression's cruel pride may blight,
By flashing TRUTH's full blaze on deeds long hid in night!

H. H. DUGMORE

A Reminiscence of 1820

In the lone wilderness behold them stand,
   Gazing with new strange feelings on the scenes
Now spread around them in a foreign clime,
Far from the sea-girt home that gave them birth.

They had been landed on a cheerless shore,
Dreary and solitary; and the hope
That erst had brighten'd all their visions, when,
O'er the blue waters looming afar,
They had seen Afric's mountains rise to view,
Had nigh been quench'd again. But they had left
The barren strand, and over hill and dale
Had slowly toil'd to reach a place of rest,
And give their children once again a home.

And this is now their home.
               'Tis lone and wild;
But there is beauty in its wildness.   See!
Yonder are mountains; in their deep ravines
Dark woods are waving, whence in noisy flight
While parrots issue forth, while loories hide
Amidst their deep recesses. Water springs
Send limpid streamlets down the mountain side,
Fring'd with bright evergreens, and brighter flowers.

   Issuing from yonder dark and craggy gorge,
Where lurks the stealthy leopard, and where shouts
With loudly echoing voice the bold baboon,

22

Kareiga winds its devious course along
Between its willow'd banks; while here and there
The dark leav'd yellow wood lifts its proud head
In stately dignity. Along the vale
The wildwood's sheltering covert stretches, where
The bushbok barks; the duiker, sudden, springs;
The timid bluebok through the moonlight glides;
And monkey mimics chatter saucily.

And there are feather'd songsters in the groves;
Not with the thrush's or the blackbird's notes,
That flood Old England's woods with melody;
But short, and sharp, and ringing in their tones,
Responsive to each other from afar,
While telling of a life of light and joy.

In the green pastures on the sunny slopes,
Where the mimosa's golden blossoms shed
Gales of perfume around; and fertile soils
Promise the husbandman a rich return
To cheer him in his toil.
                              'This is our Home!
'A spot on earth we now call our own;
'A starting point for a new life's career.
'Wake all our energies afresh! A brighter day
'Has dawn'd at last upon us. Let us raise
'A song of gratitude to Heaven,
'And gird us for our duties.'

R. M. BOWKER

Lieut. T. C. White, R.I.P.

*These lines are said to have been written in the ground with the point
of a ramrod by one of the Bathurst Volunteers on the Banks of the
Kei River, 19 May 1835.*

A Patriotic Man, to all a friend,
A firm defender of the people's right,
Who served his country for no private end
And left no stain upon his name; 'twas White.

A. G. BAIN

Kaatje Kekkelbek
or
Life among the Hottentots

My name is Kaatje Kekkelbek,[1]
    I come from Katrivier,[2]
Daar is van water geen gebrek,   There is no lack of water there
    But scarce of wine and beer.   But there is of wine and beer
Myn A B C at Ph'lipes[3] school
    I learnt a kleine beetje,   a little bit
But left it just as great a fool
    As gekke Tante Meitje.   dotty Aunt

But a b, ab, and i n, ine,
    I dagt met uncle Plaatje,   I thought with
Aint half so good as brandewyn,   brandy
    And vette karbonatje.   juicy chop
So off we set, een heele boel,   a whole troop
    Stole a fat cow and sack'd it,
Then to an Engels setlaars[4] fool,
    We had ourselves contracted.

We next took to the Kowie Bush,
    Found sheep dat was not lost, aye
But a schelm boer het ons gavang,   But a cunning Boer caught us
    And brought us voor McCrosty.[5]   before
Daar was Saartje Zeekoegat[6] en ik,   There was Saartjie Zeekoegat and I
    En ouw Dirk Donderwetter,
Klaas Klauterberg, en Diederick Dik,
    Al sent to the tronk together.   gaol

Drie months we daar got banjan kos   For three months we got plenty of grub
    For stealing os en hammel,   ox and wether
For which when I again got los,   got free
    I thank'd for Capt. Campbell.
The Judge came around, his sentence such
    As he thought just and even.
'Six months hard work,' which means in Dutch
    'Zes maanden lekker leven.'   'Six months easy life!'

De tronk it is een lekker plek   The gaol would be a lovely place
     Of 'twas not juist so dry,   If only it weren't so dry
But soon as I got out again
     At (Todds) I wet mine eye,
At Vice's house in Market-Square
     I drown'd my melancholies;   sorrows
And at Barrack hill found soldiers there
     To treat me well at Jolly's.

Next morn dy put me in blackhole,   they
     For one Rixdollar stealing,
And knocking down a vrouw dat had   woman
     Met myn sweet heart some dealing.   with my
But I'll go to the Gov'nor self
     And tell him in plain lingo,
I've as much right to steal and fight
     As kaffir has or Fingoe.

Oom Andries Stoffels[7] in England told
     (Fine compliments he paid us,)
Dat Engels dame was juist de same   exactly
     As our sweet Hotnot ladies.
When drest up in my voersits pak   my chintz outfit
     What hearts will then be undone,
Should I but show my face or back
     Among the beaux of London.

---

[1] Katie Chatterbox

[2] The Kat River 'Hottentot' (Khoi-Khoi) Settlement

[3] Rev. John Philip (1775-1851). Born in Scotland. Superintendent, London Missionary Society, South Africa, from 1819 until 1850.

[4] 1820 Settler

[5] Peter McRosty, an official in the office of the C.C. & R.M., Graham's Town.

[6] Sabina Seekoegat and Christian van Donderwether are names of imaginary characters found in an unsigned humorous letter from a correspondent at Graaff-Reinet to De Zuid-Afrikaan, 2 July 1830. The style makes it attributable to Bain.

[7] A leading Kat River 'Hottentot' who, with Jan Tzatzoe, was taken to England by Dr. Philip. Gave evidence before the Aborigines Committee of the House of Commons. (Una Long, Unofficial Manuscripts.)

D. C. F. MOODIE

Storm in Tugela Valley, Natal

When once, at ev'ning's mellow close,
   The round moon lit the sky,
And all beneath in calm repose
   In slumber rapt did lie –

Seated on high upon the steep,
   Amid the moonlight glow,
I looked upon a valley deep,
   And on a river's flow.

Sudden, across the chasm wide
   The heavy thunder growled,
While far below in sullen glide
   The noble river rolled.

And now a thousand feet below,
   Betwixt me and the stream,
The thunder-cloud, with lightning's glow,
   Obscures the river's gleam.

Loud and more loud, and all about
   The echoing hills among,
The spirits of the tempest shout
   Their diapason song.

Full in the midst the cloud now parts,
   And wars on different sides,
And through the gap the light moon darts,
   Where bright the river glides.

WILLIAM SELWYN

Hymn : Written During the Zulu War

'And I, if I be lifted up from the earth, will draw all men unto me.'
John xii. 32

O Saviour throned in peace above
    Reveal Thy piercèd side,
And let the vision of Thy love
    Stay war's remorseless tide;
        Risen Saviour, hear!

For white, for black, alike didst Thou
    Low bow Thy fainting head;
For all of ev'ry clime and hue,
    Didst Thou thy heart's blood shed.
        Suffering Saviour, hear! . . .

O hear the Briton's dying groan,
    The Zulu's piercing wail;
O hear the famished orphan's moan,
    The widow's sobbing tale;
        Pitying Saviour, hear!

In mercy stay the quiv'ring spear;
    Avert the death winged ball;
Pour balm for ev'ry scalding tear,
    And breathe Thy peace o'er all.
        Mighty Saviour, hear!

Draw weary warriors round Thy feet
    By love's constraining cord;
There let the scattered nations meet,
    And hail Thee Sov'reign Lord.
        Gracious Saviour, hear!

R. M. BRUCE

The Watermaid's Cave

. . . The sunset tints fade and the evening dews fall,
And the cattle are housed in Umgolomban's kraal.
And the dusky-skinned maids in the huts brightly glance,
Or sing and clap hands while the warriors dance.
But why is such gloom in Umdevane's face?
Devane the gay, first in dance or in chase?
But old Golomban spoke, 'Oh, Devane my son,
Not a word have you said since the milking was done;
Unshaken the calabash sits by your side,
The mealies untasted, the buck-meat untried,
And high-breasted Miaseh in vain rolls her eyes;
You mark not her glances, you heed not her sighs.'
'My Father,' young Devane roused him and said,
While the sun through the branches shone straight overhead,
'This morning the forest I wandered along
Till attracted and led by the honey-bird's song,
Down krantzes I clamber'd, through bushes I prest,
Till at last near the river he gave me the nest,
In a krantz which hangs over the Watermaid's Cave.'
'Go on,' said Umgangca the old, looking grave.
'The bees' nest I found not, 'twas under the brink
Of the crag, and my heart seem'd within me to shrink.
My name, softly uttered, came plain on my ear
From under the krantzes; I shudder'd with fear,
I fled in wild terror, nor dared to return,
And since in my bosom, my heart seems to burn.'
'Alas!' said Umquira the sage and the old,
'Alas! Umdevane, why wert thou so bold?
What is all the wild honey the krantzes e'er gave,
To entice thee to roam near the Watermaid's Cave.
Golomban, watch thy son, – nay, fast bind him with ropes
Till the sun of to-morrow is hid by the slopes;
Should the Watermaid call him again to her Cave,
Umdevane may not stop till he plunge in the wave.' . . .
Devane with riems[1] to a tree stump is tied,
And his friends, watching, sit in the shade by his side.
But warm grows the day as mounts higher the sun,
And in slumber the sleepers are wrapt one by one.
And a graceful young maiden draws bashfully near;

'Tis Miaseh, the one to Devane most dear.
'Miaseh, my loved one, come sit by my side,
Not long shall it be ere I make thee my bride;
Come sit by my side while I whisper of love,
But this cord first, which checks our embraces, remove.
Nay, fear not to loose it; while near me thou art,
A tie far far stronger is fixed on my heart.'
With love thrilling fingers she loosens the band,
And round her soft neck quickly steals the freed hand.
But hark; what sweet voice softly sounds from the river,
'Devane! Devane!' she feels his nerves quiver.
'Oh my love, my Devane! oh heed not that sound!
See, I am beside thee, my hands clasp thee round.'
He heeds not – he hears not! he leaps from the ground;
He tears those soft arms from their clinging embrace,
And springs like a greyhound let loose to the chase . . .
Now start from their slumbers the watchers in vain;
They pursue his swift flight thro' the valley and plain . . .
The slow and the swift are alike left behind,
Till nought save his footprints they're able to find,
And the last print Umdevane's foot ever gave,
Dents the sand, right in front of the Watermaid's Cave.

One line, from that footprint, of bubbles and foam,
Straight crosses the stream to the Watermaid's home,
Straight over that sunless and crystal-bright river,
Which on each side is calm and unruffled as ever,
But in uneasy motion yet tosses the wave,
Which bathes the dark sides of the Watermaid's Cave.

[1]leather thongs

CHARLES BARTER

from **Stray Memories of Natal and Zululand**

xxxi
Thence onward by the well-known road
My horse's feet had often trod
In former years, when, gun in hand,
I first explor'd this border land:
When Walmsley held Tugela's side,

And all the Zulu host defied:
When under Hlatikulu's shade
The buffalos in safety play'd;
When every night, beneath the moon,
The sea cows, in the still lagoon,
Rear'd their huge heads above the stream,
Or plunged below with flashing gleam.
How chang'd the scene! The silent lane
Is clogged with loads of ripen'd cane;
For murmur of the trickling rill,
The clang and shock of throbbing mill:
And where his wives saw Tshaka die
A bustling, thriving hostelry.

XXXV
Well I remember now the scene
Through mists of years that intervene;
The wagons on the sunburnt grass,
The mounted troopers as they pass:
Oxen and mules, a mingled throng,
By naked kafirs urged along;
The drivers, with unearthly shout,
Horses with saddles and without;
Men mounting in hot haste, to gain
Their places in the length'ning train;
All is in wild confusion tost:
Another gaze – the scene is lost.
And what remains? The trodden ground,
The dusty eddies circling round;
The whitewash'd building on the hill,
The trees that look so lone and still,
The swift Umgeni rushing by,
The calmness of the winter sky.

A. BRODRICK

Jong Koekemoer

Oh! Jong Koekemoer, from Marico's come out –   young
His schimmel Paard 'Ruiter' is sterk en gezout.   roan horse strong & seasoned
And, save some peach brandy, refreshment he'd none

But he has his 'Martini', that 'Son of a gun!'
So faithful a vryer, so fluks with his roer   *lover*   *skilful*   *rifle*
There ne'er was a Kerel like the Jong Koekemoer.   *chap*

He never off saddled, nor stopped for Kanteen,   *the pub*
He swam the Hex River where no drift was seen,
But e'er he held still at old Crocodile Kraal
The bride had said 'ja' to an Englishman small –
For a wealthy old trader, who had a 'tin' store,
Was to wed the fair Sannie of Jong Koekemoer.

He entered the house just in time for the ball
Met oompies, and tantas, neefs, nichtjes, and all;   *uncles aunts nephews nieces*
Then spoke Sannie's pa – old Swart Dirk Coetzee   *Black Dick*
(A dapper old Krygsman and Raad's Lid was he).   *brave warrior*   *councillor*
'What make you now here, Hans, so warm on our spoor?   *tracks*
Will you drink, smoke, or dance with us neef Koekemoer?'   *nephew*

'Wacht Oom, waar is Sannie? her long have I vrÿd,   *Wait Uncle, where courted*
For in all Transvaal she's the mooiste meid –   *prettiest maid*
Last nachtmaal we swore on the Bible to wed –   *communion*
But now I will just drink a soopje instead –   *tot*
There are girls in Marico – who still love a Boer –
That would gladly be vrouw to Jong Hans Koekemoer.'   *wife*   *young*

The bride brought the glass (blaauw, with bloemetjes rond).   *blue flowers around*
He drank the peach brandy, but first cried 'Gezond'.   *"Your health"*
Poor Sannie, she trembled, and couldn't tell why;
Yet she smiled with her lips, and she winked with her eye
He took her warm hand, while her ma she gaat treur   *became sad*
'Now let's have a reel, kerels,' said Jong Koekemoer.   *chap*

So tall in his moleskin, so prim in her print
(While her sweet mouth was full of the Smouse peppermint).   *pedlar's*
They danced 'Afrika' to the fiddles' sharp sound,
While the guests were half blinded with dust from the ground;
And all the young nichtjes cried, 'Mag! Hans is voor,   *nieces "Heavens! Hans*
Zÿ is gek als zÿ loop niet met Jong Koekemoer.'   *is best, She's mad if she doesn't go with young*

Quick. She pinned fast her skirts, and her kapje she tied.   *bonnet*
They rushed o'er the stoep where old 'Ruiter' they spied,
He sprang in the saddle, she jumped up behind:
And away, through the thorns, they flew, swift as the wind!
'Hold on to my belt, en moet niet achter loer,   *and don't look back*
They'll never catch 'Ruiter,' said Jong Koekemoer.

There was shouting of 'Opzaal' from all the Coetzees –   "Saddle-up!"
Doof Louw, Slim Hermanus, and Scheel-oog Du Preez!   Deaf Louw, Foxy Hermanus, Squint-eye Du Preez
There was chasing on horseback, in buggy, in vain –   Preez
But they never set eyes on sweet Sannie again!
Old Dirk, he 'looked daggers', the Uitlander swore: foreigner
And now Sannie is married to Jong Koekemoer!

ANDREW LANG

Zimbabwe

Into the darkness whence they came
    They passed, their country knoweth none,
They and their gods without a name
    Partake the same oblivion.
Their work they did, their work is done,
    Whose gold, it may be, shone like fire
About the brows of Solomon,
    And in the House of God's Desire.

Hence came the altar all of gold,
    The hinges of the Holy Place,
The censer with the fragrance rolled
    Skyward to seek Jehovah's face;
    The golden Ark that did encase
    The Law within Jerusalem,
The lilies and the rings to grace
    The High Priest's robe and diadem.

The pestilence, the desert spear,
    Smote them; they passed, with none to tell
The names of them who laboured here:
    Stark walls and crumbling crucible,
Strait gates, and graves, and ruined well
    Abide, dumb monuments of old;
We know but that men fought and fell,
    Like us, like us, for love of Gold.

C. & A. P. WILSON-MOORE

A Kafir Lament

I lofe Umlungu very much,
Him much my fren' we' az.
M'ningi promise eb'ry night,
Ikona give kusas.'
It's always 'Wacht een beetje, –
Hlan' ncozana,' then
'Footsack, suka, spuk-a-spuk!
Ngi bulala wen.'

I love the white man very much,
He's quite a friend you know.
Each night he promises me a lot,
But next day – not a thing.
Its always 'Wait a jiffie,
Sit down young man,' and then
'Beat it, buzz off, moron!
Or I'll murder you.'

M'ningi much sebenza,
Pesula Baas lo mine,
Baas biza mina 'Gashli!'
'Gashli!' eb'ry time.
It's always 'Wacht een beetje, –
Hlan' ncozana,' then
'Footsack, suka, spuk-a-spuk!
Ngi bulala wen.'

We have a lot of work,
This Baas of mine is tops,
He just says 'Be careful!
Careful!' every time.
It's always 'Wait a jiffie,
Sit down young man,' and then
'Beat it, buzz off, moron!
Or I'll murder you.'

I hold him hash,' mi' biza
'Bonzela Baas, Inkos!'
He tell me 'Hamba, footsack!'
Bulala mina nose!
It's always 'Wacht een beetje, –
Hlan' ncozana,' then
'Footsack, suka, spuk-a-spuk!
Ngi bulala wen.'

I hold his horse and ask him
'Baas, Chief, a tip!'
He tells me 'Scram, buzz off!'
And gives my nose a clout!
It's always 'Wait a jiffie,
Sit down young man,' and then
'Beat it, buzz off, moron!
Or I'll murder you.'

When Baas m'ningi 'poose'
He much tagate then,
He tell me 'Suka, tcherche!'
Him, hamba ky' kusen.'
It's always 'Wacht een beetje, –
Hlan' ncozana,' then
'Footsack, suka, spuk-a-spuk!
Ngi bulala wen.'

When Baas is on the bottle
He makes a lot of trouble
'Buzz off, you lazy bones,' he says,
But *he* gets home at dawn.
It's always 'Wait a jiffie,
Sit down young man,' and then
'Beat it, buzz off, moron!
Or I'll murder you.'

Mi' biza Baas lo mali,
He tell me zonki skat;
'Nginika wen' kusas'

I ask my Baas for money,
He tells me all the time,
'I'll give you some tomorrow,

33

'Now, kookisa lo pot.'
It's always 'Wacht een beetje, -
Hlan' ncozana,' then
'Footsack, suka, spuk-a-spuk!
Ngi bulala wen.'

In-yoni, im-balasi,
Umfazi, too, I lofe! -
'Ah! spuk-a-spuk, lo piccanin'
Dlela mina skoff!'
It's always 'Wacht een beetje, -
Hlan' ncozana,' then
'Footsack, suka, spuk-a-spuk!
Ngi bulala wen.'

But now, just cook the pot.'
It's always 'Wait a jiffie,
Sit down young man,' and then
'Beat it, buzz off, moron!
Or I'll murder you.'

I love fine things and poultry
I also love my wife -
'Hey! you moron! That piccanin
Is eating up my food!'
It's always 'Wait a jiffie,
Sit down young man,' and then
'Beat it, buzz off, moron!
Or I'll murder you.'

C. & A.P. WILSON-MOORE

Augustus Adolphe Montmorency Esq., Gentleman Digger

Augustus Adolphe Montmorency!
   Though the Norman blood coursed thro' thy frame,
Thy fathers bequeathed thee but little,
   Save the family pride and their name.
You were one of the Bon Ton, Elite;
   When we met you were barely nineteen;
As a swell you were really complete,
   As a digger a trifle *too* green . . .

Adolphe Montmorency, Esquire!
   How you got there I really can't tell, -
From the Mall to our camp on the fields, -
   But you did; I remember it well!
It was evening and raining like blazes,
   We were all sitting snug at our skoff,[1]
When raising the tent flap, you gently
   Your presence announced by a cough.
Lord! how we laughed when we saw you,
   Sublime in your polished surprise,
Lifting your hat, and adjusting
   An eyeglass to one of your eyes;

In your hand, which was gloved (breath it softly!),
    A smasher from Shaw's, – such a wreck! –
Patent leathers, and inches of linen
    Artistic'ly draped round your neck.
Poor chappie! we smothered our laughter,
    For we saw you were wet through and broke,
So we gave you some skoff, a drink and a bed,
    And left you alone till you woke.
Then you worked for a while on our claims, Sir, –
    But we never could leave you alone,
Mocking you always, thinking your ways
    Should have been rough as our own.

And then came the floods at the river,
    When Bob's child fell in at the race;
Nobody stirred, – 'twas folly, we said,
    With the river running that pace.
You were into the flood in a second,
    Our hearts stopped each time that you sank,
We thought you were gone, till we saw you,
    With the child in your arms, on the bank.
We left you alone after that, Sir,
    For we knew that your heart was bigger
And better by far than any of ours,
    Though you *were* the 'Gentleman Digger'!

¹food

OLIVE SCHREINER

'The Morning Sun is Shining'

The morning sun is shining on
    The green, green willow tree,
And sends a golden sunbeam
    To dance upon my knee.
The fountain bubbles merrily,
    The yellow locusts spring,
Of life and light and sunshine
    The happy brown birds sing.

The earth is clothed with beauty,
  The air is filled with song,
The yellow thorn trees load the wind
  With odours sweet and strong.
There is a hand I never touch
  And a face I never see;
Now what is sunshine, what is song,
  Now what is light to me?

ALICE GREENER

The Four Roads

*A young Dutch lady from one of the midland towns of Cape Colony
said recently to the writer: 'We have had four sets of executions in
our town. They always made known the sentence on Saturday and
carried it out on Monday. Sunday was a terrible day. A great black
cloud seemed to hang over the town, and at church our hearts were
filled with prayer for the dying men. The executions were carried
out at earliest dawn, before the town was awake, and the bodies were
buried in the four roads leading out of the town, so that we shall
always have to tread on their heads. The exact spot where they lie
is unmarked in any way, and is never made known.'*

*Fourie, one of 'the rebels three,' was a farmer of 50, who was much
respected as a good and kind man, and left behind him a wife and
eight children. The youthful 'rebel' of the third execution was said
by the authorities to be 20, but is known to have been only 16, as is
proved by the birth-register of his own village. (1900)*

Four roads lead out of the town,
  And one of them runs to the West,
And there they laid the rebels twain
  With the bullets in their breast.
And the English Commandant laugh'd low,
  As he looked at the sleeping town,
'Each road shall bear its vintage soon,
  And your feet shall tread it down!'

Four roads lead out of the town,
   And one of them runs to the East,
And there they laid the rebels three,
   When their stout hearts' life-beat ceased.
They had looked their last at the bright, bright sun,
   As he rose o'er the eastern hill,
They had prayed their last for the wife and babes
   Who are weeping and praying still.

Four roads lead out of the town,
   And one of them runs to the South,
And there they led the 'rebel bold,'
   With a smile on his gay young mouth.
Sixteen years he had lived on earth
   When they led him forth to die,
And there he lies, with his white young face
   Turned upward to the sky!

Four roads lead out of the town,
   And one of them runs to the North,
And there they led the dying man
   In the Red-Cross wagon forth.
And a bullet has stopped the glorious life,
   And stayed the gallant breath.
And Scheepers lies 'neath the road that leads
   To the land he loved till death.

Four roads lead out of the town,
   And for ever and for aye
Our feet must tread on the noble dead
   Till the trump of the Judgment Day.
But the blood of martyrs is still the seed
   Of the Church that is to be,
And rebel blood still bears the fruit
   Of a nation's Liberty!

Four roads lead out of the town,
   – God's sun shines on them still,
Though our brothers' blood cries from the ground,
   And echoes from hill to hill.
And our hearts cry out to the quiet dead,
   Where they keep safe watch and ward,
'Blest are the dead, the noble dead,
   The dead who die in the Lord!'

ALICE BUCKTON

At Welbedacht

'The stallions I must have, good wife! the red one and the brown.
Twill be to your advantage, too, to send them saddled down
Into the camp tonight; if not, be sure I come at morn!'

She stood at the open door, alone, in her widow's dress;
She saw them ride away – she knew her loneliness,
And turned and wrung her hands, 'My God – spare me this!'

'The red and the brown, he said? Nay, take the rest o' the stall!
Foals my husband bred, and prized the most of all,
To bear strange men, and ride to the enemy's bugle call!'

. . . . She sat till the sun went down; and waited for the night:
She looked to the distant camp, where the fires flickered bright;
Then silently she rose, and fetched a stable light.

The children slumbered both: she bent above the bed;
She took the leathern case from under the mattress head,
And slowly turned her steps behind the cattle-shed.

The creatures heard her foot, and whinnied to see her stand:
She loosed the halters, and gave the open fondling hand . . . .
Nay, finer foals were never foaled in any land!

She led to the open manger; she tethered the lantern fast,
And mixed the ready mash. 'Though it should be our last,'
She cried, 'we will have to-night our joy of this repast!'

Their lips and nostrils quivered to feel the wholesome corn;
She combed their massy manes with a comb of yellow horn:
'We must be ready, ready to meet the coming morn.'

She looked abroad from the threshold: the dawn was very near!
The manger-meal was done: why did she linger there?
She turned her into the stable, steady, without a fear . . . .

Four pistol-shots rang out in the silence of the night –
The cow-boy started forth from his hut in sudden fright,
And met a reeling woman bearing a stable-light.

Two troopers came at dawn, with a sergeant at their head.
'Yield us the stallions, woman! the brown one and the red!'
She gazed as one that wanders: 'Take them,' was all she said.

EDGAR WALLACE

Cease Fire

The fight was done an hour ago:
    The whole brigade has fallen back,
And I've been wand'rin' to and fro,
    A-askin' any – white or black,
    'Say – have you seen my brother, Jack?
    His troop was first in the attack!'

I should have seen him here by now:
    An hour ago the 'cease fire' went.
He isn't wounded any'ow,
    'Cos with the stretcher squads I went,
    An' all my other time I've spent
    A-hangin' round the doctor's tent.

Among the huddled, fallen men
    I picked a way across the plain.
I got a dozen yards, an' then
    Came back for fear I'd turn my brain . . . .
    The mangled horrors of the slain!
    O Christ! I can't go *there* again!

Say, have *you* seen my brother Jack?
    Don't know! an' damn you, don't much care! –
But 'scuse me, chum, a-talkin' back,
    I'm sorter flustered with the glare.
    These sands are hot, an' so's the air –
    Perhaps he's doin' guard somewhere! . . .

They're layin' out our dead just now,
    He can't be – no, that – that ain't sense,
An' when he comes there'll be a row!
    A-keepin' me in this suspense!
    'Tis here our line of killed commence,
    I'll sorter look – for make-pretence!

Pretendin' some one's here I know –
    I'm half inclined to turn aback –
But one by one, along I go,
    And see the crimson clottin' black . . . .
    His troop was first in the attack!
    What! Jack! Is this – this Thing our Jack?

THOMAS HARDY

Drummer Hodge

I

They throw in Drummer Hodge, to rest
  Uncoffined – just as found:
His landmark is a kopje-crest
  That breaks the veldt around;
And foreign constellations west
  Each night above his mound.

II

Young Hodge the Drummer never knew –
  Fresh from his Wessex home –
The meaning of the broad Karoo,
  The Bush, the dusty loam,
And why uprose to nightly view
  Strange stars amid the gloam.

III

Yet portion of that unknown plain
  Will Hodge for ever be;
His homely Northern breast and brain
  Grow to some Southern tree,
And strange-eyed constellations reign
  His stars eternally.

RUDYARD KIPLING

Bridge-Guard in the Karroo

'and will supply details to guard the Blood River Bridge.'
District Orders: Lines of Communication – South African War.

Sudden the desert changes,
  The raw glare softens and clings,
Till the aching Oudtshoorn ranges
  Stand up like the thrones of kings –

Ramparts of slaughter and peril –
　　Blazing, amazing, aglow –
'Twixt the sky-line's belting beryl
　　And the wine-dark flats below.

Royal the pageant closes,
　　Lit by the last of the sun –
Opal and ash-of-roses,
　　Cinnamon, umber, and dun.

The twilight swallows the thicket,
　　The starlight reveals the ridge;
The whistle shrills to the picket –
　　We are changing guard on the bridge.

(Few, forgotten and lonely,
　　Where the empty metals shine –
No, not combatants – only
　　Details guarding the line.)

We slip through the broken panel
　　Of fence by the ganger's shed;
We drop to the waterless channel
　　And the lean track overhead;

We stumble on refuse of rations,
　　The beef and the bisuit-tins;
We take our appointed stations,
　　And the endless night begins.

We hear the Hottentot herders
　　As the sheep click past to the fold –
And the click of the restless girders
　　As the steel contracts in the cold –

Voices of jackals calling
　　And, loud in the hush between,
A morsel of dry earth falling
　　From the flanks of the scarred ravine.

And the solemn firmament marches,
　　And the hosts of heaven rise
Framed through the iron arches –
　　Banded and barred by the ties,

41

Till we feel the far track humming,
    And we see her headlight plain,
And we gather and wait her coming –
    The wonderful north-bound train.

(Few, forgotten and lonely,
    Where the white car-windows shine –
No, not combatants – only
    Details guarding the line.)

Quick, ere the gift escape us!
    Out of the darkness we reach
For a handful of week-old papers
    And a mouthful of human speech.

And the monstrous heaven rejoices,
    And the earth allows again,
Meetings, greetings, and voices
    Of women talking with men.

So we return to our places,
    As out on the bridge she rolls;
And the darkness covers our faces,
    And the darkness re-enters our souls.

More than a little lonely
    Where the lessening tail-lights shine.
No – not combatants – only
    Details guarding the line!

RUDYARD KIPLING

Chant-Pagan

Me that 'ave been what I've been,
Me that 'ave gone where I've gone,
Me that 'ave seen what I've seen,
'Ow can I ever take on
With awful old England again,
And 'ouses both sides of the street,
And 'edges two sides of the lane,
And the parson and gentry between,

And touchin' my 'at when we meet –
Me that 'ave been what I've been?

Me that 'ave watched 'arf a world
'Eave up all shiny with dew,
Kopje on kop to the sun,
And as soon as the mist let 'em through
Our 'elios winkin' like fun
Three sides of a ninety-mile square,
Over valleys as big as a shire –
Are ye there? Are ye there? Are ye there?
And then the blind drum of our fire –
And I'm rollin' 'is lawns for the Squire,
                  Me!

Me that 'ave rode through the dark
Forty mile, often, on end,
Along the Ma'ollisberg Range,
With only the stars for my mark
And only the night for my friend,
And things runnin' off as you pass,
And things jumpin' up in the grass,
And the silence, the shine, and the size
Of the 'igh, inexpressible skies –
I am takin' some letters almost
As much as a mile to the post,
And 'Mind you come back with the change'!
                  Me!

Me that saw Barberton took
When we dropped through the clouds on their 'ead
And they 'ove the guns over and fled,
Me that was through Di'mond 'Ill,
And Pieters and Springs and Belfast,
From Dundee to Vereeniging all,
Me that stuck out to the last
(And five bloomin' bars on my chest)
I am doin' my Sunday-school best,
By the 'elp of the Squire and 'is wife
(Not to mention the 'ousmaid and cook)
To come in and 'ands up and be still,
And honestly work for my bread,
Me livin' in that state of life
To which it shall please God to call
                  Me!

Me that 'ave followed my trade
In the place where the Lightnings are made,
'Twixt the Rains and the Sun and the Moon,
Me that lay down and got up
Three years with the sky for my roof,
That 'ave ridden my 'unger and thirst
Six thousand raw mile on the hoof,
With the Vaal and the Orange for cup,
And the Brandwater Basin for dish –
Oh, it's 'ard to be 'ave as they wish
(Too 'ard, and a little too soon),
I'll 'ave to think over it first –

Me!

I will arise and get 'ence;
I will trek south and make sure
If it's only my fancy or not
That the sunshine of England is pale,
And the breezes of England are stale,
And there's something gone small with the lot;
For I know of a sun and a wind,
And some plains and a mountain be 'ind,
And some graves by a barb-wire fence;
And a Dutchman I've fought 'oo might give
Me a job were I ever inclined,
To look in and offsaddle and live
Where there's neither a road nor a tree,
But only my Maker and me,
And I think it will kill me or cure,
So I think I will go there and see.

Me!

RUDYARD KIPLING

The Burial 1902

C. J. Rhodes, buried in the Matoppos, 10 April 1902

When that great Kings return to clay,
   Or Emperors in their pride,
Grief of a day shall fill a day,
   Because its creature died.

But we – we reckon not with those
  Whom the mere Fates ordain,
This Power that wrought on us and goes
  Back to the Power again.

Dreamer devout, by vision led
  Beyond our guess or reach,
The travail of his spirit bred
  Cities in place of speech.
So huge the all-mastering thought that drove –
  So brief the term allowed –
Nations, not words, he linked to prove
  His faith before the crowd.

It is his will that he look forth
  Across the world he won –
The granite of the ancient North –
  Great spaces washed with sun.
There shall he patient make his seat
  (As when the Death he dared),
And there await a people's feet
  In the paths that he prepared.

There, till the vision he foresaw
  Splendid and whole arise,
And unimagined Empires draw
  To council 'neath his skies,
The immense and brooding Spirit still
  Shall quicken and control.
Living he was the land, and dead,
  His soul shall be her soul!

A. S. CRIPPS

Resurgat

for C. J. Rhodes

God be with you in your need!
When God's mills have ground you through –
All the coarse cruel chaff of you –

Be there left one grain to sow,
Which in season may unfold
Your visionary might of old!

Vine-dresser of the world-to-be,
Leave not one branch, yet leave the tree
Its life abounding, leave it free
Like some fecund vine to sprawl
On the widths of Sion's wall
In penitence imperial!

A. S. CRIPPS

To the Veld

Ragged brown carpet, vast and bare,
Seamed with grey rocks, scathed black with flame!
Stage-carpet, foil for all that's fair!
O'er thy grim stretches dance in air
Sun, moon, and stars in dazzling wear,
Enhancing splendours by thy shame.

Poor, unloved! Take my love and praise,
Not most because so faery-fine
Heaven peeps at poverty of thine,
Nor because thy mute exile days
Teach best the worth of greenwood ways,
And meadows where deep waters shine.

Nay, most for all the weariness,
The homeless void, the endless track,
Noon-thirst, and wintry night's distress;
For all tense stretchings on the rack
That gave me my lost manhood back.

A. S. CRIPPS

The Black Christ

At Easter in South Africa

Pilate and Caiaphas
They have brought this thing to pass –
That a Christ the Father gave,
Should be guest within a grave.

Church and State have willed to last
This tyranny not over-past;
His dark southern Brows around
They a wreath of briars have bound;
In His dark despiséd Hands
Writ in sores their writing stands.

By strait starlit ways I creep,
Caring while the careless sleep,
Bearing balms, and flow'rs to crown
That poor Head the stone holds down:
Through some crack or crevice dim
I would reach my sweets to Him.

Easter suns they rise and set,
But that stone is steadfast yet:
Past my lifting 'tis, but I
When 'tis lifted would be nigh.

I believe, whate'er they say,
The sun shall dance one Easter Day,
And I, that through thick twilight grope
With balms of faith and flow'rs of hope,
Shall lift mine eyes, and see the stone
Stir and shake, if not be gone.

A. S. CRIPPS

In Deserto

Afternoon

God's Fire-ball rolling smooth o'er heavens of glass,
God's Hand-fed hawk with wide unfluttered gait,
Are o'er me – as feet wrench'd and worn I pass
By black-burnt clods, by sandy furrows strait.
They do their best so lightly, bird and sun,
But all my struggling leaves my best undone.

F. C. SLATER

Lament for a Dead Cow

Chant by Xhosa family on the death of Wetu, their only cow

Siyalila, siyalila, inkomo yetu ifile![1]
  Beautiful was Wetu as a blue shadow,
That nests on the grey rocks
About a sunbaked hilltop:
Her coat was black and shiny
Like an isipingo-berry;
Her horns were as sharp as the horns of the new moon
That tosses aloft the evening star;
Her round eyes were as clear and soft
As a mountain-pool,
Where shadows dive from the high rocks.
No more will Wetu banish teasing flies
With her whistling tail;
No more will she face yapping curs
With lowered horns and bewildered eyes;
No more will her slow shadow
Comfort the sunburnt veld, and her sweet lowing
Delight the hills in the evening.
The fountain that filled our calabashes
Has been drained by a thirsty sun;

The black cloud that brought us white rain
Has vanished – the sky is empty;
Our kraal is desolate;
Our calabashes are dry:
And we weep.

[1] We weep, we weep, our cow is dead!

F. C. SLATER

Clay Cattle

Once on a day of sunshine in the deep-grooved vale
    of the Tyumie,
River that draws its milk from the breast of the blue
    Amatola,
Riding along toward Hogsback I saw, close by the
    roadside,
Laughing and flashing white teeth a sprinkle of Xhosa
    herdboys.
Cast aside were their clouts, their tattered blankets of
    sheepskin,
Naked they squatted and shaped in clay, moist, pliable,
    yellow,
Oxen to plough the maize-fields, sinewy, long-horned
    oxen;
Big-uddered cows to fill the round-bellied, red cala-
    bashes;
Sturdy humpbacked bulls and heifers with silken
    haunches.
Naked they sat in the sun, those pigmy gods and
    creators,
Moulding from worthless mud the coveted wealth of
    the Xhosa –
Cattle to dapple the plains and loom like rocks on the
    hillside,
Cattle whose sweet soft lowing gladdens the hills in the
    evening:
Laughing they sat in the sun, those gay bronze-coloured
    herdboys,

Shaping in dull, dead earth their dreams of riches and
    beauty.
Haply, while moulding the mimic, their real kine had
    escaped them,
Haply, unheeded, their herds had strayed into fields of
    mealies;
They would repent at night when an irate father would
    greet them,
Stinging their shrinking rumps with strokes of his well-
    known 'swazi,[1]
'Swazi that bites like a bug and stings like an angry
    hornet.
– Laughing they sat in the sun, those light-hearted,
    heedless herdboys,
Moulding in dull brown earth their dreams of beckon-
    ing beauty.

[1]switch

CULLEN GOULDSBURY

From **The Rhodesian Rubaiyat**

A Book on Cattle-sickness, and a Cow,
A flask of Dop,[1] some Bully-beef – and Thou
Beside me, swearing at the Wilderness,
That is the Real Rhodesia, here and now.

Ah, my Beloved, fill the cup that clears
To-day of past Regrets and future Fears –
To-morrow? Why to-morrow I may be
Running some Institution like De Beers![2]

[1]brandy
[2]The name of a farm in Griqualand West on which diamonds were discovered in
the 1870's; subsequently the name of a large corporation which mines and
markets these stones.

CULLEN GOULDSBURY

The Slaying of Mtikana

Out of the annals of forgotten days
   When Lobengula held the reins of state,
And tall, proud impis ruled the forest ways,
Wandering through the land with spears ablaze,
   Come chronicles of ancients, that relate
The doom of Chief Mtikana The Cloud,
And how he spoke with Death, and laughed aloud . . . .

It chanced, Mtikana – or so 'tis sung –
   Had wedded Makwa, daughter of the King –
One knows the venom of a woman's tongue!
The dainty snake his warming breast had stung,
   Tainting his honour with his slandering,
And, leagued with jealous Chiefs, who sought his fall,
Bore ill report to Lobengula's kraal.

Whereon, the King took council, and decreed
   That messengers should seek the Chieftain out
And hale him to his presence, that indeed
Test might be made, and punishment at need
   Be meted to him; also, captains stout
Were sent to summon in a wizard wise,
To cast the bones, and lend a shrewd surmise.

So came Manenga to the council place
   (Forebribed by Makwa with a lordly steer)
Cunning and crafty, of the wizard race,
Lord of the 'Smellers-out' – his ferret face
   Gleamed wolfishly among his feather gear,
And amulets, and charms and carven wings
Lent weightiness unto his whisperings.

'Oh King!' he mumbled, 'Lord of earth and sky!
   The bones have spoken, and the fates are plain,
Mtikana, empowered from on high
Shall smite – and lo, the Elephant shall die –
   Potions, and charms and spells, alike are vain;
His guardians are the moon and stars and sun,
King shall he be ere many days are run.'

51

'In proof whereof, Oh King, the facts are clear –
The regiments are his servants to a man,
And loud 'Bayede!' strikes upon the ear
Whene'er the Chief Mtikana draws near –
Thus rings the royal salute – your kingly ban
Avails but little to divorce your trust,
Or trample down the traitor in the dust.'

Then rose Mtikana, and all were still.
'My King,' he said, 'I pray you slay me now
It is not meet that one, whose only will
Has been the King's, whose deeds are clear of ill,
Should languish in your prison huts, and bow
Long days before your gaoler's look of scorn!
Come, slay me, ere my honour be foresworn!'

But Lobengula spoke him soft and fair,
Disclaiming aught of envy – 'Hie you hence
Gallant Mtikana! we cannot spare
So brave a warrior – my gifts shall bear
Meet tribute to your noble innocence.'
The Chieftain bowed, and answered murmuring –
'You crave my death? then slay me here, oh King!'

Howbeit, they prevailed on him to go,
And, bending till his feathers swept the ground,
He left the place with haughty tread and slow;
Thereat the King in council, speaking low,
Gave order to his captains – swift around
Mustered the Amanxusa Regiment, they
Whose province is to track the spoor, and slay.

With nodding plumes, and spears and shields of hide,
They stood like statues, and the King came forth
Without the kraal enclosure; at his side
Stood captains of his regiments, and they cried,
'Men of the Amanxusa! the King's wrath
Has fallen on Mtikana, the Chief –
Swift on his trail, and let your work be brief!'

'Bayede!' came the cry; and once again
'Bayede!' and the spear-stocks smote the ground;
Then, like a writhing serpent o'er the plain,
The Regiment of the Slayers fled amain,

And silence reigned in all the hills around;
But Lobengula turned, with set, pale face,
And paced awhile about the open space.

Meanwhile the Chief, his durance at an end,
    Had camped that evening at Dukate's kraal,
And with him rode Mabamba, a good friend
Who chafed, for friendship's sake, the night to spend
    In slumber where such danger might befall,
Crying: 'The Amanxusa are a-trail
Hot-foot and eager; what may two avail?'

'Be warned, Mtikana! Nor halt we here!
    'Twere wiser far to seek to reach your home.
If die we must, why then, 'tis better cheer
To die at home, with friendly kinsmen near
    Than here upon the veld, where jackals roam
To pick your bleaching bones!' The Chief replied:
'Death is but Death – so let the issue slide.'

Now, ere the curtains of the night were drawn,
    Or timid buck had stirred upon the vlei[1]
Mtikana arose – the quiet dawn
Slumbered within the hills, and, overborne
    By shadows still, the dim white river lay
Across the valley, like a silver thread
Drawn out amid the labyrinth of the dead.

So stood Mtikana in thought awhile,
    Gazing and peering outward through the mist;
Then, smiling, clenched his hand – but half a mile
There lay between the hills a dark defile,
    A narrow gorge, where frowning boulders kissed.
Thence, as he scanned the vlei from west to north,
The Regiment of the Slayers issued forth.

Twining like snakes amid the grass, they came
    A long brown line – the Chief stood cold and still,
Though horses grazed at hand – his eyes aflame
He gazed upon them, for he deemed it shame
    To flinch, when death was Lobengula's will,
And so they halted, while 'Bayede!' rang
Loud in the hills, and drowned the weapon's clang.

'Men of the Amanxusa!' said the Chief,
   With firm, set lips, and quiet, steady hand –
'Ye come upon an errand? lo, be brief
And workmanlike, I pray! leave futile grief
   Unto the womenfolk!' – the soldier-band
Stood fast, and speaking low in very shame
Vowed 'twas upon no errand that they came.

Then spake again the Chief: 'My lads, it needs
   No speech of yours to school me to my fate!
Obedience is the soul of valiant deeds,
And duty but the spirit-voice that leads
   The steadfast soldier to the sable gate
Where Gods sit throned and smile – come, slay me now
Ere dull delay beguile ye from your vow.'

So saying, he turned aside with quiet eyes,
   And steady mouth that seemed to cloak a smile,
Then, with a shout that almost cleft the skies,
They leaped upon him, and the assegais
   Drank of their fill in silence for a while,
Till, sated with the lust of blood, they ceased
And left the wheeling vultures to their feast.

[1]small shallow lake

E. BERLEIN

Rachel

I shall lie quiet, quiet,
   On either hand a son,
And wait in timeless patience
   Till time's long night be done.

As in the days of living
   They'll lie close by my side,
And time shall be forgotten
   And space, wherein they died.

And in the sightless darkness
  My yearning hands shall reach
To make sure of their nearness,
  And take my love to each.

I shall not draw them closer,
  Nor stir their slumber deep,
For fear a flash of memory
  Might stab the dark of sleep.

I shall lie quiet, quiet,
  One knowledge in my breast,
That close beside me, sleeping,
  Lie my two sons, at rest.

IAN COLVIN

To His Readers

Where o'er smooth floors of violet seas
  Long wedges of black duikers fly;
Where on the mountain's mighty knees
  The mists of the Antarctic lie;

Or where beside the furrow'd stream
  The vines their purple harvest bear;
Where through green oaks white gables gleam –
  Meerlust, Dauphine, Morgen Ster;

Or where upon the wide Karoo
  The lonely shepherd, far withdrawn,
Beholds – monotonously new –
  The rose of sunset and of dawn,

'Tis all one land; one people we –
  If not completely reconciled,
If we must quarrel, let it be
  But as a lover or a child.

On the contracted brows of hate
  Let our satiric sunbeams dance,
And if the frown is obstinate,
  Let's laugh it out of countenance.

PERCEVAL GIBBON

Jim

An Incident

From the Kei to Umzimkulu
  We chartered to ride,
But before we reached Umtata
  Jim turned in and died.
By Bashee I buried Jim.
Ah! but I was fond of him;
An' but for the niggers grinning,
I'd – yes, I'd have cried.

'Twas a weary trek through Griqualand,
  And me all alone;
Three teams and a dozen niggers
  To boss on my own.
And I felt a need for Jim;
It was just the job for him,
Hazin' the teams and the niggers,
  Hard grit to the bone.

I lost a load at Kokstad:
  An axle fell through;
I hadn't heart to tinker it,
  So pushed on with two.
If I'd only had old Jim!
Axles never broke with him;
But I never could handle waggons
Like Jim used to do.

I came to Umzimkulu
  With a pain in my head;
I ought to ha' bought med'cine,
  But I liquored instead:
Never used to drink with Jim;
There's a girl that asked for him;
But the jackals root at Bashee –
An' Jim, he's dead!

EUGÈNE MARAIS

Home

I know the place; –
Just where the river starts to race
And where within the murmur of the gorge
The old-time hunters built their forge –
Peace to their happy souls!

There let me sleep
Where all the wild things peer and peep
With silent footfalls
Round my cairn of stones.

BRIAN BROOKE

Smoke of the Camp Fire

'Say, where did you get that spear there?' I asked of the hunter old,
As we sucked our pipes one ev'ning, when out on the search for gold.
He slowly removed his briar, and spat in the dancing flame,
Then after a minute he answered, 'You'll reckon my story's tame; –
But it once belonged to a nigger, whom I saw a "Jumbo" kill,
And somehow I've always kept it, and probably always will.'
Then lapsing again to silence, he reckoned he'd said enough;
He was never a man for talking, was Timothy John McDuff.

But the moon was full above us, and the night was cold and clear,
And we'd got our Christmas boxes, and opened a case of beer;
We had seen no drink for a quarter, and it happened to loose his
    tongue,
And I kept on opening bottles, till I managed to get him sprung.
Then he started to tell his story, in his usual drawling way:
'Well, it happened like this, my sonny: twelve years ago today
I woke in a darned bad temper, for things had been working wrong,
– My life had been somewhat reckless, my liver was none too strong.

57

'My horse had a cold that morning, and two of my boys were ill,
The sheep which had strayed and wandered are lost in the bushveld
    still!
My pistol I found was dirty, and the sight of my rifle bent,
So I flogged it out of my tent-boy, till the most of my rage was spent.
Then I got on the spoor of a tusker, and told him to keep behind;
If he wanted no more kiboko, he'd bloomin' well have to mind.
But he never said "Yea" or "Nay, sir", his face was as hard as stone,
So he carried my second rifle, and we started away alone.

'It was getting late in the evening, when we sighted the tusker first;
We'd been on his spoor since sunrise with nothing to quench our
    thirst.
And somehow I missed my target and hit him a bit too high;
As he charged away in the brushwood he uttered a piercing cry.
I was young and daresay foolish, and followed the bloodstained trail;
I followed for half an hour, till I came on the grand old male.
Then I quickly aimed for his brain-box and drew on him fair and
    square,
He moved as I squeezed my trigger, – I missed it by half a hair.

'It all took place in a second, or possibly rather less;
He charged, and my gun misfired: it usu'lly did in a mess.
So I stood there and watched him coming – you'll find it a certain
    rule,
When you know that the game is over you'll never be quite so cool.
A scurry took place behind me, the sound of a nigger's oath;
I found myself hustled and tumbled down in the undergrowth.
He blazed with my second rifle as he pushed me safe aside,
Then the elephant crashed upon him – and with one long moan they
    died.'

The story was short and finished, I silently sat and smoked;
A fly had got into his bottle and Timothy John had choked.
I felt I should ask him something, to show that I'd heard him
    through,
So I pulled out my plug tobacco and cut off a bit to chew.
Then I said, 'Was the white stuff heavy, and what did they weigh the
    pair?
And what did you do with the nigger? Did you bury or leave him
    there?'
'Say what did I do with the beggar? – Well, what do you really think?
He was only a blasted nigger, so shove me another drink.'

WILLIAM HAMILTON

The Song of an Exile

I have seen the Cliffs of Dover
    And the White Horse on the Hill;
I have walked the lanes, a rover;
    I have dreamed beside the rill:
I have known the fields awaking
    To the gentle touch of Spring;
The joy of morning breaking,
    And the peace your twilights bring.
But I long for a sight of the pines, and the blue shadows under;
For the sweet-smelling gums, and the throbbing of African air;
For the sun and the sand, and the sound of the surf's ceaseless thunder,
The height, and the breadth and the depth, and the nakedness there!

I have visited your cities
    Where the unregenerate dwell;
I have trilled the ploughman's ditties
    To the mill-wheel and the well.
I have heard the poised lark's singing
    To the blue of summer skies;
The whirr of pheasants winging,
    And the crash when grouse arise.
But I sigh for the heat of the veldt, and the cool-flowing river;
For the crack of the trek-whip, the shimmer of dust-laden noon:
For the day sudden dying; the croak of the frogs, and the shiver
Of tropical night, and the stars, and the low hanging moon.

I have listened in the gloaming
    To your poets' tales of old;
I know, when I am roaming
    That I walk on hallowed mould.
I have lived and fought among you
    And I trow your hearts are steel;
That the nations who deride you
    Shall, like dogs, be brought to heel.
But I pine for the roar of the lion on the edge of the clearing;
For the rustle of grass snake; the birds' flashing wing in the heath;
For the sun-shrivelled peaks of the mountains to blue heaven rearing;
The limitless outlook, the space, and the freedom beneath.

HAROLD GOODWIN

Glorious?

*In the 'Eastern Province Herald' of 21 September 1955, mention was
made of the glorious battles of the Somme, Arras and Delville Wood,
in which the First South African Infantry Brigade took part.*

In the days long gone by when the 1st S.A.I.
Took part in a battle arboreous,
Mid Delville Wood's trees with a vertical breeze
I don't recollect feeling glorious.

When the battle was o'er and we counted the score
We didn't feel very victorious.
With most of our band in a far better land
Not one of us said it was glorious.

When a pal fell down dead with no top to his head
We may have used language censorious,
But whatever we said as we looked at our dead
I'm certain we never said glorious . . .

JOHN RUNCIE

Crossing the Hex Mountains

At Tweefontein in the moonlight the little white tents shine,
And a cry comes out of the darkness from those who guard the line;
The panting heart of the engine pulsed through the resting cars,
And beyond are the quiet mountains, and above are the quiet stars.

Sinister rise the mountains, jagged and bleak and bare,
Cloven and rent and fissured by fire and torrent there;
But the moon is a tender lady that loves not sights like these,
And in her spell transfigured, all things must soothe and please.

Far on the veldt behind us shone the steel-drawn parallels,
And beneath was the famished river fed by the famished wells,
And behind the shuttered windows, and beneath the hooded light,
Folk in the train were sleeping through all the wondrous night.

But I was out on the platform waiting the whistle shrill
That would break in a lustre of echoes right on the face of the hill:
Break on the face of the mountain and lose themselves in the pass,
Where the rails are like threads of silver, and the boulders smooth
    as glass.

Forth with the grinding of couplings, the hissing and snorting of
    steam,
Till the rails spun out behind her like spider-threads agleam,
Till she roared at the foot of the mountain, and brawled through the
    echoing glen,
Roaring, rocking, and ringing out her pæan of conquering men.

Right to the edge of a boulder, ominous, big, and black;
Plucking our hearts to our parching throats with fear for the open
    track;
Then forth like a driving piston straight from its iron sheath,
Till the wind stormed down on our faces, and we could not see nor
    breathe.

Looping, climbing, and falling, panting and swooping she sped,
Like a snake at the foot of the mountain, with her great white lamp
    ahead;
Shouldering the heavy gradients, heedless of breathing spells,
And racing away like a maddened steed down the sloping parallels.

Then out of De Doorns she thundered and over the starved Karroo,
Dwindling the hills behind her, farther and farther she flew;
And I know not which to praise the more – these moon-shot hills of
    God
Or the genius of the men who planned and made the glorious road.

ROY CAMPBELL

from **The Flaming Terrapin**

i. Invocation to the African Muse
Far be the bookish Muses! Let them find
Poets more spruce, and with pale fingers wind
The bays in garlands for their northern kind.

My task demands a virgin muse to string
A lyre of savage thunder as I sing.
You who sit brooding on the crags alone,
Nourished on sunlight in a world of stone,
Muse of the Berg, muse of the sounding rocks
Where old Zambezi shakes his hoary locks,
And as they tremble to his awful nod,
Thunder proclaims the presence of a god!
You who have heard with me, when daylight drops,
Those gaunt muezzins of the mountain-tops,
The grey baboons, salute the rising moon
And watched with me the long horizons swoon
In twilight, when the lorn hyaena's strain
Reared to the clouds its lonely tower of pain,
Now while across the night with dismal hum
The hurricanes, your meistersingers, come,
Choose me some lonely hill-top in the range
To be my Helicon, and let me change
This too-frequented Hippocrene for one
That thunders flashing to my native sun
Or in the night hushes his waves to hear
How, armed and crested with a sable plume,
Like a dark cloud, clashing a ghostly spear,
The shade of Tchaka strides across the gloom.
Write what I sing in red corroding flame,
Let it be hurled in thunder on the dark,
And as the vast earth trembles through its frame,
Salute with me the advent of the Ark!

ii. *The Voyage of the Ark*
Skittles to Noah's axe, the great trunks sprawled,
And with the weight of their own bodies hauled
Their screaming roots from earth: their tall green towers
Tilted, and at a sudden crack came down
With roaring cataracts of leaves and flowers
To crush themselves upon the rocks, and drown
The earth for acres in their leafy flood;
Heaped up and gashed and toppled in the mud,
Their coloured fruits poured forth their juicy gore
To make sweet shambles of the grassy floor.

When star by star, above the vaulted hill,
The sky poured out its hoarded bins of gold,
Night stooped upon the mountain-tops, and still

Those low concussions from the forest rolled,
And still more fiercely hounded by their dread
Lost in the wastes the savage tribesmen fled.

Out of its orbit sags the cratered sun
And strews its last red cinders on the land,
The hurricanes of chaos have begun
To buzz like hornets on the shifting sand.
Across the swamp the surly day goes down,
Voracious insects rise on wings that drone,
Stormed in a fog to where the mountains frown,
Locked in their tetanous agonies of stone.
The cold and plaintive jackals of the wind
Whine on the great waste levels of the sea,
And like a leper, faint and tatter-skinned,
The wan moon makes a ghost of every tree.

The Ark is launched; cupped by the streaming breeze,
The stiff sails tug the long reluctant keel,
And Noah, spattered by the rising seas,
Stands with his great fist fastened to the wheel.
Like driven clouds, the waves went rustling by,
Feathered and fanned across their liquid sky,
And, like those waves, the clouds in silver bars
Creamed on the scattered shingle of the stars.
All night he watched black water coil and burn,
And the white wake of phosphorus astern
Lit up the sails and made the lanterns dim,
Until it seemed the whole sea burned for him;

Beside the keel he saw the grey sharks move,
And the long lines of fire their fins would groove,
Seemed each a ghost that followed in its sleep
Those long phantasmal coffins of the deep;
And in that death-light, as the long swell rolled,
The tarpon was a thunderbolt of gold.
Then in the long night-watches he would hear
The whinnying stallions of the wind career,
And to their lost companions, in their flight,
Whine like forlorn cicalas through the night.

By day the sky put on a peacock dress,
And, from its far bewildering recess,
Snowed its white birds about the rolling hull –

The swift sea-swallow and the veering gull
Mixed in a mist of circling wings, whose swoops
Haloed her with a thousand silver hoops;
And from the blue waves, startled in a swarm,
On sunlit wings, butterflies of the storm!
The flying-fishes in their silver mail
Rose up like stars, and pattered down like hail,
While the blunt whale, ponderous in his glee,
Churned his broad flukes and siphoned up the sea,
And through it, as the creamy circles spread,
Heaved the superb Olympus of his head . . .
O, there were demons in the wind, whose feet,
Striding the foam, were clawed with stinging sleet:
They rolled their eyes and lashed their scorpion tails
And ripped long stripes into the shrieking sails.
High on the poop the dim red lantern glowed,
And soaring in the night, the pale ship rode:
Her shadow smeared the white moon black: her spars
Round wild horizons buffeted the stars,
As through the waves, with icicles for teeth,
She gored huge tunnels, through whose gloom to flee,
And down upon the crackling hull beneath
Toppled the white sierras of the sea!
On fiery Coloradoes she was hurled,
And where gaunt canyons swallowed up the light,
Down from the blazing daylight of the world,
She plunged into the corridors of night
Through gorges vast, between whose giant ribs
Of shadowing rock, the flood so darkly ran
That glimpses of the sky were feeble squibs
And faint blue powders flashing in the pan
Of that grim barrel, through whose craggy bore
The stream compelled her with explosive roar,
Until once more she burst as from a gun
Into the setting splendour of the sun:
Down unimagined Congos proudly riding,
Buoyed on whose flow through many a grey lagoon,
The husks of sleepy crocodiles went sliding
Like piles of floating lumber in the moon;
Then with the giddiness of her speed elate,
With sails spread like the gold wings of a moth,
Down the black Amazon, cresting the spate,
The smooth keel slithered on the rustling froth:
She moved like moonlight through the awful woods,

And though the thunder hammered on his gong,
Half-dreaming, as beneath their frail white hoods
Sail the swift Nautili, she skimmed along –
Till, raftered by the forest, through whose thatch
The moon had struck its faint and ghostly match,
She saw the monsters that the jungle breeds –
Terrific larvae crawled among the weeds
And from the fetid broth like horrid trees
Wavered their forked antennae on the breeze,
And panthers' eyes, with chill and spectral stare,
Flashed their pale sulphur on the sunless air:
While phosphorescent flowers across the haze,
Like searchlights darted faint unearthly rays:
And gleaming serpents, shot with gold and pearl,
Poured out, as softly as a smoke might curl,
Their stealthy coils into that spectral light
There to lie curved in sleep, or taking flight,
Trundle their burnished hoops across the leaves,
Till the stream, casting wide its forest sleeves,
Heaved out its broad blue chest against the sea,
And from their leafy bondage they were free . . .
Smooth as a lover's hand, ere sleep, may slide
O'er the gold sunburn of a woman's side
To drain the moonlight smouldering from her hair –
She stroked the water with her keel, and where
She passed along, it silvered into foam
And burned to take her roving beauty home.
She, whose white form had been the splendid theme
Of chanting hurricanes in their supreme
And wildest inspiration: she, whose white
Virginity appeased the lust of Night,
When in his star-slung hammock, worked with red
Stitches of lightning as with scarlet thread,
She swayed to his embraces as she lay
Dandled in thunder, cosseted in spray!
Now from his couch of terrors borne apart,
She glides alone; the silence on her heart
Weighs down with all the precious weight of gold,
While through the shades, serene and chaste and cold,
She rears aloft her moon-emboldened form,
With child of high endeavour by the Storm.

New signals greeted now the flying ship,
Like lambs the merry waves were seen to skip,

As shepherd winds drove forth their foamy sheep
To rustle through the verdure of the deep:
No more the cruising shark with whispers thin
Through their crisp fleeces sheared his sickle fin
Beside the keel, portending death and woe:
But joyful omens in unceasing flow
Saluted her, as racing with the gales,
She rolled escorted by the rolling whales.

Now far along the skyline, like a white
Signal of triumph through the muffled light,
An Albatross, wheeling in awful rings,
Spanned the serene horizon with his wings,
And towering upward on his scythes of fire,
Smote the thick air, that, strung with beams of light,
Clanged to his harpings like a smitten lyre
Tolling the solemn death-knell of the Night.
Till, rearing higher, he caught the blinding glow
Of sunlight frozen in his plumes of snow,
As his ethereal silver soared to fade
Into the light its own white wings had made,
And, fusing slowly, Albatross and sun
Mingled their two faint radiances in one . . .

iii. The Ark discharges its Cargo
Out of the Ark's grim hold
A torrent of splendour rolled –
From the hollow resounding sides,
Flashing and glittering, came
Panthers with sparkled hides,
And tigers scribbled with flame,
And lions in grisly trains
Cascading their golden manes.
They ramped in the morning light,
And over their stripes and stars
The sun-shot lightnings, quivering bright,
Rippled in zigzag bars.
The wildebeest frisked with the gale
On the crags of a hunchback mountain,
With his heels in the clouds, he flirted his tail
Like the jet of a silvery fountain.
Frail oribi sailed with their golden-skinned
And feathery limbs laid light on the wind.
And the springbok bounced, and fluttered, and flew,

Hooping their spines on the gaunt karroo.
Grey zebras pranced and snorted aloud –
With the crackle of hail their hard hoofs pelt,
And thunder breaks from the rolling cloud
That they raise on the dusty Veldt.
O, hark how the rapids of the Congo
Are chanting their rolling strains,
And the sun-dappled herds a-skipping to the song, go
Kicking up the dust on the great, grey plains –
Tsessebe, Koodoo, Buffalo, Bongo,
With the fierce wind foaming in their manes.

ROY CAMPBELL

The Theology of Bongwi, the Baboon

This is the wisdom of the Ape
   Who yelps beneath the Moon –
'Tis God who made me in His shape
   He is a Great Baboon.
'Tis He who tilts the moon askew
   And fans the forest trees,
The heavens which are broad and blue
   Provide him his trapeze;
He swings with tail divinely bent
   Around those azure bars
And munches to his Soul's content
   The kernels of the stars;
And when I die, His loving care
   Will raise me from the sod
To learn the perfect Mischief there,
   The Nimbleness of God.

ROY CAMPBELL

The Sisters

After hot loveless nights, when cold winds stream
Sprinkling the frost and dew, before the light,
Bored with the foolish things that girls must dream
Because their beds are empty of delight,

Two sisters rise and strip. Out from the night
Their horses run to their low-whistled pleas –
Vast phantom shapes with eyeballs rolling white
That sneeze a fiery steam about their knees:

Through the crisp manes their stealthy prowling hands,
Stronger than curbs, in slow caresses rove,
They gallop down across the milk-white sands
And wade far out into the sleeping cove:

The frost stings sweetly with a burning kiss
As intimate as love, as cold as death:
Their lips, whereon delicious tremors hiss,
Fume with the ghostly pollen of their breath.

Far out on the grey silence of the flood
They watch the dawn in smouldering gyres expand
Beyond them: and the day burns through their blood
Like a white candle through a shuttered hand.

ROY CAMPBELL

The Serf

His naked skin clothed in the torrid mist
That puffs in smoke around the patient hooves,
The ploughman drives, a slow somnambulist,
And through the green his crimson furrow grooves.
His heart, more deeply than he wounds the plain,
Long by the rasping share of insult torn,
Red clod, to which the war-cry once was rain
And tribal spears the fatal sheaves of corn,

Lies fallow now. But as the turf divides
I see in the slow progress of his strides
Over the toppled clods and falling flowers,
The timeless, surly patience of the serf
That moves the nearest to the naked earth
And ploughs down palaces, and thrones, and towers.

ROY CAMPBELL

The Zebras

To Chips Rafferty

From the dark woods that breathe of fallen showers,
Harnessed with level rays in golden reins,
The zebras draw the dawn across the plains
Wading knee-deep among the scarlet flowers.
The sunlight, zithering their flanks with fire,
Flashes between the shadows as they pass
Barred with electric tremors through the grass
Like wind along the gold strings of a lyre.

Into the flushed air snorting rosy plumes
That smoulder round their feet in drifting fumes,
With dove-like voices call the distant fillies,
While round the herds the stallion wheels his flight,
Engine of beauty volted with delight,
To roll his mare among the trampled lilies.

ROY CAMPBELL

The Zulu Girl

To F. C. Slater

When in the sun the hot red acres smoulder,
Down where the sweating gang its labour plies,
A girl flings down her hoe, and from her shoulder
Unslings her child tormented by the flies.

She takes him to a ring of shadow pooled
By thorn-trees: purpled with the blood of ticks,
While her sharp nails, in slow caresses ruled,
Prowl through his hair with sharp electric clicks,

His sleepy mouth plugged by the heavy nipple,
Tugs like a puppy, grunting as he feeds:
Through his frail nerves her own deep languors ripple
Like a broad river sighing through its reeds.

Yet in that drowsy stream his flesh imbibes
An old unquenched unsmotherable heat –
The curbed ferocity of beaten tribes,
The sullen dignity of their defeat.

Her body looms above him like a hill
Within whose shade a village lies at rest,
Or the first cloud so terrible and still
That bears the coming harvest in its breast.

ROY CAMPBELL

Horses on the Camargue

To A. F. Tschiffely

In the grey wastes of dread,
The haunt of shattered gulls where nothing moves
But in a shroud of silence like the dead,
I heard a sudden harmony of hooves,
And, turning, saw afar
A hundred snowy horses unconfined,
The silver runaways of Neptune's car
Racing, spray-curled, like waves before the wind.
Sons of the Mistral, fleet
As him with whose strong gusts they love to flee,
Who shod the flying thunders on their feet
And plumed them with the snortings of the sea;
Theirs is no earthly breed
Who only haunt the verges of the earth
And only on the sea's salt herbage feed -
Surely the great white breakers gave them birth.
For when for years a slave,

A horse of the Camargue, in alien lands,
Should catch some far-off fragrance of the wave
Carried far inland from his native sands,
Many have told the tale
Of how in fury, foaming at the rein,
He hurls his rider; and with lifted tail,
With coal-red eyes and cataracting mane,
Heading his course for home,
Though sixty foreign leagues before him sweep,
Will never rest until he breathes the foam
And hears the native thunder of the deep.
But when the great gusts rise
And lash their anger on these arid coasts,
When the scared gulls career with mournful cries
And whirl across the waste like driven ghosts:
When hail and fire converge,
The only souls to which they strike no pain
Are the white-crested fillies of the surge
And the white horses of the windy plain,
Then in their strength and pride
The stallions of the wilderness rejoice;
They feel their Master's trident in their side,
And high and shrill they answer to his voice.
With white tails smoking free,
Long streaming manes, and arching necks, they show
Their kinship to their sisters of the sea –
And forward hurl their thunderbolts of snow.
Still out of hardship bred,
Spirits of power and beauty and delight
Have ever on such frugal pastures fed
And loved to course with tempests through the night.

ROY CAMPBELL

from **The Wayzgoose**[1]

Attend my fable if your ears be clean,
In fair Banana Land we lay our scene –
South Africa, renowned both far and wide
For politics and little else beside:
Where, having torn the land with shot and shell,

Our sturdy pioneers as farmers dwell,
And, 'twixt the hours of strenuous sleep, relax
To shear the fleeces or to fleece the blacks:
Where every year a fruitful increase bears
Of pumpkins, sheep, and millionaires –
A clime so prosperous both to men and kine
That which were which a sage could scarce define;[2]
Where fat white sheep upon the mountains bleat
And fatter politicians in the street;
Where lemons hang like yellow moons ashine
And grapes the size of apples load the vine;
Where apples to the weight of pumpkins go
And donkeys to the height of statesmen grow,
Where trouts the size of salmon throng the creeks
And worms the size of magistrates – the beaks;
Where the precocious tadpole, from his bog
Becomes a journalist ere half a frog;
Where every shrimp his proud career may carve
And only brain and muscle have to starve.
The 'garden colony' they call our land,
And surely for a garden it was planned:
What apter phrase with such a place could cope
Where vegetation has so fine a scope,
Where *weeds* in such variety are found
And all the rarest *parasites* abound,
Where pumpkins to professors are promoted
And turnips into Parliament are voted?

[1]This phenomenon occurs annually in S.A. It appears to be a vast corroboree of journalists, and to judge from their own reports of it, it combines the functions of a bunfight, an Eisteddfod and an Olympic contest.'
[2]Example: 'Wanted: a good short-horn typist.' S.A. newspaper. (Campbell's notes – Eds.)

ROY CAMPBELL

Poetry & Rugby

from **The Georgiad**

Nor at his football match is Squire[1] more gay –
Heart-rending verse describes funereal play;
While swarming adjectives in idle ranks,

As dumb spectators, load the groaning planks,
See the fat nouns, like porky forwards, sprawl
Into a scrum that never heels the ball –
A mass of moving bottoms like a sea,
All fatter than his head, if that could be;
While still attentive at their clumsy calves
The adverbs pine away, dejected halves,
The verbs hang useless by, like unfed threes
With trousers idly flapping in the breeze,
And while they strike their arm-pits for some heat
Or idly stamp their splayed trochaic feet,
The two full-backs of alternating rhyme
Walk sadly up and down to kill the time.

[1]J. C. Squire: minor English poet.

ROY CAMPBELL

On Some South African Novelists

You praise the firm restraint with which they write –
I'm with you there, of course:
They use the snaffle and the curb all right,
But where's the bloody horse?

ROY CAMPBELL

On the Same

Far from the vulgar haunts of men
Each sits in her 'successful room',
Housekeeping with her fountain pen
And writing novels with her broom.

ROY CAMPBELL

A Veld Eclogue : The Pioneers

On the bare veld where nothing ever grows
Save beards and nails and blisters on the nose,
Johnny and Piet, two simple shepherds, lay
Watching their flock grow thinner every day –
Their one joint Nanny-goat, poor trustful thing,
That by the fence had waited since last spring
Lest any of the stakes that there were stuck
Should sprout a withered leaf for her to suck.
Rough was the labour of those hardy swains,
Sometimes they lay and waited for the rains,
Sometimes with busy twigs they switched the flies
Or paused to damn a passing nigger's eyes:
Sometimes, as now, they peeled them off their hose
And hacked the jiggers¹ from their gnarly toes.
At times they lay and watched their blisters heal,
At others, sweated forth a scanty meal
Prone on their backs between their Nanny's shins –
After the manner of the Roman twins.
What wonder then, at such a flurry kept,
That sometimes – oftenest of all – they slept?
Yet for all that their simple hearts were gay.
And often would they trill the rustic lay,
For though the times were hard they could not bilk
Their brains of nonsense or their guts of milk;
And loud upon the hills with merry clang
The grand old saga of 'Ferreira'² rang,
Till the baboons upon the topmost krans
Would leap for joy, career into a dance,
And all their Simian dignity forgot
Would hold a sort of Nagmaal³ on the spot,
Or, if to such comparisons we stoop –
A special rally of the Empire Group.⁴
Think not that I on racial questions touch,
For one was Durban-born, the other Dutch.
I draw no line between them: for the two
Despise each other, and with reason too!
But, in this case, they had both forgave the sin,
Each loved the other as a very twin –
One touch of tar-brush makes the whole world kin.

That they were true-bred children of the veld
It could as easily be seen as smelt,
For clumsier horsemen never sat astride,
Worse shots about their hunting never lied –
Though Piet once laid a lioness out straight,
I must confess – through aiming at its mate;
And Johnny, though he stalked extremely well,
Even against the wind the game could smell:
Even a pole-cat wheezing with catarrh
Could have perceived his presence from afar.
One knew them at a glance for Pioneers
Though Piet, but two years since, had washed his ears:
Their musty jackets and moth-eaten hair
Showed them for children of the Open Air;
Besides red tufts, there shone upon their faces
That 'nameless something' which Bolitho[5] traces
To gazing out across the 'open spaces' . . .
As for that 'nameless something', it was there
Plain as the grime upon their ragged hair –
Bolitho calls it an 'inspired alertness'
And so it seemed (in spite of their inertness) –
A worried look, as if they half-expected
Something to happen, or half-recollected
Anything having happened there at all
Since old Oom Jaapie's heifer calved last fall.
As for the 'boundless spaces' – wild and free
They stretched around as far as eye could see,
Which, though not very far, was yet enough
To show a tree, four houses, and a bluff.
Geographers, who say the world's a sphere,
Are either ignorant, or mazed with beer,
Or liars – or have never read two pages
Of any of our novelists or sages
Who tell us plainly that the world's more wide
On the colonial than the other side,
That states and kingdoms are less vast and grand
Than ranches, farms and mealie-planted land,
And that wherever on the world's bald head
A province or protectorate is spread
The place straightway to vast proportions jumps
As with the goitre or a dose of mumps –
So that in shape our cosmos should compare
Less with an apple than a warty pear.
For all our scenery's in grander style

And there are far more furlongs to the mile
In Africa than Europe – though, no doubt
None but colonials have found this out.
For though our Drakenberg's most lofty scalps
Would scarcely reach the waist-line of the Alps,
Though Winterberg, besides the Pyrenees,
Would scarely reach on tip-toe to their knees,
Nobody can deny that our hills rise
Far more majestically – for their size!
I mean that there is something grander, yes,
About the veld, than I can well express,
Something more vast – perhaps I don't mean that –
Something more round, and square, and steep, and flat –
No, well perhaps it's not quite that I mean
But something, rather, half-way in between,
Something more 'nameless' – That's the very word!
Something that can't be felt, or seen, or heard,
Or even thought – a kind of mental mist
That doesn't either matter or exist
But without which it would go very hard
With many a local novelist and bard –
Being the only trick they've ever done,
To bring in local colour where there's none:
And if I introduce the system too,
Blame only the traditions I pursue.

[1]*Jiggers:* subcutaneous parasites.

[2]*Ferreira:* a smutty folk-song in Afrikaans.

[3]*Nagmaal:* a reunion of South African peasants and their families for purposes of social festivity, commerce and religious debauchery.

[4]*Empire Group:* a society whose meetings are mentally and morally analogous to the above.

[5]*Bolitho:* Hector, not William. Prolific and popular interpreter of the 'New Earth,' the 'Open Spaces,' etc., to which he even relates the present writer's poems. Accounting for the mental and physical 'superiority' of the Colonial to the European, B. writes – ' "It's the distance that does it," said my millionaire, looking at me with his rather fine head chiselled on a background of cream madonna-lilies, "it's the distance that does it." ' (Campbell's notes – Eds.)

ROY CAMPBELL

Rounding the Cape

The low sun whitens on the flying squalls,
Against the cliffs the long grey surge is rolled
Where Adamastor[1] from his marble halls
Threatens the sons of Lusus as of old.

Faint on the glare uptowers the dauntless form,
Into whose shade abysmal as we draw,
Down on our decks, from far above the storm,
Grin the stark ridges of his broken jaw.

Across his back, unheeded, we have broken
Whole forests: heedless of the blood we've spilled,
In thunder still his prophecies are spoken,
In silence, by the centuries, fulfilled.

Farewell, terrific shade! though I go free
Still of the powers of darkness art thou Lord:
I watch the phantom sinking in the sea
Of all that I have hated or adored.

The prow glides smoothly on through seas quiescent:
But where the last point sinks into the deep,
The land lies dark beneath the rising crescent,
And Night, the Negro, murmurs in his sleep.

[1]Spirit of the Cape of Good Hope

ROY CAMPBELL

Luis de Camoes[1]

Camoes, alone of all the lyric race,
Born in the black aurora of disaster,
Can look a common soldier in the face:
I find a comrade where I sought a master:

For daily, while the stinking crocodiles
Glide from the mangroves on the swampy shore,
He shares my awning on the dhow, he smiles,
And tells me that he lived it all before.
Through fire and shipwreck, pestilence and loss,
Led by the ignis fatuus of duty
To a dog's death – yet of his sorrows king –
He shouldered high his voluntary Cross,
Wrestled his hardship into forms of beauty,
And taught his gorgon destinies to sing.

[1]Great Portuguese poet of the 16th Century who used Vasco da Gama's discovery
of the sea-route to India as the theme of his epic poem *The Lusiads*.

J. J. R. JOLOBE

The Battle of Amalinda

from **Thuthula**

The *Ndlambe* tribe in counsel did consult.
The messengers of war from royal kraal
Took news to all the sub-chiefs of the tribe,
A day was named for *impis* to report. — regiments
The warriors sharpened *izikempe* spears, — short stabbing assegais
Ijozi too and ox-hide shields were tried. — large assegais
The women ground *utshongo*, food for war, — ground-up, half-cooked mealies
And then the hordes held muster at Great Place.
They came in bands, each as a regiment,
According to their clans. The chieftains led.
Soon all have come, there sounds the war song grave.
There stands the chief, the army to address.

'*Thuthula*'s gone, the woman of the tribe. — woman of exceptional beauty, Ndlambe's wife
Her track is said to cross the River Fish.
As you all know, no ill was done by me;
My fault was only to bring up a child . . .
All you who gather here, I send you on.
I say prevent this branch from hitting me,
I do not know the cause; the same with you.
Look there he is, ye sons of *Phalo* great,
Ye sons of *Tshiwo* bold and *Ngconde* brave.' — Xhosa chiefs

With feeling spake *Rarabe's* son that day. Chief Ndlambe
court poet
Imbongi too a string of praises sang,
As he did strut around the royal folds.
In course of speech he said, 'What seek ye more.
Chief *Ndlambe* great his charge has given out:

'Who is the topic of the day,
The hoer of the weeds of land,
The heeder not of timely word,
The grower of the forest thorn,
The cruel thorn which pricks him now
The *Basho* of *Xukashe* land.'

The war song grave once more was sung by all.
Itola too his rites mysterious made   army doctor
And in the river all the army washed.
Then like a *mamba* black the swarm uncoiled.   poisonous snake
They go to fight to win the beauty home,
To right the wrong against the *Ndlambe* tribe . . . .
One thing they knew, *Thuthula* stolen was.
The *Ngqikas* all had done this shameful deed.

They burned the huts and left no kraal untouched.
Destroying, plundering, they drove the spoil,
And like a forest fire they left a waste,
Until one day they face to face did meet,
These armies of related chiefs by birth,
On that great plain, the bloody plain of death,
A swarm of dusky forms in multitudes.
The spears against the sun did dazzle eye.
The shield was man's sole hiding-place that day.
The vanguards of the armies led the hosts,
The scouts behind in *Xhosa* fashion true,
Intshinga and *iQauka* army main.   royal section   commoner's section
The flanks were held by the *inkongo* swift.   the flying column
Uqoqo braves the rearguard did compose.   reserve
The men of royal blood were there that day
And heroes brave, the *izithwala-ndwe*.   men honoured for bravery
They stood not sizing up each other long.
A man was heard to say, 'Tsi ha! the arms   a war cry
Of Chief *Rarabe*.' Slaughter red began.
The *indwe* man another *indwe* met,   men honoured for bravery
The common man another commoner.
'Right into battle,' urged the voice of man,
With fury slaying right and left with might . . . .

And when the sun did seek the western hills
The *Ngqika* wall collapsed, the brave were done.
They beat retreat; defeated remnants fled.
Courageous *Umrotshozo* heroes fell.   Chief Ngqika's regiment
For these Chief *Ngqika* shed some bitter tears,
His braves, the bodyguard, the trusted men,
They were propitiation for the wrong –
        . . . *Thuthula* was the cause.

ALAN PATON

The Hermit

I have barred the doors
Of the place where I bide,
I am old and afraid
Of the world outside.

How the poor souls cry
In the cold and the rain,
I have blocked my ears,
They shall call me in vain.

If I peer through the cracks
Hardly daring draw breath,
They are waiting there still
Patient as death.

The maimed and the sick
The tortured of soul,
Arms outstretched as if
I could help them be whole.

No shaft of the sun
My hiding shall find,
Go tell them outside
I am deaf, I am blind.

Who will drive them away,
Who will ease me my dread,
Who will shout to the fools
'He is dead! he is dead!'?

Sometimes they knock
At the place where I hide,
I am old, and afraid
Of the world outside.

Do they think, do they dream
I will open the door?
Let the world in
And know peace no more?

WILLIAM PLOMER

The Scorpion

Limpopo and Tugela churned
In flood for brown and angry miles
Melons, maize, domestic thatch,
The trunks of trees and crocodiles;

The swollen estuaries were thick
With flotsam, in the sun one saw
The corpse of a young negress bruised
By rocks, and rolling on the shore,

Pushed by the waves of morning, rolled
Impersonally among shells,
With lolling breasts and bleeding eyes,
And round her neck were beads and bells.

That was the Africa we knew,
Where, wandering alone,
We saw, heraldic in the heat,
A scorpion on a stone.

WILLIAM PLOMER

The Explorer

Romantic subject of the Great White Queen,
See him advancing, whiskered and serene,
With helmet, spectacles, and flask of brandy,
(That useful stimulant, he always keeps it handy),
Unmoved by cannibals, indifferent to disease,
His black frock-coat rocks sadly in the tropic breeze.

He never shows emotion, least of all surprise.
Here nothing meets his fat and hopeful eyes
But big game, small game, fur and fin and feather,
And now he dreams of daisies, Scotland and the Flag,
The nimble corncrake in his native heather,
The handy corkscrew in his leather bag.

WILLIAM PLOMER

The Pioneers:
Or, Twenty Years After

The street, the store, the station, especially the bar,
Show what the fathers of this tin-town hamlet are:
Moustaches waxed, these mammoths lean on counters,
Old rotting whales ashore and thick with flies,
Their blubber proof to bullets and to kicks,
Fill up their lungs with beer and blow out spouts of lies,
Tales of rebellions, cannons and encounters,
Before their brains dried up in nineteen-six.

WILLIAM PLOMER

The Boer War

The whip-crack of a Union Jack
In a stiff breeze (the ship will roll),
Deft abracadabra drums
Enchant the patriotic soul –

A grandsire in St. James's Street
Sat at the window of his club,
His second son, shot through the throat,
Slid backwards down a slope of scrub,

Gargled his last breaths, one by one by one,
In too much blood, too good to spill,
Died difficultly, drop by drop by drop –
'By your son's courage, sir, we took the hill.'

WILLIAM PLOMER

Johannesburg

Along the Rand in eighty-five
Fortunes were founded overnight,
And mansions rose among the rocks
To blaze with girls and light;

In champagne baths men sluiced their skins
Grimy with auriferous dust,
Then oiled and scented, fought to enjoy
What young men must;

Took opportunities to cheat,
Or meet the most expensive whore,
And conjured up with cards and dice,
New orgies from new veins of ore;

Greybeards who now look back
To the old days
Find little in their past to blame
And much to praise –

Riding bareback under stars
As lordly anarchs of the veld,
Venison feasts and tribal wars
Free cruelty and a cartridge belt;

Pioneers, O pioneers,
Grey pillars of a Christian State,
Respectability has turned
Swashbuckler prim and scamp sedate;

Prospecting in the brain's recesses
Seek now the nuggets of your prime,
And sift the gold dust of your dreams
From drifted sands of time.

WILLIAM PLOMER

The Devil-Dancers

In shantung suits we whites are cool,
Glasses and helmets censoring the glare;
Fever has made our anxious faces pale,
We stoop a little from the load we bear;

Grouped in the shadow of the compound wall
We get our cameras ready, sitting pensive;
Keeping our distance and our dignity
We talk and smile, though slightly apprehensive.

The heat strikes upwards from the ground,
The ground the natives harden with their feet,
The flag is drooping on its bamboo pole,
The middle distance wavers in the heat.

Naked or gaudy, all agog the crowd
Buzzes and glistens in the sun; the sight
Dazzles the retina; we remark the smell,
The drums beginning, and the vibrant light.

Now the edge of the jungle rustles. In a hush
The crowd parts. Nothing happens. Then
The dancers totter adroitly out on stilts,
Weirdly advancing, twice as high as men.

Sure as fate, strange as the mantis, cruel
As vengeance in a dream, four bodies hung
In cloaks of rasping grasses, turning
Their tiny heads, the masks besmeared with dung;

Each mops and mows, uttering no sound,
Each stately, awkward, giant marionette,
Each printed shadow frightful on the ground
Moving in small distorted silhouette;

The fretful pipes and thinly-crying strings,
The mounting expectation of the drums
Excite the nerves, and stretch the muscles taut
Against the climax – but it never comes;

It never comes because the dance must end
And very soon the dancers will be dead;
We leave by air to-morrow; how
Can ever these messages by us be read?

These bodies hung with viscera and horns
Move with an incomparable lightness,
And through the masks that run with bullocks' blood
Quick eyes look out, dots of fanatic brightness.

Within the mask the face, and moulded
(As mask to face) within the face the ghost,
As in its chrysalis-case the foetus folded
Of leaf-light butterfly. What matters most

When it comes out and we admire its wings
Is to remember where its life began:
Let us take care – that flake of flame may be
The butterfly whose bite can kill a man.

WILLIAM PLOMER

A Transvaal Morning

A sudden waking when a saffron glare
Suffused the room, and sharper than a quince
Two bird-notes penetrated there
Piercing the cloistral deep veranda twice.

The stranger started up to face
The sulphur sky of Africa, an infinite
False peace, the trees in that dry place
Like painted bones, their stillness like a threat.

Shoulders of quartz protruded from the hill
Like sculpture half unearthed; red dust,
Impalpable as cinnamon softly sifted, filled
With heaped-up silence rift and rut.

Again those two keen bird-notes! And the pert
Utterer, a moss-green thrush, was there
In the veranda-cave, alert,
About to flit into the breathless air.

The strangeness plucked the stranger like a string.
'They say this constant sun outstares the mind,
Here in this region of the fang, the sting,
And dulls the eye to what is most defined.

'A wild bird's eye on the *qui vive*
Perhaps makes vagueness clear and staleness new;
If undeceived one might not then deceive;
Let me', he thought, 'attain the bird's-eye view.'

H. C. BOSMAN

Seed

The farmer ploughs into the ground
More than the wheat-seed strewn on the ground
The farmer ploughs into the ground

The plough and the oxen and his body
He ploughs into the ground the farmstead and the cattle
And the pigs and the poultry and the kitchen utensils
And the afternoon sunlight shining into the window panes of the
    voorhuis[1]
And the light entangled in the eyes of his children
He ploughs into the ground his wife's brown body
And the windmill above the borehole
And the borehole and the wind driving the windmill.
The farmer ploughs the blue clouds into the ground;
And as a tribute to the holocaust of the ploughshare –
To the sowing that was the parting of the Juggernaut –
The earth renders the farmer in due season
Corn.

[1]sittingroom

THELMA TYFIELD

I Confess

The day's blond brilliance
Tempts me. Even I
Look out

Through Phoenix-eyes

Calling, from habit, you
You and you.
No replies.

I am old. I confess

The falcon-sun's
Brass plumage
Draggles.

Wildfire dies.

THELMA TYFIELD

Gifts

You bring me (neighbourly)
sprays
of sweet-pea and
jasmine –

bring me (quite
unaware of it)
sprays
of yourself.
The gifts
have sweetened my house
and beckoned all
things – floral and
human – near me.

NOEL BRETTELL

Harvest at Horsebridge, Hampshire

a Rhodesian ruminates

The restless combines fret and clack
Beside the ancient Roman track;
The jigging cutter saws and fusses,
Tosses out the fragrant trusses,
Blocks of odorous masonry
To raise the stack and bed the sty,
And, trampled in the reek of byres
To feed the hungry old desires
Stirring in the womb of earth
Bursting with the green of birth,
To regiment the spears of grain
Along the ancient track again.

Beside the ancient Roman road
The waggoners toss up the load;

The chronicles of fifty farms
Are written large across their back,
And legends live along their arms
And grey eyes under eyebrows black
As conifer or blond as barley,
While consonant and vowel parley
Across the honest Hampshire tongue –
Larynx and lips that could belong
To ealdorman or carl or yeoman
To swarthy sire or flaxen woman –
But not a lineament of the Roman.

How the blind centuries forgot
The terse and close-cropped overlord;
Did he once think how time would rob
The burnish from his idle sword,
When his little hog-maned cob
Jogged his dangling buskined foot
Jogged his clipped unsmiling pate
Through the fluted villa gate:

And while the moody shadows draw
Across the latifundia,
He'd bar the door and chase the damps
And trim the scared reluctant lamps
Along the echoing portico;
And while the draughty tapers dripped
Unrolled the precious manuscript,
Revolving for an hour or so
For bees or beeves some curious plan
Adapted from his Mantuan –
While the cold nostalgia stirs
Through the bright hexameters.

How the bright sun illumines the dark years.
The voltage of the old forgotten storm
Striding the cathodes from the south to north
With instantaneous brilliance split the dark
And caught the wild intruders –
Dirk in the mouth and one leg over the wall:
And did the glimpse suggest, uneasy sir,
That time your tall imperium had bespoke:
Mud in a reedy field at Silchester,
Shards on a shelf in Basingstoke?

It's time to return –
The whistle shrieks across the soaring larks,
The tractor's crimson flames at another turn –
Time to go back, cross the forgotten track;
Back in our exiled southern summer
The monstrous sickles of our question marks
Lay the long swathes the swart sun will burn.
The slow cracks widen in the wall,
The footprints harden in the mud,
And through our sour refusals crawl
The infiltrations of the blood.
The concrete towers fall, the markets topple,
Percentage flounders down to score and dozen,
And through the crevices the arc-lights double
The stares and spears of the barbarian.

O walk across the centuries, my cousin,
My black or pale or tawny antiquarian:
Explore us from your quaint antipodes,
And in your unimaginable matters
Label my mysteries:
My few bright words
My tarnished taps and platters
My potent sulphonamides and frustrated rhyme.
O will they seem so pitiful, wry with rust,
Beneath your alien curiosity?
Deal kindly with me as you sift the dust
And from my story scrape the crust of time.

NOEL BRETTELL

Skid

The back wheels spun and the tall bank
came suddenly to life and leapt upon us
spouted above us like a mounting wave
hung menacing for one congealed second
horribly etched and bright
ragged heraldic clawed and dragon-angry
old Hokusai in a second across league and century ranging

all its eyes stared
the startled martin hung there frozen in flight
we saw his bead of eye his sliver of beak
the strata line of pebbles bared its teeth
the harebell's nod clove frozen to its stem.

Such brightness only lives in ecstasy:
the wheel responds
and hearts slipped back again and grip went slack
and the old ruts stretched out again before us.

R. N. CURREY

Halo

Pastor Mgadi's startling blackness
In my father's study, taking tea,
His smile for me as white as the saucer
Balanced like a privilege on his knee.

Pastor Mgadi in the drab location
Reading his letter by his gap of door;
Waiting by my horse, I watched his pigeons
White as the paper from my father's drawer.

Pastor Mgadi's brilliant blackness
Laughing in the sun by his pigeon-cote,
Wearing his fluttering halo of fantails
White as the celluloid about his throat.

R. N. CURREY

Chosen People: Our History Teacher

Mrs van Rensburg, in her short square person,
Re-lived for us the myths of her dour nation.

Her close-set eyes surveyed, as from a trance,
The history which, she told us, was romance.
It was the Will of God: a small boy's hand
Thrust in a dyke preserved the parent land.
It was the Will of God: the Portuguese
Discerned a rock of hope in stormy seas;
Diaz, da Gama, sailing round the Cape,
Gave the long continent its perfect shape;
Tacked down a carpet to the East, in stages;
Created a round globe in seven pages.

So far the dim, romantic origin –
And then her trumpets blew the Dutchman in!
When Jan van Riebeeck landed to be warden
Of a few cattle and a kitchen-garden,
She stood beside him, privileged to see
In that small bargaining group the land to be;
The Tavern of the Seas, the half-way station,
Hung out as sign a fine new constellation,
The Southern Cross, her focus from now on –
The Great Bear dropped into oblivion.

We saw her bosom rise, her nostrils swell –
And now she welcomed Simon van der Stel;
His exiled Huguenots, their first sour wine,
Were further details in the Grand Design;
The Flying Dutchmen of this coaching stage
Seemed to be blowing in a golden age.
Alas! their white-walled Groot Constantia dream
Was splintered on a clumsy English scheme
To free the slaves, to draw the frontiers in.
She held her shoulders back, thrust out her chin;
Gallows and trust collapsed at Slachter's Nek –
She cursed, and spat, and went with the great Trek.

The great Land-hunger March – the sixteen-spanned
Waggons that pointed to the inner land.
In calico bonnet and complexion-veil
She trudged by hooded wheels that ground a trail
Over the Dragon-passes to the high
Wine-heady emptinesses endlessly
Rolling towards a northern Promised Land –
Met the invading hosts and made her stand.

Like those far dykes with which her ancestors
Had faced the sea, the waggon-rings and squares
Fronted the tide of tribes that crossed the plain –
And she was in the thick of it again,
Packing in thorn-bushes with bleeding hands
Between chain-fastened wheels. And now she stands
Passing the loaded muskets to her men:
Pour in the powder, ram it down, and then
The wad, and last of all the leaden shot –
And now, wet rags because the barrel's hot!
But we had been there with her since the crust
Of the horizon's rim broke into dust:
The running impis with their silver line
Of assegais, their short-shaft discipline,
Striding towards us under plumes of dust;
The great bull's forehead low, his long horns thrust
Curving to right and left to close us in,
The full-chest bellow swelling to a din
That swayed around, above us – nerves like wire
Waiting to see the markings clear – and fire.

She told us how her father once had lain
Hidden, and watched an impi cross the plain:
The mat-boys first, in running rank on rank
With rolled-up mats and cooking-pots, their lank
Long limbs and bodies moving easily –
The squires these, the warriors-to-be;
And then the knights themselves, with shield and spear
And loping ankle-tufted stride, were there.
They passed for hours, ran forty miles that day –
And won a battle at the end – he'd say.

Mrs van Rensburg had us with her there;
She lifted loaded muskets till her hair
Fell from its pins about her glowing face –
She stopped the war to put it back in place.

> Old Colley had his try
> Of course he had to die;
> No Englishman shall ever cross the Vaal!

She did *not* have me with her when she fought
A British column ambushed in some poort
Or helped to stalk them on Majuba Hill –
Crouching behind their beards they reached the rim

To find the naked square drawn up for them –
The graves of Colley's men are white there still!

Or when she side-slipped continents and read
Of 'British regulars' who 'fired and fled'
At Lexington, from Longfellow's *Paul Revere;*
But when her history had come this far
God's will, romance and documents were one;
There was no pardon underneath the sun
For any side but God's. I jibbed once more
When she was *veldkornet* in Kruger's war:

> Joubert and his sons
> Kruger and his guns
> No Englishmen shall ever cross the Vaal!

Still in my mind her monologue of wrongs
Is mingled with the words of burger songs
In Dutch and English – making clear
That words, like blood, can mingle and cohere.

> *Hoera ! Hoera ! Die burgers het gestaan*
> *Die Engels wil die* franchise *hê*
> *En* Equal Rights *daarby*[1]
> No Englisman shall ever cross the Vaal!

[1] Hurrah! Hurrah! the burgers stood their ground,
The English want the franchise
And Equal Rights as well.

R. N. CURREY

Remembering Snow

To-day I think of a boy in the Transvaal
Spending his Christmas Day at the krantzes
Where the khaki drought of veld, cleft open,
Held festivals of water in a fern-green canyon.

We dived fork-naked into crystal pools,
Explored behind the maidenhair waterfalls,
Eating our Christmas pudding beneath the grace
Of feminine willows on the vivid grass.

My mother lured the pony with lumps of sugar;
We coaxed him into his creaking cat's-cradle of leather,
My father, all that tawny homeward run,
Remembering snow as I remember the sun.

NORMAN DE LA HARPE

It's No Good Looking at Lovely Women

It's no good looking at lovely women like
Peaches behind plate-glass.

It's no good if they walk about on limbs
Soft as the flesh of pears:
Ordained ripeness accurately shaped.
No good.

Sit still. Tune your heart to listen.
For she is also a song;
Also half the universe.

Then only, my fine Cockalorum,
Then only
Wonder links the gapped selves

And loneliness heals

And wings fold.

ADÈLE NAUDÉ

Memling's Virgin with Apple

She is a person here in her own right.
This one forgets when the Child, the three wise men,
holy angels and shepherds share the light

with her. So often she's but part of the composition,
part of the scene.
                  But here she's the centrepiece.
There's a Child, it's true, reaching a hand
for a glossy apple and rich embroideries
on His cushion. There's a cameo of a distant land.
But the landscape's far away, the trees
fading from the picture, the towers of the town
withdrawing themselves. The Child one hardly sees
although He is near. It is the blue of her gown
with the jewels, twin rivers of hair
held with a pearl-starred coronet, the glow
of the red cloak, the flowing hands. All is there
of purity in the lowered lids, the wide brow.

But there's a detachment and a strange withdrawal,
an aloneness in her serenity
taking her far away from us. It's unusual,
for mothers holding their children are not easily
disentangled. But she was different, I know.
There was no one quite like her. That's why,
Perhaps, the painter depicted her so –
a mother, but aloof, made lonely by the high
rôle she was playing. Special people would be
like that – kings and queens and very great
artists. Perhaps in this moment she,
for the first time, realizes her state
of separation. She was engaged before
with His hourly needs and the unfolding wonder
of motherhood. But here He is wanting more,
for He's older, wanting the shining object beyond her.
From this moment in the picture, onwards, her road
will be skirting the market-places, the cheering,
gossipy exchanges where a load
of strangeness might be lightened in the sharing.
From now onwards her state will be a lonely one
all through her life and when the chapter ends
in darkness, she'll stand with the other Marys, alone
and weeping in a wilderness of friends.

ELISABETH EYBERS

Narrative

A woman grew, with waiting, over-quiet.
The earth along its spiralled path was spun
through many a day and night, now green, now dun;
at times she laughed, and then, at times, she cried.

The years went by. By turns she woke and slept
through the long hours of night, but every day
she went, as women go, her casual way,
and no one knew what patient tryst she kept.

Hope and despair tread their alternate round
and merge into acceptance, till at length
the years have only quietness in store.

And so at last the narrative has found
in her its happy end: this tranquil strength
is better than the thing she's waiting for.

CHARLES MADGE

Delusions VIII

Placed in a country on a desert verging
But under southern skies, richer in stars,
I spent my solitary years observing
Their forms, more bright and numerous than ours.

They date from childhood, and the first dissection,
The bleached skull and the spiny xerophyte,
Those tastes, which taking gradual direction
With more mature experience unite.

My voyage in the ocean, where the lead
Was dropped into an unknown gulf profound
Explained some features of the secret bed:
In those domains I was the first to sound.

CHARLES MADGE

Obsessional

No justice can be done
To the sunlost tribes
Where they sit musing
In their stony arbours

Whose brains are yolks
The ages have matured
Into their existence
As selfish primaries

Communications for them
Link up their eyes
Those stones that gaze
In unrestricted emptiness

The rule of myriads
The counting of souls
The range of classes
Absorption of being

On their forked brows
Hunger and lightning
Reveal the mountain
Of the supersensible.

H. I. E. DHLOMO

Chorus from the Past

Sweet are these dales,
These lucent vales!
Beauteous the flowers
Like lingering hours
Of dreamful thought
With visions caught!

Here are no tears,
No haunting fears.
Tall men rise up
To fill the cup
Of joy and wine,
To dance and dine.
Warm shines the sun
On skins all dun
And beautiful,
With health ripe full.
Here pleiades
Pour song and ease.
This land of hills
    (Praise!)
And leaping rills!
    (Praise it!)
This land which fills
    (Sing!)
With joy that kills
    (Sing it!)
By loving arts
All evil hearts.
Here is no strife,
No vices rife.
In harmony
Dwell such as we.
We seek no gains
And know no pains.
But Beauty bred,
On love and truth
And goodness fed,
We keep our youth.
Our virgin maids
Pursue no trades
Of sin and shame;
They love the name
Of purity!
And youth is free,
Not bound in chains
Of greed, but trains
To do its part.
All labour's art!
Art love, love truth –
Eternal Youth!

199096

Our race feels young!
Great and far-flung
Our Rule will be
When we rise free
From 'prentice long
To sing our Song
Of manhood strong!

F. T. PRINCE

The Babiaantje

Hither, where tangled thickets of the acacia
Wreathed with a golden powder, sigh
And when the boughs grow dark, the hoopoe
Doubles his bell-like cry,
Spreading his bright striped wings and brown crest
Under a softening spring sky, –
I have returned because I cannot rest,
And would not die.

Here it was as a boy that, I remember,
I wandered ceaselessly, and knew
Sweetness of spring was in the bird's cry,
And in the hidden dew
The unbelievable keen perfume
Of the Babiaantje, a pale blue
Wild hyacinth that between narrow grey leaves
On the ground grew.

The flower will be breathing there now, should I wish
To search the grass beneath those trees,
And having found it, should go down
To snuff it, on my knees.
But now, although the crested hoopoe
Calls like a bell, how barren these
Rough ways and dusty woodlands look to one
Who has lost youth's peace!

F. T. PRINCE

False Bay

She I love leaves me and I leave my friends
In the dusky capital where I spent two years
In the cultivation of divinity.
Sitting beside my window above the sea
In this unvisited land I feel once more
How little ingenious I am. The winter ends,
The seaward slopes are covered to the shore
With a press of lilies that have silver ears.
And although I am perplexed and sad I say
'Now indulge in no dateless lamentations;
Watch only across the water the lapsed nations
And the fisherman twitch a boat across the bay.'

F. T. PRINCE

In a Province

Because of the memory of one we held dear
Call to mind where she lived and the ruins there
Among the silken shrubs. I have dismounted where
Her children played and watch the pale sky grow clear.

And as for me, standing between the silken shrub and the broom
And tasting the breath of the blue sage, I must stay
Though my friends are setting out with the first of the day
And they murmur to me, 'Do not linger in that gloom,
Remember that tears make whole the heart.' But I say
'Is there nowhere I may rest among the shells
Of the ruins and the droppings of white gazelles?
However brief my hours are, I would delay.'

The tears that fall from my eyes have wet my hands
Holding the reins of my horse. How many hours
Were sweet to me because of women! These showers
Bring to my mind that day among pale sands,

101

Call to mind how one came with me unwillingly
On an evening warm as another country's noons
And all seemed of long ago among those dunes
And under a clear sky, under a clear green sky.

F. T. PRINCE

To a Man on his Horse

Only the Arab stallion will I
Envy you. Along the water
You dance him with the morning on his flanks.
In the frosty morning that his motions flatter
He kindles, and where the winter's in the wood,
I watch you dance him out on delicate shanks.
And lashes fall on a dark eye,
He sheds a silvery mane, he shapes
His thin nostrils like a fop's.
And to do honour to his whiteness
In remembrance of his ancient blood,
I have wished to become his groom,
And so his smouldering body comb
In a simple and indecorous sweetness.

F. T. PRINCE

The Moonflower

The secret drops of love run through my mind:
Midnight is filled with sounds of the full sea
That has risen softly among the rocks;
Air stirs the cedar-tree.

Somewhere a fainting sweetness is distilled.
It is the moonflower hanging in its tent
Of twisted broad-leaved branches by the stony path
That squanders the cool scent.

Pallid, long as a lily, it swings a little
As if drunk with its own perfume and the night,
Which draws its perfume out and leaves the flower
The weaker for its flight.

Detached from my desires, in an oblivion
Of this world that surrounds me, in weariness
Of all but darkness, silence, starry solitude
I too feel that caress –

Delicate, serene and lonely, peaceful, strange
To the intellect and the imagination,
The touch with which reality wounds and ravishes
Our inmost desolation:

All being like the moonflower is dissatisfied
For the dark kiss that the night only gives,
And night gives only to the soul that waits in longing,
And in that only lives.

F. T. PRINCE

Soldiers Bathing

The sea at evening moves across the sand.
Under a reddening sky I watch the freedom of a band
Of soldiers who belong to me. Stripped bare
For bathing in the sea, they shout and run in the warm air;
Their flesh worn by the trade of war, revives
And my mind towards the meaning of it strives.

All's pathos now. The body that was gross,
Rank, ravenous, disgusting in the act or in repose,
All fever, filth and sweat, its bestial strength
And bestial decay, by pain and labour grows at length
Fragile and luminous. 'Poor bare forked animal',
Conscious of his desires and needs and flesh that rise and fall,
Stands in the soft air, tasting after toil
The sweetness of his nakedness: letting the sea-waves coil
Their frothy tongues about his feet, forgets

His hatred of the war, its terrible pressure that begets
A machinery of death and slavery,
Each being a slave and making slaves of others: finds that he
Remembers lovely freedom in a game
Mocking himself, and comically mimics fear and shame.

He plays with death and animality.
And reading in the shadows of his pallid flesh, I see
The idea of Michelangelo's cartoon
Of soldiers bathing, breaking off before they were half done
At some sortie of the enemy, an episode
Of the Pisan wars with Florence. I remember how he showed
Their muscular limbs that clamber from the water,
And heads that turn across the shoulder, eager for the slaughter,
Forgetful of their bodies that are bare,
And hot to buckle on and use the weapons lying there.
– And I think too of the theme another found
When, shadowing men's bodies on a sinister red ground,
Another Florentine, Pollaiolo,
Painted a naked battle: warriors, straddled, hacked the foe,
Dug their bare toes into the ground and slew
The brother-naked man who lay between their feet and drew
His lips back from his teeth in a grimace.

They were Italians who knew war's sorrow and disgrace
And showed the thing suspended, stripped: a theme
Born out of the experience of war's horrible extreme
Beneath a sky where even their air flows
With *lacrimae Christi*. For that rage, that bitterness, those blows,
That hatred of the slain, what could it be
But indirectly or directly a commentary
On the Crucifixion? And the picture burns
With indignation and pity and despair by turns,
Because it is the obverse of the scene
Where Christ hangs murdered, stripped, upon the Cross. I mean,
That is the explanation of its rage.

And we too have our bitterness and pity that engage
Blood, spirit, in this war. But night begins,
Night of the mind: who nowadays is conscious of our sins?
Though every human deed concerns our blood,
And even we must know, that nobody has understood,
That some great love is over all we do,
And that is what has driven us to this fury, for so few

Can suffer all the terror of that love:
The terror of that love has set us spinning in this groove
Greased with our blood.
                              These dry themselves and dress,
Combing their hair, forget the fear and shame of nakedness.
Because to love is frightening we prefer
The freedom of our crimes. Yet, as I drink the dusky air,
I feel a strange delight that fills me full,
Strange gratitude, as if evil itself were beautiful,
And kiss the wound in thought, while in the west
I watch a streak of red that might have issued from Christ's breast.

NORMAN CLOTHIER

Confession

Yes, I have killed
And I was wild with pride
And anger as they died.
High exultation filled
My heart and head like wine
With the sweet savage glory of success
And surging thankfulness
The forfeit was their lives, not mine.

And when I soberly surveyed
The things of silent horror they became,
Dead in the sunshine, things that I had made,
No pity stirred in me, I felt no shame.
Coldly I looked at them and coldly thought,
'This is the end to which their striving led.
These were my enemies. We fought.
I live and they are dead.'

NORMAN CLOTHIER

Zero Hour

Above us in the mist our shells
Tear at the slopes whose summit we must climb
Up to the silent spandaus and grenades
That wait for us. Perhaps this time –
Well there's no future in the thought.
It's so long since I dared to think or feel
Disuse has almost atrophied my nerves.
It's better so. No need to conceal
My glum reluctance for the task ahead
And all the shoddy senseless tasks of war.
I gave them pride and courage once, but now –
I've done it all so many times before . . .

CHARLES EGLINGTON

The Vanquished

With treble vivas and limp hedgerow flags
The children welcome us: again we meet
The fearful sons and daughters of defeat.
And through the town our dull compassion drags
The scarecrow of our greeting.
                              Brown-eyed brat,
Your dusty face and sapless, sapling limbs
Start in my blood a wave of anger that
Breaks hotly on my eyes in spray that dims
Your hungry, haunted smile but cannot drown
The image of a child you bring to mind
Who might be mine: If ever, thin and brown,
She, too, must some day wait to find
Bread and forgiveness on the conquerors' way,
May they advance defeated – as today.

CHARLES EGLINGTON

Meeting

Confederates in this white field –
Our callings are allied – we will
Lie in rough comradeship until
Our flesh and spirit softly yield.

Then as your natural sympathy
Meets mine, the fierce caress
Is warm with sudden tenderness
And pacifies us utterly.

The unfamiliar room grows warm
As our heat radiates; the rain
Sobs like desire on the pane;
We rock together in the storm . . . .

Until exhaustion stills us. First
You, falling suddenly asleep
On my slack arm, I plunging deep
Into the filled pool of my thirst,

And waking, later, find the chill
War-haunted city in the room:
And we, the spectres of its gloom,
Apart and yet together still.

Your naked breasts, untenderly
Loved, lie abandoned, but your face
Is tired and gentle with such grace
As I had never thought to see.

Madonna of the one-night bed,
Between revulsion and desire
I touch the limbs I have on hire
And stroke your tousled head.

But sleep divides us, so I muse:
Perhaps in every war it's we
Who in our love alone are free,
With least to win and least to lose.

CHARLES EGLINGTON

Cheetah

Indolent and kitten-eyed,
This is the bushveld's innocent –
The stealthy leopard parodied
With grinning, gangling pup-content.

Slouching through the tawny grass
Or loose-limbed lolling in the shade,
Purring for the sun to pass
And build a twilight barricade

Around the vast arena where,
In scattered herds, his grazing prey
Do not suspect in what wild fear
They'll join with him in fatal play;

Till hunger draws slack sinews tight
And vibrant as a hunter's bow:
Then, like a fleck of mottled light,
He slides across the still plateau.

A tremor rakes the herds: they scent
The pungent breeze of his advance;
Heads rear and jerk in vigilant
Compliance with the game of chance

In which, of thousands, only one
Is centred in the cheetah's eye;
They wheel and then stampede, for none
Knows which it is that has to die.

His stealth and swiftness fling a noose
And as his loping strides begin
To blur with speed, he ropes the loose
Buck on the red horizon in.

CHARLES EGLINGTON

Old Prospector

Old men with eyes like his are right to claim
They know the country better than the palms
Of their own hands: they are not eyes that seek
The eagle's view, to read in distances
The cantos of a continent: they are
Diviner's eyes that read in cryptic signs
The formula for rich discoveries:
A scale of lichen or a patch of moss,
A rocky outcrop, the minute
Activity of ants, a garnet chip –
The small things, close to earth, that other men
Think trivial or do not see.

I ask him and he tells me: 'Over there
There should be diamonds . . .;' then falls silent, for
He has no language to explain the signs –
And he is secretive: his singleness
Has made him inarticulate, and shy
Of those who do not share the veld's
Arcana; yet his tongue that hesitates,
And stumbles over simple words to tell
His simple science, can roll lustrous nouns
And adjectives (as he would roll
The iridescent gems in his rough hand)
To voice his solitary life-long love.

CHARLES EGLINGTON

Rocks

Below me on the beach
The waves write, scramble and rewrite
Their rocky syllables;
They leave no final word,
No testament.

Those I remember best –
Who went from other beaches to their end –
Wrote, scrambled and rewrote
My generation's page
In rocky vocables.

I have remembered them too long
For peace or resolution:
What they knew and wrote
Upon the living rock
Time, like the sea, abrades.

Nerved by the alcohol of height,
As I look down
My resolution hardens; and the waves
Write, scramble and erase
The rocky syllables.

C. LOUIS LEIPOLDT

The Zombie

His face was like a bleached bone
    The desert wind unsands,
And cold and white, like marble stone,
    Were both his mummied hands.

His eyes were clouded like the eyes
    Of fish no longer fresh;
No glint of anger or surprise
    Within their depths did flash.

Heedless like a noctambulant
    He passed along his way,
And little children as he went
    Ran crying in from play.

The women crossed themselves and held
    Their eyes upon the ground,
Until his passing had dispelled
    The fear his presence found.

And old men, very close to death,
  But still afraid to die,
Gabbled a spell beneath their breath,
  Until he had passed by.

Only the stranger, unaware
  Of evil's awful might,
Looked at him with a curious stare,
  And wondered at the sight,

And asked a native lad who ran
  Some twilight tryst to keep,
'What is that dreadful-looking man
  Who walks as if asleep?'

With startled glance the home-born youth
  Spoke with averted head,
As if he feared to tell the truth,
  'A Zombie, sir,' he said.

I went into a crowded hall,
  And heard an old man speak
Of ending wars, 'which, after all,
  Were hopeless for the weak.'

With an old man's garrulity
  He glibly drooled along.
The future, so he said, would be
  Made peaceful by the strong.

All little nations would obey
  The greater ones above.
The greater ones would have their say,
  And rule the world by love.

I whispered to my neighbour man
  (Who seemed to pray or weep),
'What is this awful charlatan
  Who talks as if asleep?'

Tear-stained bi-focals fixed my eyes;
  He slowly shook his head,
And whispered back in mild surprise,
  'A Statesman, sir,' he said.

JACK COPE

from **Maríe**

*In the 300th year of our nationhood the origin of the race is described;
Our founder, Jan van Riebeeck, an official; The growth of the race
and its components; A belief which may do injustice to the great
Official; How an historic controversy arose and the decision to settle
it; The Country renamed.*

Our dawn three Centuries ago
Sing Muse! the trippling measures flow!
Frill out our immemorial span,
That age since history began;
For arts and culture must agree
In policy, like Emperor Chi
Who sanely had the books destroyed,
That, till Van Riebeeck, all was void.

Vast clashed the universal Night,
Worlds reeled as drunken soldiers fight,
And then the gods vouchsafed some light,
Raised mountains from the Ocean floor
And Jan van Riebeeck stepped ashore.
(Our private legend of creation
Is rightly hazy by tradition.)

In colonies Jan was no novice
For first he built himself an office;
His needs were water and green veg
And round his plot he grew a hedge.
But from his garden Jan soon sallies
To pick the pockets of the valleys:
Earth, erven, drostdys, farms and rocks,
While Hottentots picked up the pox.
Mercy had lent his gentle heart
Some wisdom in the healing art,
For many ills he knew the answer,
To leech a vein or lance a cancer;
Blood to the elbows, he'd begin
To saw a sailor's mangled shin,
But should the races choose to mix
Alas! that break he could not fix.

An Ishmael true to prophesy
In wastes his seed did multiply,
And morgens filled with sturdy sons
Armed with their Bibles and their guns.
Some were great hunters, steely-eyed,
Others as jacks-in-office vied,
Some were bards or on ramkies[1] twanged,
Some warred, some whored and some were hanged.
The tribes still came and still they grew:
Tough Dutchman, Englishman and Jew,
Malayans, Zulus, Huguenots,
And how they came, or why, God knows.

The legend runs Jan never died
But rose, like Nepos, deified
In swift promotion great and glorious
Till high in Heaven like Pretoria's
Proud Departmental heads he sits,
The god of servants and slow wits;
And on some koppie's drilled and cut rocks
A chair is burnished by his buttocks.

In time, the Nation's literati
Fell out in feuds of blood and party:
The one side grasped for the sole right
To favours in the idol's sight
Thus owning it was no obsession
That God's a national possession;
The other held *all* should be free
(Except the great majority)
To lay a dutiful oblation
Before the Founder of the Nation,
As if to say he was as much
A Saxon hero as a Dutch.
From editors' and learned chairs,
From pulpits and from Brothers' lairs
Shouts rose, authorities declaimed,
So, with hot heads still more inflamed
No mightier battles raged round Ilion
And words fell slaughtered by the million . . .

But first with general acclaim
It was resolved by all debaters
To give the land a fitter name
In keeping with her classic status . . .

For seven days the savants sucked
Their thumbs, their hair and eyebrows plucked
And chewed their nails and picked their noses,
So grave the stress that thought imposes,
But though they knew this labour vital
Not one could frame a worthy title.
They pored through books of ancient cultures
And watched the ominous flight of vultures;
One analysed a dead goat's guts,
Another wrote to Marshal Smuts.
With bones, horoscopes and black magic
Their impotence assumed the tragic:
Then Prestwick, passing their enclosure,[2]
Said smiling: Call the land EROSIA![3]

Dumb with amazement, numbly wrung
With pleasure the professors flung
Their bays from shining brows to greet
Their master, prostrate at his feet.
But he escaped, not being in mind
For suffocation from their kind.

One Savant set himself to prove
The title claimed the God of Love –
Where none fear over-population
Love brings eternal generation
And makes the Kalahari teem,
Breeding like frogs in every stream;
And love inclines the gentle Boer
Towards his British conqueror;
Love knits the burgesses of Durban
With the dark wearers of the turban
The flame that every heart imbrues
Endears the Burger to the Jews
And in beloved harmony
The Black man *passes* with the free.
Enfranchised from the curse of Babel
Our leaders build, well found and stable,
The multi-tribal Continent
With love's strong binding for cement.

A second thought the name implied
The praise of heroes, the due pride
A noble generation places

Sprung from a line of mighty races.
A Third, whose brain was scored and wrecked
With endless cycles of neglect,
Complained that Prestwick might have chosen
A name less prompted by erosion.

None heard; a great philologist
Was charged in the national interest
To probe in etymologies
Erosia's roots and pedigrees
And bring the work to public ears
With all dispatch in fifty years:
Meanwhile the clamour rings: Farewell
South Africa – Erosia hail!

[1]home-made guitar
[2]Mr. Prestwick was the wit who coined this sonorous title impromptu during a so-called 'brains trust', thus by a single shaft of humour saving a tedious parlour game from complete boredom.
[3]'Erosia.' *Pro Patria, inversique mores !* – Horace.
  (O name of country once how sacred deemed,
  O sad reverse of manners, once esteemed.) (Cope's notes – Eds.)

ELIAS PATER

from Coons Carnival

When I was young and my father still alive,
He used to take me to see the Malay brides
Being driven around in an open coach,
Drawn by four white horses, from the palm-trees
In Long Street, all the way across the town;
Then we'd walk along, strolling, to the Pier.

Younger folk have not heard about the Pier:
It has disappeared these many years;
But I recall with ease the old fakir,
Bearded and turbaned, squatting at the entrance,
Playing his bulbous pipe to a swaying cobra,
Whose nether part lay coiled up in black coils
At the bottom of a broad wicker-basket.
From where he sat, one could hear the band,

When the wind blew in the right direction,
Blaring over the bay from the band-stand;
Or watch the tide suck at the mussel-covered pillars
Of the jetty. In the pull and splashing
Of those dark-green waters, I recognized
A world which was certainly not me.
Behind us rose the grey bulk of Table Mountain,
Majestic background for the rest of his life
To the dreams of any boy born in its shadow . . .

ELIAS PATER

My Grandmother

The servant-girl found her in the morning,
The bottle of heart-pills clasped in her hands,
Empty. It was the Feast of Our Lady's entry
Into Heaven and Her Crowning by God.

Perhaps the meaning of the omen was
That She, who deigned to speak to Bernadette
In patois, leaned forward to welcome her
With a smile and a greeting, in Yiddish.

ELIAS PATER

The Poets

I have often taken down old volumes
From long shelves crowded with conversations
That have ceased, the interlocutors now
Standing stiffly side by side, in silence.

But these others, they quarrelled with themselves
About terrible things like love and death;
And you can hear their passionate murmur
Inside the covers, like bees in a hive.

ELIAS PATER

The Damned

Man: Oh! voice of one weeping in the desert,
       Before you fade, leaving behind a stillness
       As extended as the moonlit sands,
       What word have you to offer to a man
       Who has strayed to the boundaries of the camp
       At evening, to meditate by the well?

Voice: I lost myself in the place where I lived,
       Because I did not overflow my place

       I lost myself in the time I lived,
       Because I did not lord over my time

       I wandered in the maze of the multiple,
       Mislaying the ancient map to singleness

       I lost my soul, because I judged it right
       To place bounds on possibility.

           Now I go weeping to a place
           No stream, no desire overflows

           I go weeping into a time
           Whose moments tighten like a noose

           I go to be separated
           Into pieces without centre

           I go to where possibility
           Is caged in these three burning hoops.

ELIAS PATER

Silence

Your throne is amongst the stars;
    It glitters quietly;
It has grown very lovely
    In my sight.

Your haze hangs over deserts
    And remote hills;
There you may be seen abroad
    Only at dawn.

You swell strangely-shaped boulders
    With hardness from within,
To resist intrusion
    Into your privacy.

You dwell in ocean depths,
    Where fish glide in darkness,
Like ships at night whose portholes
    Are all lit up.

Your delicacy is extreme,
    Fragile as glass;
A dove taking to wing
    Could break it.

You are also sacred;
    Perhaps you are God!
Since your friends are so few,
    Count me among them.

ELIAS PATER

The Stranger

You spoke forcibly to the company,
Though it seemed you sounded too emphatic
Dwelling heavily on your certitudes;
The Stranger remained silent to the end.

He was en route to where the high mountain
Signs a new alliance with the sky,
And rock-born streams clothe the desert sand
In striped robes of fresh significance.

He left us when the wild bird cried in passing.
You remain to praise professionally
The static beauties of a marble shrine,
Lying in a white dream under moonlight.

ELIAS PATER

Lemon Tree

For twelve years you have stood outside my window
Under a sky persistently seeming,
Beneath stars I could blow out with a breath;
Now I bring you into my room, beside
A table loaded with too many books,
To remind me of the earth your roots embrace
While I pretend to be busy reading;
The raging storms which beat your bare branches
While I sit snug behind thick walls watching;
And the flood rolling down yellow nuggets,
So to be held in your green estuaries,
That young girls stop in summer pleading:
'Please let me pick a lemon, please, just one!'

ELIAS PATER

The Generations

The way the young pause in distant respect
When you enter the room which had been yours –

The way it will be taken for granted
That you cannot understand their patois –

The way their eyes will fill with a faint stare
When you mention a once reigning poet –

The way they reduce to oblivion
All that your contemporaries had known

Of suffering and love, of hot debate
And times of creative development –

The way they ignore the family secrets,
How the passing Angel of Destruction

Found no red paschal sign on the lintel –
How like they are to what you once had been.

119

ELIAS PATER

St Thérèse of Lisieux

You would not have traded that moment
For an empire, tending a hand
To steady the gait of an old nun –
Acts to measure against Death,
Or other profound abysses;
But what could I pretend to know
Of such extreme tenderness,
Whom no young god has ever kissed.

Bathed and perfumed, like Esther,
With oil of myrrh, and spices, and lotions,
You step into the perfect garden,
Where peacocks rustle their thousand-eyed tails.
There Ahasuerus waits for you.

Let me therefore sing your soul's beauty,
The scalloped shell upon a mythic sea
Holding love aloft in full panoply;
So shall I deepen all my meanings,
For what may poets add to the rose,
Except its red engender song.

ANTHONY DELIUS

The Gamblers

The Coloured long-shore fishermen unfurl
their nets beside the chilly and unrested sea,
and in their heads the little dawn-winds whirl
some scraps of gambling, drink and lechery.

Barefoot on withered kelp and broken shell,
they toss big baskets on the bitter turf,
then with a gambler's bitter patience still
slap down their wagering boat upon the surf.

Day flips a golden coin – but they mock it.
With calloused, careless hands they reach
deep down into the sea's capacious pocket
and pile their silver chips upon the beach.

ANTHONY DELIUS

Emerald Dove

The Xhosa say
When the emerald dove
Sits sobbing in the bush
She is thinking of the terrible wars
And she cries
My father is dead
My mother is dead
My sisters are dead
My brothers are all dead
And my heart goes
Doem Doem
Doem doem doem doem
doem
doem.

ANTHONY DELIUS

Deaf-and-dumb School

On the black tarmac playground dark
Nuns, a white statue of the Virgin watch
Bare feet of the muted children jerk
And scuffle over endless silence. Such

Is their element. Though I have heard
Them flute like evening swallows in the sky
The sounds were sad, irrelevant, absurd
And could not pierce the silences of play,

Nor break the glass that frames their world.
A soundless quality of painting grips
A small boy leaning from a bench enthralled
In thoughts that dance on other finger-tips.

One with the cry and stiffness of a crane
Dances before a dumb-struck clientele,
Beyond, some cheerless footballers bemoan
A speechless player's bungled goal.

And all around communication glimmers
From hand to eye, and each attentive face
Turns to a dream of mimicry and mummers,
Like songless planets signalling through space.

Sound there is, but silence underlies
The fire-flies of gesture. One cannot catch
Exactly what the muffled outcry says,
Or what it is the nuns and children watch.

Silence like a window shows the room
Of minds that make their signs and mouth their cries,
But what leans out to touch you from the dream
Only the white statue and the darkness realise.

ANTHONY DELIUS

These Million English

from **The Last Division**

These million English are a vague communion
Indifferent to leadership or goal,
Their most accomplished children flee the Union,
Search other countries for their cause and soul,
And to the pioneer premise of their fathers
Add on no better moral, finer story,
Leave our crude glaring sun and savage weathers
To bask, reflect in other people's glory.
Most able men, not all, who stay behind
Fix loyalty to man upon shareholders,
The other whites are voters of a kind

And blacks are some statistics in their folders.
Man may diminish while they make their pile,
Black generations brew in new diseases,
What if the legislation stinks of guile?
What? If the supertax reduction pleases . . . .
Their language is looked after by the Jews,
Their politics thought out by Afrikaners,
Their colleges embalm enlightened views,
While they get on with business and gymkanas.

ANTHONY DELIUS

The Ethnic Anthem

from **The Last Division**

'Ethnasia will last a thousand years,
Our land is studded with its glories,
Its monuments are separate bars
And segregated lavatories.
'God has through us ordained it so!
Post Offices are split in two
And separate pillar boxes fix
That correspondence does not mix,
No-one has ever managed better
To guard the spirit – and the letter.

'On ethnic trains and buses daily hurry
Divided hues to earn divided bread,
The races may not fornicate or marry;
They even lie apart when they are dead.

'God may award his just damnation
For mixed or unmixed fornication;
Down here we warn the citizen
With whom it is a crime to sin,
And no man takes, with our cognizance,
A liberty without a licence.

'Yea, in our law men stand or fall
By rule of thumb or finger-nail;
So sensitive's our Roman-Dutch
It notes if lips protrude too much.

'We've split all difference so fine –
No wider than a hair or skin, –
To foil the trick of traits and needs
So shockingly the same inbreeds –
For such success in our researches
We thank Thee, Lord, in separate churches.

'How wondrous is our work, our way,
And thine as well, Great Separator,
Who separating night from day
Left us to sort the rest out later.'

ANTHONY DELIUS

Distance

The Gods of Africa regard me
From the edge of my suburban lawn.
They have the tall thick legs of tree-trunks,
And tiny white faces of the stars.

I do not grovel at their sprouting toes,
But stand in my Euclidian door
And hope the centuries of grass
Are far too wide to leap across.

ANTHONY DELIUS

from Black South Easter

But Makana[1] fluttered a hand, tapering
And delicate as a bat's wing, brushed
Woltemade[2] lightly on the sleeve,
And said, 'My friend, the blow, the spear,
The heart, cannot ignore the wind
That blows from ancestors to the unborn.

124

There are those who must sit still
And hear what the wind will bring
Under the sky, or the hut's thatch.
To one searching the earth or entrails
The inwardness of the Great Spirit then,
And for time to come, is made plain.
To be brave without this truth of time
Is to be an elephant approaching a game-pit,
Suddenly his world is gone from under him . . . .
When first I saw the sea,
And how it ended in a white unrest,
It seemed to me a sickness, a leprosy
Gnawing inward at the edge of our country.
The bony sand was edged with bush,
A brow the vultures had picked clean
Of flesh. Even the rivers ended
Like the dead, their mouths stopped up
With sand. Three days I watched
The spirits rising from the trembling water,
Going inland over the bush,
Over the crouching thousands of my people.
Three days I listened while the sea
Spoke with its ceaseless spirit's voice,
Until I knew the words within it.
Far as the gulls I heard the cry
Of women, the soft sound of assegais
Sighing in the air to break on stone.
On grey rocks I saw the broken
Shells, the huts burst open
To the sun, and all their dark life
Withered beneath the roofless light.
Was it a woman's or a child's cry, I heard?
The pale spirits crossed the path
From sea to land, from sea to land
Steadily as a great white army
Slipping inland. I was no more to them
Than a single berry of buck's dung.
On the third day I stood up and shouted,
'Hear me! Go back to the sea!'
Makana, the crafty, the left-handed, would
Shrivel their dampness in a Karoo-wind
Hissing with tongues of a thousand heated
Spears, trap them in the hot bush,
In the mountains, in the steep green valleys.

I, Makana, was the land
And all its people . . . Oh that laughter!
That laughter followed me, 'Ha-ha',
A far-off laughter in the plains,
A sudden laughter from behind a stone
Rang around the hills and in the forests.
The courage, numbers, manhood, hope
Of warriors grew sapless as millet
In drought, and rustled with a dry despair.
The smoke had a smell not known before.
We whispered that our foes had powders far
More powerful than mine. Were they ghosts?
Does a ghost smell? These beings
Stank if we crept close enough
To see them sweating from their fiery faces.
And when they died, the fire died
And left a face of ash behind.
Like ash was this powder in which their power
Lay waiting, waiting till it burst
Out laughing and we died. The smell
Was never of rain flowering in the dust,
To promise life, but sharper, as of lightning
Splitting a green tree, a rock,
Sperming the raped earth, with a molten
Egg of death. And our hearts were raped.
All my witchcraft could do nothing
To stop it. Nothing. I went to the Whites
Saying, 'Kill Makana, for his people.
Your God gave up his Son,
And I have boasted that I was the people.
Let the vultures turn me into dung.'

'They took me away to that flat island
Across the sea from a flat mountain,
A place of seals, lepers, madmen . . . .
All day I watched the spirits
Going inland over the mountain,
Endlessly over the mountain and inland.
Many would watch as their hearts withered.
'Xhosa, the rain is theirs!' I cried.
'Do not let its plenty deceive you.
Its overflow will drown the Ancestors'
Graves, the cattle, the Great Places,
The huts on the green hill-tops

And fields blanketing the valley sides,
A flood swilling all to the sea.
This rain is the sea-python's spittle.'

'Despair bore hope, and a plot.
One day we rowed for the rocky shore,
But the sea had another way for me.
It dragged me down from my last day
To a green world. My shouting blood
Became a cool and tranquil silence.
Now I do not know what to say
Of prophecy. For forty warring years
My people remembered me. A girl[3] foretold
The sun's madness, my return and triumph.
This hope made its own drought,
The herds lay with bone faces,
The unreturning Ancestors were left
With villages of white skulls for descendants.
The past destroyed itself in a dream:
The Xhosa grew tamer than their cattle
For a century . . . . Perhaps in their secret places
They wanted this yoke, and powers they knew
Were greater than mine. Prophecy knows
Only half the truth, the other
Lies in those coming after.
Who would give a piece of meat
For a prophet's kaross? . . . .'
                              He looked away
Eastwards searching a remembered valley
For lost followers.

[1]Makana (Links – the left handed) (d. 1820) Xhosa prophet and leader. After the failure of the attack on Grahamstown in 1819, he surrendered and was imprisoned on Robben Island. He was drowned while attempting to swim to the mainland. For more than fifty years his followers refused to believe that he was dead.

[2]Woltemade, Wolraad. Cape Dutch farmer who was drowned while rescuing the crew of a stranded vessel at the mouth of the Salt River, 1773.

[3]Nongquase. See Christopher Hope: 'The Flight of the White South Africans', and note p. 256.

GUY BUTLER

Stranger to Europe

Stranger to Europe, waiting release,
My heart a torn-up, drying root
I breathed the rain of an Irish peace
That afternoon when a bird or a tree,
Long known as an exiled name, could cease
As such, take wing and trembling shoot
Green light and shade through the heart of me.

Near a knotty hedge we had stopped.
'This is an aspen.' 'Tell me more.'
Customary veils and masks had dropped.
Each looked at the hidden other in each.
Sure, we who could never kiss had leapt
To living conclusions long before
Golden chestnut or copper beech.

So, as the wind drove sapless leaves
Into the bonfire of the sun,
As thunderclouds made giant graves
Of the black, bare hills of Kerry,
In a swirl of shadow, words, one by one
Fell on the stubble and the sheaves;
'Wild dogrose this; this, hawthorn berry.'

But there was something more you meant,
As if the trees and clouds had grown
Into a timeless flame that burnt
All worlds of words and left them dust
Through stubble and sedge by the late wind blown:
A love not born and not to be learnt
But given and taken, an ultimate trust.

Now, between my restless eyes
And the scribbled wisdom of the ages
Black hills meet moving skies
And through rough hedges a late wind blows;
And in my palm through all the rages
Of lust and love now, always, lie
Brown hawthorn berry, red dogrose.

GUY BUTLER

Sweet-water

While packing gold butter, lace doilies, buck biltong,
spring chickens, frilled aprons, cut flowers, dried peaches
into the boot and back seat of the car,
Aunt Betsy, convener of twenty committees
and big queen bee of the church bazaar
barked gently at the garden 'boy':
'Boesak! Where's master? Find him! Tell him
that we are waiting.' Then, smiling, to me:
'Just like your Uncle, selfish old dreamer.'

When Uncle Danby took the wheel,
his hands would hover, seize it, feel
it for tension like one who tries
the reins of a horse who sometimes shies;
his legs, once expert with stirrups and spurs,
had never quite mastered these brakes and gears.
As the clutch was released the back wheels sprayed
the hens with a shrapnel of gravel; dismayed
they took to the trees, while parcels galore
rocketted onto the Buick's floor.
No word of comment from the old folk:
was this start normal? Or beyond a joke?

In silence we sailed with white winter grasses
swishing the mudguards; silence, enlarged
by the drone of the engine, by a startled korhaan
rising, clattering, into the sky: silence
seeping from petrified seas in the sandstone, so huge
that when I opened a gate the squeak of its socket
sounded small and sharp as a cricket
where grumbling breakers smother the old Cape granite
at dusk when a long Southwester falls.

'So you're going to 'Vahsity?
That's what they called it,
them Pommie Awficers
in the Bah Wah.'

He chuckled, remembering
accents and mannerisms
of elegant red-necked subalterns
whose blue-blood pedigrees
went back to the Battle of Hastings
rather than Eighteen Twenty.

''Vahsity!'

'Yes, Uncle.'

'Man, I only made standard four.
Dad called us back to the farm.
He had his reasons –
a run of bad seasons
locust swarms in the sky
dark as the day of doom –
Oh long, Oh long before
the ostrich feather boom.'

At the word 'feather' Aunt Betsy's hand
unconsciously fluttered towards her antique hat.

Ironstone koppies like dead volcanic islands
rising purple and black from oceans of grass,
fawn-soft grass lapping the parallel shales
of mountains thrusting daring capes and headlands
from continents still hidden over either horizon.

And here and there, as light as a drift of flotsam,
a store, an avenue, a kraal or a farm;
or a new-shorn flock of merinos like a trail of spume.

Not far ahead the Kwaai River
trailed its tawdry fringe of mimosas across the flats.
Soon our red-road-ribbon
would cross the stream, on the brand-new causeway,
the pride of the district:
opened last month by our M.P.C.
with a speets on nashonil prowgriss
followed by braaivleis and brandy –
O concertinas and moonlight
and singing of Sarie Marais.

'Along this road,
come rain, come shine,
my brothers and me
we drove stock to the fair.
What I remember best
was dust.
Man, I must
of swallowed a muid or two
of good Karoo soil in my time.
But there was also
the sweetest water.'

He ran his tongue round his bearded lips.

Approaching the river we saw the causeway,
concrete, white, with neat crenellations
like a Beau Geste fort fronting the river,
but wide enough for one-way traffic only.
Carefully he eased the car down the slope,
then, slap in the middle, switched off the engine.

Aunt Betsy sat up with a start: 'What? –'

'Man, when I was a boy,' he said.

'Danby!' she cried, 'We're half an hour late!'

His blue eyes quelled her.
'When I was a boy,' he said,
'we always outspanned for the night,
here, among these trees.
There's no sweeter water
in all the district.'

The way he said it, with a smooth small gesture
of the arm from the elbow with the palm flat, downwards,
sent the mind's eye reeling over
the whole Fish River catchment
down South from Dassiedeur and Daggaboer
in a great arc North to Teviot
and West-by-North to Spitskopvlei.

'But Danby dear, we're half an hour late!'

I don't think he heard her. Sometimes a greybeard
leaning, listening down the deep well of his years
turns stone-deaf to the fractional present.
Seventy winters through his bones
since first he stopped at Kwaai River.

At the end of the new-fangled causeway
he clambered over the ironstone boulders
and strolled up the river bed to a bend
where seventy centuries had scooped a bowl
in the crazily-cracked substratum of gravel.

Fringed with palest sand, a large pool in the blue gravel
with a fine and feathery dust upon it
and water boatman tracing
lazy arcs and circles in the sun;
their legs, no longer than an eyelash,
were shaking the reflected sky and making
the far-off images of mountains quake.

I heard a crescendo of hooting
and pictured the chaos at the causeway.
But he was oblivious, busy with things that mattered.

On the sand near the water's edge
he spread his handkerchief, and knelt.
I could hear his old joints creak.
Embarrassed, I knelt nearby.
'Now,' he said, 'you must first
blow the dust from the surface, like this.'

The floating film gave way like wax off apple skin.
The frantic water beetles scattered so quickly
they left the eye blinking at ripples and ripples only.

'Now scoop the water with your hand, but never,
no matter how thirsty you are,
swallow the first.
That's to rinse the dust from your mouth.'

He did so, spitting the water behind him.

'Now,' he said, 'now,
Oh taste how sweet it is.'

Delicately, three times,
the huge and trembling hand
cupped the sweet waters of the Angry River
to his lips, to sip it with a little noise
softer than the whirr of starling wings
from their nest-holes in the bank above us.

When we got to the causeway a dozen cars,
some hooting, were waiting; and old Aunt Betsy
sunk in shame and sulks. Unabashed
he lifted stiff legs onto the pedals
and said, with an ice-breaking twinkle:
'But don't you want to rinse your mouth, my dear?'

Laughter and fury broke together from her:
'When I was a boy, indeed! When
were you ever anything else?'

Turning, he grinned at me. The blue eye said:
'Oh, she don't understand us boys.'

He's dead now, and I am left,
bereft, wondering
to what stream I could take whom
and kneel like that, and say:
Taste how sweet it is.

GUY BUTLER

The Divine Underground

Souls *in flagrante delicto* or *in extremis*,
stretched on the rack or Cleopatra's bed,
you have no news for me,
me, not fit to tread
where hawk-sure men of the media
zoom lenses down on your limbs in spasm
or claw at your grunts or ululations
with glittering microphones.

No, I go hungrily slumming for those who wear
a habit of discipline on every gesture, armed
in still affection, steel-bright after years.

I find them poorly disguised as morons,
under distorting stars,
lost in their lands of birth, quite ousted by
smooth bastards or daughters in gorgeous gowns:
in the cold, in the shade,
like lepers, like untouchables, in whose eyes
our storms of guilt dissolve in their light of forgiveness:
they know what they have lost,
they guess at what they've gained;
divining an innocent justice, they endure
our grand and murderous razzmatazz
as if they were God's spies.

GUY BUTLER

Home Thoughts

I

Strange rumours gripped Olympus. Apollo's hand
Paused at its work, set plummet and rule aside;
Then glittering in clean-cut bronze he sped
To rout the brash disturbers of that peace
Which year by year had raised archaic Greece
Nearer his vision of the poised and planned.
Oh barbarous with drums, with dancing drums,
Amid a snarl of leopards through whose hide
Shimmer disastrous stars, the drunkard comes,
Black Dionysus roaring in his pride!

Ten thousand times they fought, wrestling before
Both gods and men; it seemed the very rocks
Watched those wild bouts among the barley shocks,
The brown vineyards, the dusty threshing floor.
If pressed Apollo side-slipped to the sun,
Striking his rival blind, while he in turn
Would slink instinctive into copses, run

Underground like roots, and hoot weird scorn
From his nocturnal world: but neither could
Conquer the force in which the other stood.

The spectacle gave poets double sight;
Their nerves grew keen to catch at brightest noon
Rumours of drums; in dark, ecstatic night
Could wake to shafts not quivered in the moon.
At last, at Delphi, half in love with him,
Apollo gave the drunkard elbow room;
But though his pride of leopards purred, near tamed,
And he himself grew decorous, he might
Still breathe a deep, vibrating gloom
Round anything the Bright One named.

At length, when peasants, through his autumn trance
Stirred slow pavans for summer on soft drums,
He cried aloud, (his leopards stretched their limbs):
Kill me, Apollo, or join the tragic dance!
Instead the Bright One watched: the flexing knees,
The raving, rending; heard the ecstatic crying;
But mirrored on his mind's white dancing floor
Dark dancers sighed and swayed like cypress trees
Around a man on whose defiant dying
Cracked clouds of knowing never moist before.

II
Why do I hanker homewards, falter?
Because in Arno's flood the stars
Cavort with neon signs, headlights of cars?
The Centaur, snapping its human halter,
Demolishes baroque façades;
The Great Bear runs amok
Among our maps, tugging the Pole awry;
Oh all things heave and buck
Since Dionysus slipped Apollo's guards
And let his leopards range the earth and sky!

Stupid of me to brood and cry
These barbarous confusions where
Triumphant marble effigies defy
The moody turmoils of the air;
But, as at home, I here discern
The predatory shade;

Asleep all day in ivy or that fern
Which smothers the balustrade
It sniffs the night and pads the cracked parterre
Between dry laurels and the shattered urn.

Man's task is to get such dark things clear.
Old Galileo, that empiricist
Through gothic tombs, antiphonies of psalms
Smuggled a serpent-sharp idea;
Smooth linen cordage looped in his swinging fist
Chilled the ascending stairs;
The sceptre-grasping ikons round the dome
Shook as his ape-like palms
Paid out that system-smashing metronome
Whose jazztime spoilt the slow waltz of the spheres.

Long years drifting through African dark
Bred dreams that I might find, once here
A burning beacon, a gyro-setting mark –
That cord would ruck and tangle where
The rough stone of a leopard's bark
Ripples the scrub with fear.
What pendulum can trace the mind's unseen
Sharp arcs, its blind man's reach
Round knots of being that have never been
Subdued to slip through flaming hoops of speech?

Never so clearly have I known
That though the sharp mind's eye was made
To sever struggling shape from strangling shade
These shapes and shades cannot be mine.
O African creatures, across this night
I glimpse in our primitive storm
Of thunder, whirlwind, mirage-twisted light
A lifted limb or glance
Which I might free, give consciousness and form
Dared I but stare into your furious dance!

III
Old Galileo's heirs can cite
How stubborn atoms may become
Open to change in unimpeded light,
Or round a rod of platinum
May curtsy, open arms and start
Dancing a different dance;

But the catalyst remains itself, apart,
Waits like a hermit there
Through dull khamsins of accident and chance
To set one crystal, get one colour clear.

These images at which I stare
Beneath such slow, myth-burdened stars,
Virgilian forests shedding mortal tears,
Might blind me in my native air.
Unless for some loved principle one strips,
As the desert fathers did,
The soul of gaudy accidents, and grips
A Mosaic serpent or rod
One's deepest cries come from Egyptian lips
Blowing dead bubbles on a Red Sea flood.

IV
I have not found myself on Europe's maps,
A world of things, deep things I know endure
But not the context for my one perhaps.
I must go back with my five simple slaves
To soil still savage, in a sense still pure:
My loveless, shallow land of artless shapes
Where no ghosts glamorize the recent graves
And every thing in Space and Time just is:
What similes can flash across those gaps
Undramatized by sharp antithesis?

I boast no quiet catalytic wand
Nor silently swinging, tell-tale pendulum
To civilize my semi-barbarous land;
A clearer love is all that I bring home:
Little, yet more than enough. Apollo, come!
Oh cross the tangled scrub, the uncouth ways,
Visit our vital if untamed abysm
Where your old rival in the lustrous gloom
Fumbles his drums, feels for a thread of rhythm
To dance us from our megalithic maze.

Nervous he wanders staring-eyed among
Barbarous forms unknown to the northern muse.
Leaves, granites touch him; in ear, on tongue
New sounds and tastes, so many they suffuse
His sense with a blur of heat: delirium
That neither sleep nor sweat can clarify.

Oh let the lightning of your quickening eye
And his abounding darkness meet and mate,
Cleave, crack the clouds! From his brimming drum
Spill crystal waves of words, articulate!

GUY BUTLER

'Body Grows Old, Heart Stays Young'

Guga mzimba sala nhliziyo – Zulu proverb

Before we troubled
The Cape of Storms
Or shook the Highveld
With horses and arms,
Before the births
Of Shaka, Retief,
Old Zulus were chanting
This joy-in-grief:
'Body grows old,
Heart stays young.'
Such was the heartsease
In their song.

Now, as we drive
Or are driven apart
Till none dare give
Of the love in his heart,
As bodies grow chill
As spears to each other
And clouds drift still
Through ominous weather,
'Hearts grow old
In bodies yet young,'
Runs like a shudder
Through our song.

In ages of iron
Gilded with gold
The Cross and Orion

Swing high and cold.
Great Hunter, Great Lover,
Swing low, shine warm
Till our tongues recover
That ancient charm:
'Body grows old,
Heart stays young'
Again be the sequence
Of all song.

GUY BUTLER

Epitaph for a Poet

He strove, both in and out of season,
To use his modest gift aright;
Still went on rhyming without reason
Far into the night;
Rhymes of the desperate word,
Absurd
As the flounderings of a beheaded bird.

He hammered for help on the doors of the sky,
He heard the dead silence of God;
Lost in the syntax of how and why
To and fro he trod.
At last he halted, numb,
Struck dumb
By his long suspended sentence to the tomb.

RUTH MILLER

Honey

The helicopter bee fines down
His motor to a midget drone.
The creamfurred throat engulfs him. Soon
His legs grow pantaloons of gold.

His thousand brothers sing and thrust
Their piston legs, their pinion gauze,
Blind to the plundering soft raid
On catacombs of murmuring halls.

Now cool long jars gleam with the taste
Of amber hours suavely stolen
From summer swooning in the heat;
Till smooth and pale, and pale and golden,
There slides like bliss upon the tongue
A bawd's red kiss, a drudge's song.

RUTH MILLER

Fruit

These were the distant fruits of a garden childhood:
Yellow fluff on the hard astringent quince –
Finger-scratched to smooth small streets and lanes;
Cornelian-coloured ball of pomegranate,
Split in shining cups of pirate rubies
Set each against each like bee-cells in white silk;
Figs that we shredded, pulpy soft and purple,
Throwing aside the dry and skeined imposters,
Their milkflesh stained with russet short-cut threads.

Sunday fruit was silver-bought. But these
Grew in the garden, formed a roadside hedge,
Concealed us from the coinage of the world.
Amongst the quince, the fig, the pomegranate
We hid away with glossy greensprung secrets;
Lay quiet and heavy, sweet with an edge of bitter
Under the lazy heat, the languorous season:
Breathless to be plucked and by love consumed.

RUTH MILLER

Plankton

Remember the day the sea turned red:
The breakers ruddy as though the sun
Had fallen, Icarus-spent, too soon;
We watched it from a white dune

And marvelled that the changing element
Could be so changed. Russet-tinged,
The rollers crimsoned; but inshore
Were cats-eye green as before.

From floating seethe of miniscules,
A billion in each drop, the pale
Profusion blossomed rose again
In one far blood-red stain.

Breasting the inshore waves, we speared
Through them, cleansed and clean as air.
Huge seas lifted, took us, leaping,
By the hands, and drew us in;

Drew us further, deeper, into
And beyond the next and next
Massive, smooth, unclenching green.
One step more – we would have been

Engulfed beneath the swinging crests
Curving in a rush of rose.
Back we forced – the ominous tide
Away from us, flowered, and died.

Away from us, died too
The bright day, a fallen feather.
Apart, we left the strange sea
Within each other.

RUTH MILLER

Birds

The lion, even when full of mud, with burrs
On his belly tangled, his great pads heavy
And cracked, sends such a message on the dry air
As makes all smaller animals wary, their fur
Rising in silken shivers, their horned heads
Up with the wind, reading its tragic story.

There is nothing majestic about death. Yet the king
Remains royal, and knows it; is accepted,
Though fled. Only the tiniest things –
The birds, whirr down from the tall sky, fling
Their feathered softnesses at shadows, dare to move
In his company, dare to sing.

Suppose a million birds could once shake loose
From the tops of trees, from the white horizon,
Veering in a soft outflinging noose,
Clouds in their clouds, lightning in their claws –
To peck out his sagging heart. How royally they would bedizen
His beggarman bones with the charity of their wings.

RUTH MILLER

Spider

No spider struggles to create
The beautiful. His tensile arc
Knows mathematics in the dark;
A Michael Angelo of air
Who weaves a theory that states
Ultimatums on a hair.

Born to the purple of his need
He has no unsolved problems. He
Suffers no dichotomy,

But wakes to work and works to kill;
Beauty empiric in his greed,
Perfection in a villain's skill.

Ragblown summit of the ooze
Of soft warm mud that split and stirred –
I hold within my skull the word
Sealed and socketed; yet my hands
Fashion with artifice and ruse
Not wily web, but witless strands.

But when the poor cold corpse of words
Is laid upon its candled bier,
I, vindicate, will shed the tear
That falls like wax, and creep unheard
To weave in silence, grave and bowed,
The pure necessity – a shroud.

RUTH MILLER

Penguin on the Beach

Stranger in his own element,
Sea-casualty, the castaway manikin
Waddles in his tailored coat-tails. Oil

Has spread a deep commercial stain
Over his downy shirtfront. Sleazy, grey,
It clogs the sleekness. Far too well

He must recall the past, to be so cautious:
Watch him step into the waves. He shudders
Under the froth, slides, slips, on the wet sand,

Escaping to dryness, dearth, in a white cascade,
An involuntary shouldering off of gleam.
Hands push him back into the sea. He stands

In pained and silent expostulation.
Once he knew a sunlit, leaping smoothness,
But close within his head's small knoll, and dark

He retains the image: oil on sea,
Green slicks, black lassos of sludge
Sleaving the breakers in a stain-spread scarf.

He shudders now from the clean flinching wave,
Turns and plods back up the yellow sand,
Ineffably weary, triumphantly sad.

He is immensely wise: he trusts nobody. His senses
Are clogged with experience. He eats
Fish from his Saviour's hands, and it tastes black.

RUTH MILLER

Blue-mantled Mary

Blue-mantled Mary
Bloody in the byre
Brought forth. The hawthorn was as white
As milk, the berries all on fire.

Nine months waiting.
Nine months waiting.

Now I remember
The months ago annunciation –
First feathery thrust of the angel
Nine months ago, this December.
The tall touch of the stranger
On my breast, on my skin,
His insupportable maculate breath
Breathing as I did, out and in,
Out and in
Waiting for the time of birth.

Untouched by man, blue-mantled Mary ran
Ran on her pencilled feet into the light
Of the cathedral window, serene as snow.
How was she then to know
What would be done? Whose Will it was she knew.

And I remember
Unhallowed, un-Mary'd, this seed must grow
Slowly toward its day – though each day is holy –
Toward the windowless
Breathless lusty breath
Of a full-term Death.

RUTH MILLER

The Floating Island

Down the glutted river's throat
Jut the jagged trunks of trees,
Giddily the bubbles float;
The dead drowned buck have wounded knees.
The basket nests ooze mud in sodden trees.

Swirling in a giddy gyre
Down the brown Zambesi flood
Comes an island – torn entire
With tendon reeds and brackish blood,
Prised from its moorings in the silent mud,

Bearing on its swinging arc
A herd of buck, alive, aground,
With anguished eyes, their wet flanks dark
With sweat. The water gabbles round.
Their sucking hoofprints moon the mud with sound.

The sliding scenery repeats
The gliding greenery of fear.
A newborn buck gropes for the teats;
Green to terror, he does not hear
The lipping tongues around his mother's feet.

Head back flat, with seashell horns
Against the wind the leader strains.
Around him lean the does and fawns:
They can remember summer rains –
But not like these. Not these obliterated plains.

Do they smell the tumbling doom
Scarved in silken spray that slides
To the falling ledge, that looms
But one nightfall on? Their sides
Bulge and flatten. Their eyes darken and grow wide.

Along the gorged Zambesi swims
In a slow insensate dance
Frieze of buck with dervish limbs
Frozen in a dreamer's trance.
Anarchy has leapt beyond mischance.

A nightfall on the Smoke that Thunders[1]
Will spring to gulf their leaping sides.
Wrenched from our continent, we blunder
And lacking weather-sense for guide
Our green uncharted islands sink in ravelled floods, blind-eyed.

[1]Victoria Falls

RUTH MILLER

from **Cycle**[1]

To eat pain like bread is a condition,
A part of living
Which is the condition of dying;
But how slowly. The delicate tissue
Fails where it is fronded; how slowly.

  We have a shell light as cocoon, internal,
  Within which you beat like a promise.

There was a sort of heaven in all you failed
To see, yet saw: that which was hidden
Apt to the touch. The secret garden
With dreaming effacement fashioned
For heroes; brain and heart beating purely
In the old man like a child, and in the child
Beating like age.

146

Finding music in counterpoint of worlds
In shapes as old as rock, you took the star
In your fingers and drew it over the strings,
Listening with passion to the murmur
That leapt from the secrets of the great man, deaf.
Two hundred of you sang in the Messiah.

In the centuries back of the questioning, you met,
Parted and met, in aloneness, no ears hearing together.
No eyes seeing the same.
Yet you saw: rhythm and speech of harmony
In a statue with loops of nothing, a circle of air,
Statement of colour on colour which, each mis-reading,
Read purely, if intention is a grace:
Spread in patterns of brightness, later in patterns
Of doomknowing darkness like a circle of nothing
On circles of water.

Water flows forward and backward. You followed after.
Time was a stream in the spiral, a rock in the stream.
Together we followed the path which distorted, eluded.
How could it not, if the answer sought was the one
Significant beyond measure?

All the majestic vistas – you ventured down all,
Retaining the dream and the laughter. How else be fashioned
So wholly: laughter ringing the bells in my breast?

You were not good to the poor: You enriched them
With eyes and hands that knew to speak and be silent.
You were not kind to the maimed: You un-maimed them.
Remembered now by the nameless servant,
The old man fishing, the singers and doers,
The raucous young voices who fling and linger on areas
Filled with your presence.

But to eat bread like pain,
To eat pain like bread,
To wake in the morning in sunlight
Warm in the sun on the floor
And know with the only real knowledge
Complete, undivided, undoubted,
That your voice will not open the door
Your hand will not latch on the sunlight

Your footstep not ring through the dark.
Ah, Greek with the visage of horror
How can you bear it, the stopping?
How can we bear it, the cruel
Cut of the skein in the morning?

But the morning is you, and the bread
Warm from the oven; the stars
Crammed in your pocket; the singing
Hallelujahs of dreams.

To eat pain like bread is a condition
Of living, which is endless dying.
You will not allow me to refuse
My daily bread.

[1]in memory of the author's son

DAVID WRIGHT

Livingstone

My favourite myth was the legend of Dr Livingstone
With linen, salvation, beads and love in his hand,
Searching the continent for Herodotus' fountains,
And leaving after his death his heart and his guts behind.

The parson who recorded his defeat in dialectics
By an African wizard, going without a whip or a gun
In his hand, to the rivers and the inland lakes,
Among the savage and terrified, came to no harm.

Seeing the Zambesi roll like a leaf below
Him, and the valley of black humankind
Rise like an arm to religion and to their
Peace, the kindly and self-disciplined

Man in the end left their shackles forgotten,
Heard not any more the natural cry
Of the chained river. For more than freedom
He respected the curiosity

That once to glimpse the divided hill
Where the four sources of the Nile shape variously,
Was a last passion, and the final
Burial of his will and energy.

In which prayer dying, David Livingstone
Passed, and those whom he could not save
Carried his bones to Zanzibar and England,
But kept his heart and innards in their proper grave.

DAVID WRIGHT

My Grandfather

My grandfather was an elegant gentleman
Who trod behind an ox-wagon's wheels in his youth
Four hundred miles to Kimberley from Port Elizabeth,
To resuscitate the family fortune.

His love affair with money lasted a long time.
In my childhood I best remember
His glass-panelled car and European chauffeur,
And dignity in a cricket pavilion;

Or when in gardens imitating England
He in a morning-coat between two ladies
Walked. I was afraid to recognize
My father's father, and kept my distance.

Nothing became my grandfather so much as his age.
Impoverished and living in a single room,
He kept his grace and distinguished costume,
Imposing on distress an unstooping carriage.

The lady left him, but he took his congé
Like a gentleman. The old colonial
Never allowed a merely personal
Regret pour a poison in the ear of memory.

DAVID WRIGHT

For Roy Campbell

My countryman, the poet, wears a Stetson;
He can count his enemies, but not his friends.
A retired soldier living in Kensington,
Who limps along the Church Street to the Swan.

Horses and bulls, the sable and impala,
Sparkle between his fingers, and a sun
That sleeps and rises from the Indian Ocean
Gongs the images of his passion.

He never loved liberty for her name,
Or wept on the disastrous ashes of Guernica,
But he fought for her where he could find her,
Knowing she was not lying in a newspaper column,

But bound, still bound in the aboriginal fall
From Eden and of Adam. His ancestors who came
Out of the eighteeenth century and Scotland
Taught him to have no truck with the liberal.

Horses and bulls, the sable and impala,
Thunder between his fingers; as they run,
He hears another thunder in the sun,
Time and the sea about Tristan da Cunha.[1]

[1]Volcanic island in the South Atlantic, subject of a poem by Roy Campbell.

DAVID WRIGHT

Cape Town, 1937: Embarking for England

Under the African lintel, Table Mountain,
The violet ship at the quay
Casts off, the laughing sentimentalists hold her
Momentarily with coloured streamers

As she moves out to sea.
The paper ribbons part and flutter; and the crowd
Puts forth its handkerchiefs like leaves.

The African continent leans against the peninsula.
In hallways at Kalk Bay
Fishing-tackle waits beside a salt-stained surf-board;
The electric trains flicker by
Washed colonial gables, rainweary oakwoods,
And expensive small hotels,
Stucco villas elbowing for maritime vistas.

O spectacular home of mediocre visionaries,
The mailboat draws away
From one of the more terrifying middleclass paradises
Of the shut mind and eye.
I wave from the deck of the Union-Castle liner,
And an exile waves from the quay.
Why do we love the places we were born in?

DAVID WRIGHT

Game Reserve
from **A Voyage to Africa**

How gentle, courteous, and noble is nature
Whose beasts, when visible, appear dumb and good,
And whose prospects, munificent but pure;
Or she is cruel if that should be the mood,
May be dressed in or divested of allure.

A mirror more perfect than any of glass
She is: when looked in, the looker sees a shape
Of his emotion, and of what really was
There, looking in; of an angel or an ape.
If her mountains lean toward beguiling us –

In whom, once, we saw a visage of our fright,
Though long ago, and in another country,
Whereas today they flatter us with their height –
O nature, mirror or mishandled pantry,
Or medicine, goddess, enemy, what you like –

I love you, and knowing whom I really love,
I find it difficult not to love you more;
Either in a city's confines, at one remove,
Or when I, travelling past in train or car,
Touch the innocence your wildernesses prove.

As for the human spectators there on show
(Whose stink of worry, effectively overcome
By a scent of steel and petrol, does not now
Terrify to a stampede the herds of horn)
Become beasts by virtue of machines, they go

By Sabi in the Kruger National Park
Where the lions, mewing from Pretorius Kop,
And light-bummed impala, poised as a photograph,
Live easy as in an Eden, have no hope;
Content with joy infects with joy their dark.

Cropping under rocks depending for their fall,
Sunlit, the prelapsarian creatures move;
In their incommunicable selfish toil
They praise what made them with no need to love
Or ever to manifest that praise at all,

As we are led, by what I am now aware
Is guilt of loving not enough, to beg pardon,
Embarrassed by overmuch of love and care
And so excluded from the encircling garden,
In learning and in the laud of what moves there.

The hairy and stupid beasts that have no troubles
Beyond rinderpest and acts of God, increase.
A hippo, lulled by water, is snoring bubbles
While lion beside the zebra loll at peace;
Scavenging from heaven, an aasvogel[1] wobbles;

And intelligent babooneries alone
Who peer from behind their thrones of boulders, pierce
The simple human disguise of a machine,
Avoiding the direction of eyes and ears
And of a curiosity like their own.

[1]vulture

DAVID WRIGHT

Kleomedes

Both Plutarch and Pausanius tell a story
That is a worry to imagination.
It's of the athlete Kleomedes, a moody
Instrument for a theophanic anger
And for an outrageous justice not our own.

Plutarch reports the tale in the barest outline,
Evidently having no comment to offer,
And certainly no word of explanation
To throw light upon what happened to Kleomedes
Or the subsequent oracular non sequitur.

As for Kleomedes: at the Olympic Games he
Killed his opponent in the boxing-contest.
The ox-felling blow was not his, so he claimed; the
Fury struck through him, it was not his own strength.
He'd won, but they withheld the palm nevertheless.

The injustice of it. Nursing rage like a pot-plant,
Watering it with his thoughts, which were few and stupid,
When he drank with others he drank with his back turned
To cherish that shrub till one more bud had sprouted.
It was growing to be a beauty and he loved it.

The palm of victory, his by rights, denied him.
Well, he would go home to Astypalaea.
There they would understand; were they not his own kin?
Anger. His heart fed an ulcer. Would it disappear
At sight of the headland of his own dear island?

So Kleomedes went away; his rage didn't.
It's hard being done by foreigners, but far worse
When the people one grew up with see no harm in it.
Even the light of the noonday sun seemed altered
In the familiar market-place where fools chaffered.

Wrath. Wrath. In an excess of it he stood up.
May God damn the lot of you, he said, seizing the first
Thing his eye fell on: it was a marble column.

Ah, and he tugged. Tugged. And his brow pimpled with sweat.
Possessed, he exerted more than his might. It tumbled.

Slowly a coping-stone slid. Then the whole roof
Collapsed with a roar. Thunder. A pall of dust
Stood like a rose where had been a schoolroom of children.
Kleomedes saw their blood lapped up by the earth.
There was silence and grief. Then a cry, Murderer!

Murderer! Murderer! He was among strangers.
Hatred and anger in that man's, that woman's eye.
And now they were one eye. The eye of an animal,
Hackles up, about to rend. Its name Mob, hairy
Gorgon. Brute, it is a beast made up of us all;

May none of us ever be or see it! He saw,
Miserable quarry, lust ripple its muscles.
Act now or die! He acted. Ran for sanctuary
To the holy temple, the temple of Pallas Athena:
Mob may respect the precinct of the armed goddess.

But what does a beast know of gods? He heard baying
Hard at his heels. Saw a chest there in the forecourt.
Prayed it be empty. He lifted the lid. Stepped in
Pulling the lid behind him, and held it fast shut.
More strength than his own held it against all efforts.

I don't understand the story from this point on.
Here enters mystery. Levering a crowbar
They heaved at hinges; the wood groaned and a hasp cracked.
Now for the fellow. Kleomedes did not appear.
They looked; but the chest was empty; the man was gone.

It was anticlimax. Fear fluttered from dismay.
They were people again. The sun continued to shine
As it had done. There were the children to bury.
Catastrophe and the violated shrine
Remained; and, before them, a vacant box grinning.

Astypalaea sent to Delphi embassies
To ask the pythoness what these events forebode;
What might be their significance; where the guilt lay.
The oracle kept silence. Then vouchsafed its word.
'The last of the heroes was Kleomedes.'

154

DAVID WRIGHT

from **On the Margin**

An anniversary approaches: of the birth of god
In a stable, son of a virgin and a carpenter,
But really issued from loins of omnipotent glory:
A babe, ejected from the thighs, greased in mucus and blood,

Weeping with its first breath, suffering the cold air, high king
Of the galaxies, and powerless as a fieldmouse.
Over him breathe the oxen; shepherds who have seen a star
Honour the obscure event; and, they say, three travelling

Magi, or charlatans. This is the messenger of hope;
The military have been instructed to deal with him.
A wholesale killing, their invariable strategy,
While abolishing a generation, fails of effect.

We are asked to believe all this (it's only to start with).
What a jumble of the impossible and casual,
Of commonplace mixed with violence; ordinary muddle;
The props and characters scruffy; at best unheroic.

Yet accordant with the disposition of things holy
As we understand them; whose epiphanies are banal,
Not very aesthetic; gnomic; unremarkable;
And very much like what we have to put up with daily.

ALAN ROSS

Rock Paintings, Drakensberg

These mountains of up-pointed spears
Hold eland, oribi and rhebok
Capering over yellow rock
To sandstone caves that form a barrier

Eastward mauve and vertical,
Westward greenly gradual.
Sweet grasses swish below like silk
Torn at dark by prowling buck.

Baboons on red and scrabbling paths
Scatter dust in layers of talc,
Imitating as they stalk
Human gestures, hurling oaths.

A form of sympathetic magic
More goodnatured now than tragic,
Though practised by the bushman hunter,
Re-creating as a painter

Animals he hoped to capture,
Art was not a surplus rapture,
But a means of softening up
Hartebeest and antelope.

Here walls of cave and sky converge;
Within, the human primal urge.
Brush-pigs scuttle from cracked rocks,
Bush-girls thrust their weighted buttocks

Squatting as they chant in line
Round pots of boiling porcupine.
The painted bushman aims his bow,
The real sunset starts to flow

Across this sweeping mountain range
And still, despite ten centuries' change,
Art remains a kind of hunt
Eliminating fear and cant,

A means of pinning down
An object, by the sheer act
Of drawing animal or loved one,
Making absence into fact.

F. D. SINCLAIR

Zimbabwe

Stranger walls, that shell no violent presence,
No mask of gold, no bee-swarm in the skull,

Stand waiting, quietly, without impatience,
Their hour of mortal birth within a mind

That will exalt them in its running vision
From ruin to reality in song.

Here the sea is grass, and here its waves
Are restless hills of grass that surge to hide

What pinnacle of urgent mystery,
Serenely islanded, lies charted still

Within the eye, upon the mind's close map,
Washed by the peaceful tides of day and year.

There is no face beneath the broken stones,
No searching of decay to bring the heart

Nearer to history of blood, and cut
The desolation spun, without, within;

Only silent emptiness of wind
That covers time and crumbles down the walls.

This is a temple that has lost its god
And lies, memorial to solitude,

Fit for rededication in the mind
That gives it now a meaning and a song,

Identity from timeless non-existence,
Deeper than thought, earthed in the feeling heart.

JILL KING

Grief Plucked me out of Sleep

Grief plucked me out of sleep
(for whom? for whom?)
breaking proportions,
narrowing the room,

narrowing the room,
widening my heart,
no space for comfort,
no place apart;

widening my heart,
lowering the sky.
In grief's dimension
captive I lie,

all the world's area
shrunk to a room,
my night shaped by grief –
for whom? for whom?

BERNARD LEVINSON

Group Therapy

We were talking about love
(not daring to use that word)
as they sat about me
in a circle.
The boys and the girls
each with a puppet on one hand.

He said –
'Mine's an old man.
He's so very hungry
and so very much alone.'

And she in the softest voice –
'My puppet's ugly
everyone hates her'.

I searched for words
to form a bridge
between them.

The old man looked at the ugly puppet.
The paper heads nodded gravely
while the group waited.

And I, groping in my word-world
waited for the right words
to set them free.

On an impulse,
he stretched forward
and gently swept her hair
out of her face.

BERNARD LEVINSON

Weskoppies[1] Asleep

Weskoppies asleep.
The green roofs
float in the rising heat.
The old trees
bend to the windows
and listen –
the sick are asleep.
They are dreaming –
their tears flow
into the darkness
over the waiting trees.

On duty
I only hear
the hospital breathing,
the corridors

the wooden stairs
the warm core
of this dark world
breathing.

Somewhere in the valley
trains running northwards
call to each other.
The sound swims through the night
into the quiet
of my room.

I am no longer aware
of the sick
hiding in their lonely beds.
Only inside me
the wide questioning eyes
refuse to close.

[1]a mental hospital

ROY MACNAB

Majuba Hill

On the craggy mountain-top the mist
Held a redcoat army in its fist.
Beaten by arrogance and the sun,
They'd dragged their last uncaptured gun,

To make a fortress of the hill
And watch all night from the citadel.

The creatures of the mist, the sheep
Sniffed round the red men in their sleep,
The only sentries still awake
Who heard the yielding branches break.

For the five-day sleepless sentry stood
And snored at his post above the wood,
While down upon the stirring plain
The night brought up its Dunsinane.

The moon went skulking from the sky
And hid its face as the wood passed by,
A few score Boer and bearded trees
Scaling the mountain on their knees.

The dawn rose up from an angry bed,
Drew back the shroud from the mountain-head,
And sent the sun out over the stones
To gnaw at the sleeping soldiers' bones.

The soldiers sleeping in the sun
Could never know what the night had done,
How bitter were the blazing noons,
The defeat in dust of proud dragoons.

Only the nibbling goat and the sheep
Saw how remote were the dead asleep.

ROY MACNAB

Seven of the Clock

Seven of the clock and the day
Clean as a copybook, white
As I whistling go on my way,

Two flying feet
Hopscotch through the street
All the way down
To the end of the town,

O breathless I am and blowing
Like a whale, a spinnaker sail
On a Summer sea,

Feet and fist
Reach out through the mist
For the bridge that grows like a Roman nose
In a landscape as noble as this,

Now over I go but adagio
For this is the slow
Movement of Matins,

See far below
The ballet begins
And I make my bow
To swans on a lake,

O this is the hour when life's begun
To unfold in the flower
Face and hands to the sun,
This is the time for the hare to run
From shouts and shadows and
Shots from a gun,

When the stag in the park
Awoke with a start, antlers
Caught in the arms of an oak,

And everywhere suddenly broke
News of a day, bells and chimes
And the definite stroke

Of Seven of the Clock.

ANNE WELSH

Speech

Inland, the stream talks
To itself, to stones, to me
If I happen to pass.

Fluency from the dry hill
Is water washing rock,
The gleam below the grass
Like the forgotten sense
Of a word much used.

ANNE WELSH

That Way

That way. He went that way.
The pink road through the brown hills,
The path across the yellow grass
Towards that lifted place
In those stone folds.

Bleak, they say,
The wind has no caress
But strips and burns.

The journey will be dusty,
Footfall after footfall.
And first the ash of evening
Will put out colour
Then nightfall overtake him.
The going is blind at times
For rock engulfs.

Moments of shelter
And of peace, perhaps –
When torn land is consoled,
The broken earth grows whole
And hills are loved by light.

Those coming back?
It's difficult to say –
Worn by weather,
Exposure under stars.

But that rock marks. It makes.
They look the same but have a different shape.
They say, when nothing is withheld
Rock takes them on,
Takes over, gives itself.
They say that terror goes,
That after night,
The shining of the morning is most marvellous.

ANNE WELSH

Sight

A shine and shock
Are scarlet lilies
By sun-dazzled waters.
Storm-bloom on hills,
Rock-sparkle or bright glass –
Each colour is a cock
That crows of glory.

Sun sprays new fibres
On leaf-cool collections,
And golden butterflies
Dance on a dusty surface.
Rivers are pliant light
Or stanchions taut for sun.
Grasses, ivory, or rose,
Stones, apricot, or red
Smoulder to pale miles overhead.

Out of the crowded valley's colour
Single call-notes trumpet as I pass,
Till eyes are strutting peacocks,
And sharp mosaics
Block out distance
Where no fronds wave.

In glittering valleys
Shine is more lucid than an argument,
Horizons make an arbitrary ring,
And this closed-circuit for the eyes
Sets all the roundelays.

Distance is silent –
It is beyond the sight.
O mountains not seen, can I recognize,
Or ever discover your colours
When articulate trumpets are missing?

ANNE WELSH

Beat Red

Street tomatoes shine
Through plastic bags:
Shine where the sun strikes
On the pavements' edge.

In the complex pallor
Of concrete and winter
The shine is simple
And a common colour
For collected pulse,
Or for the abyss
In any private heart.

Red is a bright colour,
A singular colour.
And in the life of men
Incarnate colour
Is the common one.

C. A. FAIR

from **Kangra Paintings**

Krishna to Radha

Birds call and fly; leaves stream in the warm air;
Cowherds look up and whistle to their cows,
Urging them to the village.
Come under this leaf umbrella; the rain is wetting your
                                    forehead,
Plastering the black hair, clinging in drops on the
                                    lashes;
You look as if you are crying.
But storms are our delight;
Winds shake our branches;
The lightning is our joy,
Scarring the violet cloud.

The Exchange

The cowherd leans on his staff,
The girl stands at the doorway;
A tree bursts into flower,
Hills move like gentle waves;
Birds fly to the branch
And sit in cool and silence,
While these lovers meet in eyes.
Their look sustains the sky;
On its stream of ocean float
Trees, houses, hills.
Its currents hold them upright,
Forgetful of their forms,
Released and buoyant plants.
Flowing in air to each other,
Separate and one,
Their unfaltering gaze a universe
Melts and defines.

C. A. FAIR

To Mack

You and my father were friends for a lifetime,
Bright-eyed, patched, believing boys,
Scholarship children of a far London,
Breathlessly bent through its streets to your truth.

You, impatient at man's blindness,
He, not doubting that men would see;
Frugally fed, your one hunger
The lighted abstractions of number and word.

You could sing like a blackbird at ease in a cherry-tree,
And he whistle a music-hall song.
Struggle became you, because unlamented.
During, and past it, you knew how to joy.

The world darkens. The lies unsurprise you.
He is long dead; it wearies to recall.
Hear me now say the heart thinks of you and quickens:
Never believe you were anything but loved.

C. A. FAIR

Grasmere

Down a green ghyll two cuckoos spoke,
The notes chiming, not answering,
Each talking to himself alone;
And solitary flowers grew,
Sundew and violet, looking down,
Indifferent to the passing bee,
By marish track and single stone.

I like it when nature does not lie,
But underlines man's separateness.
The tree and fern, aloof and cool,
Distance our human hot distress,
And make compassion seem less good.
The undemanding here may find
A deeper peace in loneliness.

PAUL CHIDYAUSIKU

Grandpa

They say they are healthier than me
Though they can't walk to the end of a mile;
At their age I walked forty at night
To wage a battle at dawn.

They think they are healthier than me:
If their socks get wet they catch a cold;
When my sockless feet got wet, I never sneezed –
But they still think they are healthier than me.

On a soft mattress over a spring bed,
They still have to take a sleeping-pill:
But I, with reeds cutting into my ribs,
My head resting on a piece of wood,
I sleep like a babe and snore.

They blow their noses and pocket the stuff –
That's hygienic so they tell me:
I blow my nose into the fire,
But they say that is barbaric.

If a dear one dies I weep without shame;
If someone jokes I laugh with all my heart.
They stifle a tear as if to cry was something wrong,
But they also stifle a laugh,
As if to laugh was something wrong, too.
No wonder they need psychiatrists!

They think they have more power of will than me.
Our women were scarcely covered in days of yore,
But adultery was a thing unknown:
Today they go wild on seeing a slip on a hanger!

When I have more than one wife
They tell me that hell is my destination,
But when they have one and countless mistresses,
They pride themselves on cheating the world!

No, let them learn to be honest with themselves first
Before they persuade me to change my ways,
Says my grandfather, the proud old man.

LIONEL ABRAHAMS

The Issue

The enemy is clearly marked
in black or white.
The shades in between confuse the issue.
You have to be against whom you're not for:
there's no neutrality,

no switching sides – the thought
compounds your treachery
with confusion of the issue.
Doubt, change, give-and-take,
contradictions, exceptions
and fine distinctions
brake the action and confuse the issue.

Humanitarians confuse the issue
through tolerance.
Moderates confuse the issue
through compromise.
Progressives confuse the issue
through optimism.
Liberals confuse the issue
through criticism of both sides.
Partisans of common cause
confuse the issue
through indiscriminate goodwill.

Those who defect from their known place
to mingle in unwalled markets
and barter inherited science
for whatever language they can learn
have yet to understand
their profit's futile
since they confuse the issue.
Understanding is not the issue.

The issue involves attack and defence.
If you're not for the victory
of your own sort, your country,
party, ethnic category right
or wrong, you count for nothing,
you only confuse the issue.
The question of actual benefits
confuses the issue.
Reason confuses the issue.
Hope confuses the issue.

The issue is, on the set day,
having prepared, having received
the clear final word of command,
doing what is to be done to the enemy –
and he is clearly marked.

WILLIAM BRANFORD

Trooper Temple Pulvermacher

Killed in action, Mount Hope, Cape Province, 26 October 1901

I
Forgotten soldier, in the winter grass,
Still ambushed for my step, among the rocks
And creviced hills that looked upon your death,
In the reconnaissance of the hare, the mica-fleck's
Miniature helio, and the entanglements
Of thorn and sugarbush, your human stealth,
Capacity for skirmish and attack,
Seem to survive, and fascinate as if
Perpetuating you.
And in the life of beasts and vegetation,
Here, in the valley of your last day's fighting,
Strange echoes of the sterile skills of war
Almost delight me, bringing you to mind.
And yet you're nothing to me but a word
On a memorial brass, so what's your warrant
For lurking in the memory, except
Unlucky soldiership, spent in a bad quarrel?

II
Well, after fifty years, yours is an easy death
To come to terms with, as the morning's breath
Flatters the lungs, and the Long Kloof extends
A boundless country of imagined friends.
When, like a shadow or a light unsought
You come to darken or inflame my thought,
Is not narcotic pity free to dote
On agonies conveniently remote,
Or idle intellect to contemplate
Hypotheses to justify your fate?
No surer provocation it's been said
For loose emotion than the anonymous dead.

III
Morning marches into the valley, overwhelming
The strong-points of the mist; unseen
Creatures of half-light, forsaking the haunts of man,

170

Withdraw to the pathless hills.
But you, invisible inhabitant
Of thought, hold out against the thrusting sunlight.
For death is more than the rifleman's misjudgement,
More than whatever material accident,
Choice of wrong cover or failure of vigilance
Brought upon you.
Death itself is your claim to compassion.
Illusions vanish with dew, but no evaporation
Of private fiction, sentimental detail,
Breaks down the substance of your right to memory.

And I see you as guardian, sentinel over
Life's secret frontier, because you lie
Here, remote from political priestcraft
And synthetic humanism. For here indifferent rock,
Cactus and thornbush forbid irresponsible
Funeral oration, tolerant only
Of reticent sympathy:
The root's comprehension of earth, or the combatant aloe's
Grasp of essentials.

WILLIAM BRANFORD

Canonical Hours[1]

for I. A. Richards

Morning creates: Adam's experience
    Springs in me faint but true:
Spiderweb, skyline, apple-blossom, all
    My own, and new.

Noon dissipates: the world of morning splits
    Along surveyor's lines;
Bosman's potatoes, the municipal quarry
    And Gerber's pines.

Evening quickens: deep in swirling mist
   Mencius writes again:
Night-spirit slowly fills the waiting kloofs
   Sufficient to sustain.

[1]With one's day-night-what rests, dawn's spirit, one's likes-dislikes to men's difference slight; one's morning-day's what done have fettered-lost it, fettered again and again one's night-spirit not sufficient to sustain (itself); night-spirit not sufficient to sustain, then he differs from birds-beasts not far.

Mencius,
Tr. I. A. Richards.

MICHAEL MACNAMARA

Fare for a Needle

White-haired,
walking in dead leaves
he came.

As I waited for a bus
he sold me a needle-book
I didn't want:
Seventy
assorted nickel goldeye needles,
finest quality,
with threader.
Fifteen cents.

   No fare.

But, opening the book, I found
the needles were organ pipes.

   For cents
   I walked with Bach
   in autumn.

SYDNEY CLOUTS

Animal Kingdom

Spading earth
I thought of the earth. Here
and there gazelle and hog
locust and elephant
fly and frog,
collecting their light, leapt
frumped pondered and whizzed
and the river that I heard
included birdsong.

What happens when the sun
dewed with such joy, shines on, spills down
on gazelle and hog
locust and elephant
fly and frog
pond hand stalk and loquat
river and beak?

I want I have I give I love
I answer the senior core of the sun
I speed the body of the warm gazelle
I lift the elephant high in my thought
like a cloud of heaven that moves so slow,
and the fly I follow, the dustheap find
my plumtree grows from a clod of sleep.
Locust locust leap with me
water flow and mirror me.

SYDNEY CLOUTS

Dawn Hippo

The size of a cavern for men to crouch in
by fire trickling small;
for demons uttered by name
to crowd like tropical thunder
and crackle against the wall,

he domes the birth of day;
built moving on the river,
shrubless mound of weighty sheen,
a large derisive slope
hammering back each ray,
he floats his quiet hilltop
he sizes up the morning;
a zone of bubbles happens round his head,
streaks of his glitter spear them dead,
breaking the break of day.

A fine froth scums his sides like primitive acid,
birds with sharp beaks fly over him;
he bulges landward
choosing a shelved approach,
the water shallows where he wants it to,
pushes in savage rings that smash
high reeds and rock the river. Mud swarms,
mud slimes his paddling belly as he climbs
heavily wagging the water away.
The full ridiculous splendour mobs the stones:
thunder and lightning jostle on his bones.

SYDNEY CLOUTS

Firebowl

Kalahari Bushman fires flowing
in the hollows of the desert
click all night
stick stuck upright
click
click
of starlight
bowstring
toes of the eland
thk thk the big raindrops
tk tk tk the sandgrains
drinking.

Sssskla!
sparks of honey
arrowheads
we who dance
around the circle
around the circle
spoor him
find him

my arrow clings to the thick thick
grunt of darkness
my arrow sings through fire

we who dance we find
the
fire
of the fire.

SYDNEY CLOUTS

The Hawk

The hawk broods earthward
on glimmering scythes,
darkens the mountain,
darkens the field.

A white cloud goes over –
so pure I cry out
for a word of judgement
lean as a blade.

Flowers are toppling,
the earth burbles blood.
O scholars of Mercy,
interpret the flood!

SYDNEY CLOUTS

The Sea and the Eagle

The sea contains a destiny,
Also the broadwinged eagle.
Both with an equal loneliness
Devour their continents.

Bird, where are you bound,
Borne on the surfs of height?
There is nothing unknown in the air.
Why do your wings flow up and upward?

Whose silence, waters, and what wound
Do you conceal in thunder?
Your beak has worried the bones of earth
Longer than the seasons have been about
Our robes, rising and falling,
And mingling us in the flowing metre.

We have given you both a mystery.
Reveal it and we shall see ourselves
Suddenly like a rising wing,
Terribly like a swoop of water.

SYDNEY CLOUTS

Within

You look long about you
intent on the world
on a midsummer day;
the sea flames hard
it is rumpled like tin,
the sun is burning
dimension away.
If you cast a pebble down
it will clatter on the waves,
your eye can not go in.

And it cannot find a tree
standing generous and full
or a house or flower
with individual power;
and it must not look within,
hardness afflicts you,
flat is the world you'd find:
a row of wooden rooftops
that can easily topple
and bring the heart down
and bring down the mind.

SYDNEY CLOUTS

The Sleeper

For Marge

When you awake
gesture will waken
to decisive things.
Asleep, you have taken
motion and tenderly laid it within,
deeply within you.
Your shoulders are shining
with your own clear light.
I should be mistaken
to touch you even softly,
to disturb your bold
and entirely personal devotion
to the self that sleeps
and is your very self,
crucial as when you hasten
in the house and hasten through the street,
or sit in the deep yellow chair
and breathe sweet air.

Unaware of the stars
outside our window
that do not know they shine,
as well as of the wild sea

that can have no care,
as well as of the wind
that blows unaware
of its motion in the air,
sound be your rest
and gentle the dreaming
of your silent body
passionately asleep.
Can a cloud stay so still?
Can a bird be so lonely?
It seems you have found
great patience in your breath:
it moves with life,
it rehearses death.

SYDNEY CLOUTS

Poetry is Death Cast Out

Poetry is death cast out
though it gives one chance to retaliate.
Death takes it but the poem moves
a little further beyond death's gate,

and I know the proof of this. Once walking
amongst bushes and lizard stones I found
a little further than I had thought
to go, a stream with a singing sound.

SYDNEY CLOUTS

Of Thomas Traherne[1] and the Pebble Outside

Gusts of the sun race on the approaching sea.

In the air Traherne's Contentments shine.

A jewelled Garden gazed at him.

178

What shall be said of Paradise?

Obscure vermilion heats the dim pebble I hold.

The long rock-sheltered surges flash with spume.

I have read firm poems of God.

Good friend, you perceived bright angels.

This heathen bit of the world lies warm in my palm.

[1]Thomas Traherne (1634?–1704). A religious poet.

SYDNEY CLOUTS

The Portrait of Prince Henry[1]

from the painting by Nuño Gonçalves

His hatbrim's full Copernican ellipse
of cloth of night encircles him.

The long monastic face renounces land,
at Sagres, in the tower
of his life's long nightwatch:
night of the sea routes
night of the waves of God
and of the starry spice routes
round and round the sun.

His eyes forgive the possible
its stormwind its astrolabe
its monster isolation
with humility,
gazing free and full,
and only then suggest
his shorter kingdom,
Portugal.

[1]Prince Henry the Navigator.

SYDNEY CLOUTS

Prince Henry the Navigator

The Navigator

At the summit of perception
a blackness starts to rise:
raw images of darkness
unkempt alarming skies

that can torment the sturdy mind
to grief or shibboleth.
Day's daylight is the reckoned tune,
night's huge and driving breath

ordains the heart of knowledge
the spokes that spin the wheel
the meditating lantern
the star-revolving keel.

Meditation On Dry Land

Through the leafy Lisbon trees I heard
the frogless ocean whiten wild as flutes.

When I wandered in Lisbon's blossoming darkness
or sat in my house, suddenly afraid

of winged horizons perched on the prow,
strange and pure their dome of singing,

silent I prayed, my task began.
I cross the deliberate gulf of man.

SYDNEY CLOUTS

The Discovery

The heartbeat! the heartbeat! Be,
but, if, how, when, between.
Every drop of blood speaks by,

the soul in concept
storms the strings.
Here's the expedition, knot by knot,
the rigging and the prow.

Canary Islands, brightly;
Bojador, in darkness
darkness
esperança!

Rounding the Cape, the sodden
wooden grumble of the wheel.

SYDNEY CLOUTS

Salute

Very Profound Men have lived in Europe.
On the world's perimeters, sharkfins, anteaters, kangaroo,
    pearloysters, bears,
and others (fit for smiles).

It was the Wolf of Europe that went prowling.

Good morning, gentle cobra, are you well?

SYDNEY CLOUTS

Intimate Lightning

Too succulent for quinces comes
this fresh quo vadis,
    Africa

    the bud
    the blossom
    the scent
    of intimate lightning.

181

Tusks traded for cash lie somewhere staling under hessian,
to be fetched for another buyer at the coast.
Tusks, skins, rhinoceros horn.

What I want, Zambesi's
abler darkness fools with:
the full penetrant
eye, and more, much more:

eye in whose obstinate dusks and rains
the forest opens;

truths of the long lianas tense with dew.

It promised these
once, but lost them
in me. I
now, in a scooped log, ride
upon More, More, the River of Night.

SYDNEY CLOUTS

The Situation

Red mountain, red forest.

Of curious quiet the late afternoon.

Is the sun setting, is it the sun?

This chocolate sweetens thought.

When the dung-beetle scratches the noise echoes in the house.

Come wind, blow wind blow!

I stand still in my garden.

Let us elect a Minister from some wise stones.

182

Set the wine on the table.

Dead thought is swarming with tyrannical flies.

The clouds are in Congress.

Set down the fruit.

Of exultant serenity shine the firm plums.

Cleft rocks, torn fish in the sea.

SYDNEY CLOUTS

Residuum

I
My tradition is dew on a shrub.

One word is too many; many, too few.

Not for perfection though that is a part of it.

The pressure of silence is about me.

A commotion.

'History
surprise us!' is one petition.

'Society
save us!' is one petition.

Speeding the lizard.

Thingbedded mutterings delay.

Listen, listen amongst the particles.

A vigil of the land as it appears.

Open. Open.

Enter the quick grain: everything is first.

I am in the dewfall
anthole
searock flintlock killed blesbok by lion, and in lion.

I am the method of the speck and the fleck.

Dew-on-a-shrub is the name no one shall refuse.

II
One word is too many; many, too few.

Sing a paean to bacteria.

Nasturtiums dwell through many many streaks of yellow,

Red and black in the smoke of the assault.

We are on the qui vive like sparrows.

No lexicon, just one word accommodates us, quickly said.

No word is my dwelling place.

Fire! Fire!

I shall shape the music by and by.

O rhetoric of hydrogen.

Somewhere the Tuareg cameldrivers raise their tents.

A man in Klapmuts breathes the secret.

And a shack on the coast is disputed.

The nervous system ails the stars.

You leapt clothed into the river in spontaneous love for me.

SYDNEY CLOUTS

Hotknife

Hotknife

Innie pondok[1] he wait for me
he say you know wy
he say you know wy, Hotknife.

He say
you know wy, Hotknife
you know wy, you Skollie[2] baasted.

So engry, maaster.
No one say dat to me.
Ony my fa'rer say dat to me.

Nellie newwe
tol' me she was married sir
she newwe tol' me she was married sir.

It was luck
but it was bad luck, maaster.

I am Hotknife
of Capricorn
an she was in de Crab sir. It was tiekets.

She newwe tol' me she was married sir.
She was hot for me, hot.
I'm sorrie sir: are you married, maaster?

I'm a man sir
ennytime, bu' dis was ekstra special condieshns.

She say Hotknife, swietaat, you a fat man.
Sa! ten years for luff sir.
I'll newwe kiela man again

no, not till I die, maaster
not for a woman, maaster.
She can be so hot for me an I'll not kiela man sir . . . .

[1]hut
[2]hooligan

Nellie

Where you Nellie
blerrie mischiff.
Ten years is not a fency fawtnight.
God is my fa'rer Nellie
an he won't make it bad for me.
He know my tennencies is honorabll
but excep' sometimes I blow up.

Dey tol' me you were dead, Nellie
but Daantjie say you ony living somewhere else.
I don' forget I don' forget nutting.
Where you living, hey?
Where you O Marie Biskit?
God is my own fa'rer
and he giff me clearance, usstrue,
he giff me clearance.
An Hotknife is Hotknife stll an he newwe cut nutting
wort' a damn excep' baaipasses since Augus' 1952.

Come come sof' chicken
come ladybird.
Hotknife is Hotknife stll
by nummer 3a
Wil'flower Awenue.

SYDNEY CLOUTS

After the Poem

After the poem the coastline took
its place with a forward look
toughly disputing the right of a poem to possess it

It was not a coast that couldn't yet be made
the subject of a poem don't mistake me
nothing to do with 'literary history'

But the coast flashed up – flashed, say, like objections
up to the rocky summit of the Sentinel
that sloped into the sea
such force in it that every line was broken

　　and the sea came by
　　the breaking sea came by

TESS KOLLER

Go Gently Through All Green

Go gently through all green.
Be careful on each grassy slope
And where the fragrant small things grow.
Green is the garment of our hope.

Go beautifully slow
Through others' brave terrain.
From small men's meteors
We find heroic stance again.

Go so our child is not
Pushed skew or shown a cul-de-sac.
We do not own our now.
We only have the usufruct.

TESS KOLLER

Let Me Not Factory

Let me not factory on the levels
Like a tick-tock, clippety-clop
Rocking horse millionth,
Screwed and proved.
Let my grass not be mowed.

Let me not year in the shallow, safe places
Where the water grows in pools.

I'll take my carnival to the mountains
Rather, high up, never-to-stop
Zircon placed zenith
Vast with dance.
I will sing among clouds
All time in perilous flames of joy balance
And I'll reap heaven's golden glance.

Beyond the pin-pricks of street eyes will I
Fly my thoughts, the kites of my thoughts.
And when all height fails
At death halt
And my urn is upturned
Let me be purest hosanna still, let
Me be undiluted salt.

DON MACLENNAN

By Kleinemonde River

I
By Kleinemonde river I sat down and wept
knowing the world had searched
and found me incomplete.
Through dark bush
and bent stems of trees
the sound of seasmiths
beating out moonsilver sheets
their cold salt furnace roaring all night long.

II
The satyr Marsyas
inferior musician
challenged Apollo
lost
was flayed alive.
His friends so wept

(says Ovid)
it became a stream
an undeniable
perennial river
of despair and ecstasy.
A poet sees things
as they never are
perceived –
by the dark waters
unskinned
he sits down and weeps.

G. C. MILLARD

Dream

Jury of twelve men with dusty veldskoen,
Hands tied, turned in silence,
Were marched off to a scaffold
On the market square;
Vierkleur[1] and Union Jack
Hung in the dead air;
Streets away, behind a corrugated fence
I played with a wooden gun
And heard no sound of breaking necks;
There was such silence there.

[1]flag of the old Transvaal Republic

PATRICK CULLINAN

The Evangelists in Africa

Tapping a light drum,
The Evangelists
Are walking down the road

In white overalls,
Carrying branches;
Calling the world,
This Sunday morning
After the rain,
To walk slowly,
To whisper 'Hallelujah.'

Those who go with you
Seize a branch,
And somewhere deep in grass
Along the river,
Make a church
To sing the truth,
The Hallelujah;
And know at once together
More of charity,
More of other men.

You move around
The hill and the thudding
Drum grows weaker:
This is the day of praise,
The sun is stronger,
And all the people
Living here sing
The creation, or make
New men from branches
After rain on Sunday morning.

PATRICK CULLINAN

Grand Hotel

I
Younger than those around him,
His hands
Are as pale as riesling.
We are told he is in Fabrics:
'Designing' he says.

                But why
Will he not sit down?
And when will he stop talking,
So well, so knowledgeably about
The etchings of Picasso:
Or is he now
On food and wine?
                Why ask?
There's more to come.
We are to hear about
The bitter squabble
He's having this instant
With his 'darling, irrational,
Fizzpop of a Mum.'

II
Her eyes stare
From a whirlpool of wrinkles.
She likes it to be said
They are blue, blue
As the violets in Spring.

Now she will show her water colours,
Painted on soft paper,
Pale washes of pink or rose that fade
Eluctably into
Mutations of celadon.
The smallest sell for Twenty Pounds,
(She has trouble with the currency)
But if she likes you,
Something she at once *feels*
She'll let them go
For nearer Twelve.

Oh why,
Ambushed at morning tea,
Did I smile at her? Why
Was I brought up
To be nice to old ladies,
Never taught to evade
Their petal-blue, glinting,
Money mad eyes?

PATRICK CULLINAN

The Billiard Room

The play of his power,
      the living, you can smell it
in this room: the cues glitter like weapons,
      the green nap of the table
was a battleground for him where conflicts broke
      in the strategy of a game.

And I can remember hearing,
      at night above my head,
the sound of a glass breaking, and a burst
      of rich laughter; then silence,
except for the powerful tread, the pacing
      from angle to angle,
and the crack of a cannon
      as the white slammed into the red. It's

all snuffed out now of course, like a long
      Havana cigar, a Hoyo de Monterrey perhaps,
smoked down for an inch or two, and never
      much more. The act has gone, his gesture
casual on an evening thirty years ago
      is obsolete; now
only a sense of ritual pervades the room and feeds
      familiar on the tokens of power:

a German ceremonial sword
      he captured in South West stands rigid
in a shell case, against one wall an old
      propeller rots (and somewhere stuck in a drawer
there's an album showing photographs of the crash),
      so that objects of steel and brass, records
of dead encounters have made this room
      a potent place, the temple of my caste

where I must pay homage, the sour pietas
      of son to father, the unforgiving
love that looks for only one thing in the past:
      conflict as barren as dust. I have no god

but a giant who paces above my head,
   who blusters nightly that in his turn
my son shall have his saga of Fee, Fie, Fum,
   to grind my bones to make his bread.

Though I stand by a half opened window
   and breathe in the air
the dust stirs about me,
   raised by a step on the floor,
and the smell that comes up is the smell of old power,
   unbreaking love, unfinished war.

PATRICK CULLINAN

**1818. Monsieur François le Vaillant[1] Recalls his
Travels to the Interior Parts of Africa 1780–1785.**

At home in the damp hills of Champagne
I take my warmth at the fire. Official
And unofficial birds stare glassy-eyed
From cabinets, uncurious now
And oddly meditative. As flames rise a glow
Lightens their wing feathers;
They are not and I am not
In Africa now; yet we remain, we are
The artefacts of that long journey,
Survivors of a narrative:
A story that I chose to tell, solid
In parts, deliberately vague
In others. I had no choice, I found
A normal country, rather like paradise
In places, a garden
Camouflaged by scandal,
Darkened by a kind of history.

So from the very start, exploring,
Plume-hatted among the hordes,
I sought what had been lost and what I found
I made my own: birds, animals, a cave of leaves,
And men. My friends became the fearful tribes,
Unwanted half-breeds, and, by letters

From the wilderness
A lonely savant at the Cape. Only
The Colonists were not to be endured:
Vicious at times or just plain boring, sly;
Certainly not schooled enough
To leave the wild unploughed,
Brandy-sots who could not comprehend
Rare Sensibility, true Pride.

But I was clever, had a way
Of getting what I wanted; that trick . . . .
Of loading my fusee
With powder, wax and water
To bring a warbler down,
Immaculate
And flat on earth . . . .
Before I broke its neck
I named the bird
And it was mine.
I had a method, yes, because I found
Buffon's stale categories a bore.
My method was to educate,
Delight, attract:
As in the breed of *Drongos*
The species multiply . . . *Drongri.*
Drongear, Drongo Moustache,
Drongo Fingah and finest of them all
Disporting on a bough
Le Drongo à Raquettes.

To crawl to no god, command no slave:
This was the ordinary
Guide of my life; but given a want
Of Civility, common
To that land, good manners helped:
Narina stank of grease but liked
A buckle, most of my toys
And understood the gallantry,
The camouflage of teasing which
Hid the method. Item:
For the King of France. The Pelt
Of one Giraffe or Cameleopard.
Chased in the Canton of the Boshmen.
Beyond the Gariep.

II
So, in the end, it all went well enough.
A King and an Emperor both
Admired my great bird book.
The one has lost his head, the other
Studies seagulls on a lonely rock . . . .
And walking in this room today
A true Apostle of Jean Jacques,
By private conversation,
Step by step, deferring, said
What I have written nicely balances
The Good with Evil, Nature with the Perfidy
Of Man.
            Is that enough, is that
What I was looking for?
I said and say again:
The Fabulous was quite destroyed
And in its place I set the truth.
I made a country real, a normal place.
Romantic, I agree, and odd but
Savage the right way at last. I showed
There were no Giants, club-footed or one-eyed,
Who now denies that Pigmies are small men?
Monomotapa, Vigite Magna have disappeared
From the maps; and where I travelled
That continent it is not dark.
I say the best minds of the age
Have made my Africa their own: my truth
Feeds their imagination. I have shown
That men in skins move in a certain
Landscape, are men like us, have names:
Confused, they love and hate.
            Is that the truth,
Is that what I see now?
There was a night, when wandering from my tent
At the stream of the Gonaquas,
I saw the moon had covered all
That forest, all the mountains with its light.
It flowed as bland as milk, the normal landscape
Seemed to shift, to alter . . . . what I saw
Remained authentic yet I knew
It was not real.
            And here much later,
Here by the fire tonight my Africa

Is dark again. Stuffed Drongos, Trogans,
Shrikes will not flap their wings;
They sit as still as rocks. Nothing
Moves but firelight closed
In the long high room.
The world is what it seems
Always, but it can flow beneath the moon
And change, alter the staid
Sequences of vision.
Half blind amid
The humdrum panic of the herd
Or camouflage of predator and prey
I only saw what I was made to see,
Could comprehend.
Do all
Travellers into darkness know,
Their eyes half closed,
Exploring they betray themselves,
Betray what they have found?

[1]Le Vaillant, François (1753–1824). French naturalist and explorer, whose travel notes were translated into many languages. His *Birds of Africa* was one of the first works on South African ornithology. He survived the French Revolution and spent the remainder of his life editing his works.

MAZISI KUNENE

Cycle

Part I
So many are asleep under the ground,
When we dance at the festival
Embracing the earth with our feet.
Maybe the place on which we stand
Is where they also stood with their dreams.
They dreamed until they were tired
And handed us the tail with which we shall dance.
Even the weeds emerge in their praise.
Yesterday there were vast villages;
We too shall follow their path,
Our dust shall arise at the gathering place
And the child will dance alone on our grounds.

Part II
How many generations
We dance over
When we are happy at the feast.
They scream from the outskirts,
Where we shall not reach with our feet.
Our eyes break into the sea of the night
When we arrive at the disputed field
Where people fight for a resting place,
Competing with the generations of antiquity.
Their tried voices rise
Rising with their songs
That will remain after the festival.

PAMELA MAY FÖRS

In Witbank Town

I came in love to Witbank Town,
So sure my love was meant for me.
What had you then in Witbank Town,
That bade me set him free?

Deserted station in the dust,
An engine shunting mournfully.
That could not be, in Witbank Town,
What took my love from me.

A laughing child astride a gate,
An old man dozing fitfully.
But what was there in Witbank Town
That took my love from me?

A church, forbidding as a stare,
And at the fence a weeping tree.
Was that alone, in Witbank Town,
What took my love from me?

Ah no, the truth of Witbank Town
Is simply that I came to see

197

How torn my love in Witbank Town,
And so I set him free.

The streets were cold in Witbank Town.
No soul came out to comfort me.
They did not know in Witbank Town
How broke my heart in me.

I came in love to Witbank Town
So sure my love was meant to be.
How could I guess, in Witbank Town,
My bitter destiny.

DOUGLAS LIVINGSTONE

The Sleep of my Lions

O, *Mare Atlanticum*,
Mare Arabicum et Indicum,
Oceanus Orientalis,
Oceanus Aethiopicus
     save me
           from civilization,
    my pastory
           from further violation.

Leave me my magics
and tribes;
to the quagga, the dodo,
the sleep of my lions.

Rust me barbed fences.
Patrol what remains.
Accept bricks, hunting rifles
and realists, telephones
and diesels
to your antiseptic main.

Grant me a day of
moon-rites and rain-dances;

198

when rhinoceros
root in trained hibiscus borders;
when hippo flatten, with a smile,
deck-chairs at the beach resorts.

Accord me a time
of stick-insect gods, and impala
no longer crushed by concrete;
when love poems like this
can again be written in beads.

DOUGLAS LIVINGSTONE

Gentling a Wildcat

Not much wild life, roared Mine leonine Host
from the fringe of a forest of crackles
round an old dome-headed steam radio,
between hotel and river – a mile of bush –
except for the wildcats and jackals.

And he, of these parts for years, was right.
That evening I ventured with no trepidations
and a torch, towed by the faculty
I cannot understand, that has got me
into too many situations.

Under a tree, in filtered moonlight,
a ragged heap of dusty leaves stopped moving.
A cat lay there, open from chin to loins;
lower viscera missing; truncated tubes
and bitten-off things protruding.

Little blood there was, but a mess of
damaged lungs; straining to hold its breath
for quiet; claws fixed curved and jutting,
jammed open in a stench of jackal meat;
it tried to raise its head hating the mystery, death.

The big spade-skull with its lynx-fat cheeks
aggressive still, raging eyes hooked in me, game;
nostrils pulling at a tight mask of anger
and fear; then I remembered hearing
they are quite impossible to tame.

Closely, in a bowl of unmoving roots,
an untouched carcass, unlicked, swaddled and wrapped
in trappings of birth, the first of a litter stretched.
Rooted out in mid-confinement: a time
when jackals have courage enough for a wildcat.

In some things too, I am a coward,
and could not here punch down with braced thumb,
lift the nullifying stone or stiff-edged hand
to axe with mercy the nape of her spine.
Besides, I convinced myself, she was numb.

And oppressively, something felt wrong:
not her approaching melting with earth,
but in lifetimes of claws, kaleidoscopes:
moon-claws, sun-claws, teeth after death,
certainly both at mating and birth.

So I sat and gentled her with my hand,
not moving much but saying things, using my voice;
and she became gentle, affording herself
the influent luxury of breathing –
untrammelled, bubbly, safe in its noise.

Later, calmed, despite her tides of pain,
she let me ease her claws, the ends of the battle,
pulling off the trapped and rancid flesh.
Her miniature limbs of iron relaxed.
She died with hardly a rattle.

I placed her peaceful ungrinning corpse
and that of her firstborn in the topgallants
of a young tree, out of ground reach, to grow: restart
a cycle of maybe something more pastoral,
commencing with beetles, then maggots, then ants.

DOUGLAS LIVINGSTONE

Pteranodon

A seven year old herd boy,
ragged happy and vacant,
sits alone playing the stonegame,
his back to the five
thin healthy head grazing.

Across the valley
the distant warts of huts
squat on the wrist of the hill.

Long believed extinct,
there was no one
but the walleyed
stampeding clot of cattle
to see the two dozen
feet of dusty leather
wingspread, hear the wet
crush of long toothed jaws closing,
the snap of vertebrae,
and nothing, nothing at all
the flight away
with the broken rabbit boy
one limb slow waving.

DOUGLAS LIVINGSTONE

Dust

The bundle in the gutter had its skull
cracked open by a kierie.
The blunt end of a sharpened bicycle
spoke grew a solitary
silver war-plume from the nape of his neck.
I turned him gently. He'd thinned to a wreck.

It was my friend Mketwa. He was dead.
Young Mac the Knife, I'd called him,
without much originality. Red
oozed where they'd overhauled him.
An illegal five-inch switchblade, his 'best'
possession, was stuck sideways in his chest.

He had been tough: moved gracefully, with ease.
We'd bricked, built walls, carted sand;
pitting strength against cement-bags, we'd seize
and humpf, steadied by a hand.
I paid the regulation wage plus fifty
per cent, his room, his board. He wasn't thrifty.

We were extending the old house I'd bought.
Those baked-lung middays we'd swill
the dust with cans of ice-cold beer. I thought
he must be unkillable,
except by white men. Each night the beerhall
took him: stoned wide, he would not stall or fall.

I don't think he learnt anything tangible
from me. From him, I learnt much:
his mother, cattle, kraal; the terrible
cheat that repaired his watch; such
and such pleased a woman; passes; bus queues;
whereabouts to buy stolen nails and screws.

His wife in Kwa Mashu, a concubine
in Chesterville, a mistress
in town: all pregnant. He'd bought turpentine
but they wouldn't drink it. This
was the trouble with women. Letters came
we couldn't read. He found another dame.

He left – more money, walls half-done, him tight –
to join Ital-Constructions.
Perhaps it had been white men: I am white.
Now, I phoned the ambulance
and sat with him. It came for Mac the Knife;
bore his corpse away; not out of my life.

DOUGLAS LIVINGSTONE

The Lost Mine

I suppose you could almost call it romantic –
the way the dead wheel hangs there in the sky
against the rusty blood-washed banner
of a bat-stitched evening and the evening star;

Clumping about, denting a tin with a kick,
the solitudes enhanced, I might say, by the cry
of a distant fisheagle and that flaky hammer
stuck, mute and forgotten, in a hollow spar

I cannot evoke the transparent ghosts of men
although they must have lived and slept here
(whose beard bowed to this cutthroat razor's blade?
and what meteors left that shed-roof holed?)

Looking at the black pit-mouth, I wonder when
it all ceased: Saturday nights with fiddle and beer,
and sweat-stained daguerreotypes of chinny maids;
two stars up now, both peering the blank craze of gold.

To find a rock and chuck it down the open shaft
is simple stuff, as is the childish thrill
of water swallowing a stone: this maw whose food
has long been dust, perhaps a rotten cable, rats,

Whispers somewhere in its tainted throat daft
silent work-songs, the stilled smash of pick and bill
and echoed grapplings from the ancient seamy feud
of men and pits. Around me tack the triumphant bats.

DOUGLAS LIVINGSTONE

Mpondo's Smithy, Transkei

Cold evenings: red tongues and shadows
spar under this dangerous thatch
rust-patched; one weather wall of planks;

long-limbed tools, wood, coal in smoke-dimmed stacks;
a hitched foal's harness musical.

The grindstone's rasped pyrotechnic
threatens the stopped-dead angled tip
of a stripped Cape cart that waits on
the return of its motivation;
a sudden hiss as quenched irons cool.

Two cowled purple-cheeked bellows-boys
pump, or jump for smiths or furies;
files of elders sucking pipestems,
ordered by fire's old feudalism,
squat: wrinkled jury on this skill.

Horseshoes, blades, shares and lives: all shaped
to the hoarse roar and crack of flame,
by the clang of metallic chords,
hammer-song, the anvil's undertone;
nailed to one post a jackal's skull.

DOUGLAS LIVINGSTONE

Vanderdecken[1]

Sometimes alone at night
lying upon your surf-ski
far beyond the sharknet

drifting on the salt-wet belly
of your mistress the black ocean,
cool under a windless moonless sky

your dangling toes you hope
not luminous from below,
dozing to the sleepy remote

mutter of shorelusting breakers
you start hearing the thrash
of bone, foam and wake;

splintering yardage and thrumming
cords; creak, groan and rattle
of blocks – and, trembling

as you lie, wet from your own death –
salt, you hear the solitary
hopeless steady cursing in Dutch.

¹*Vanderdecken* – According to legend, Capt. Henrik Van der Decken, in the 17th
century, encountered hostile winds at the Cape of Good Hope and swore in a fit
of rage he would round the Cape if it took him till Doomsday. Providence took
him at his word, and the 'Flying Dutchman' has been sailing these waters ever
since. One variation of the legend allows him to get as far as Delagoa Bay once
a year, before contrary winds force him back. Douglas Livingstone wrote this in
Durban and remarks: 'We only get a proper seafog once or twice a year; and you
can see him all right in these!' Many seafarers have claimed to have seen him,
including King George V as a midshipman on the 'Bacchante' in 1880.

DOUGLAS LIVINGSTONE

A Flower for the Night

Where I lived for a childhood
the night grass was as magical as the moon;
coolly white and soft, like new snow beautiful,
and deeply piled by the monsoons.

There was a flower (I never learnt its name)
that bloomed one night a year,
following, with its delicate bluish face,
the arc that the full moon steered.

There was a garden of small temples,
a shrine to the wind and other deities,
where tea was served to guests in porcelain shells
carried over bridges of red-painted filigree.

On the low, carved tables scattered about
black pots stood etched with cloud-shaped trees;
each pot held a bud, each had its silent knot
from the waiting throng of, mostly, Chinese.

And then the moon rose fat-faced and yellow.
The few lanterns appeared to fade in the silver air.
In minutes, as in a spell, all the buds opened.
There were so many quiet people there.

DOUGLAS LIVINGSTONE

Splinter of the True Cross

Splinter of the True Cross
I care not whence you hail.
Pale vehement researchers

in the glummer universities
have peered and proved you false,
but with polite divergencies

of theses and radio-
active-carbon datings.
One subtle group hold you,

by a certain corner-aspect,
a piece of saddlewood
carved for a camel's back;

another shoal of adepts knows,
hinged by that same corner, you held
a Roman seadog's sea-chest closed.

Rust in this nail-hole has etched
haloes of salt-flavoured pith
where unwise theologians,

monks and sinners have probed
you with curious, sad or suppliant
tongues, tasting the centuries' blood.

Pitched and rolled in caravans,
rubbing the dingy hides raw
above trackless nights of sand,

or tossed in torpedo hulls
shuddering to oar-strokes
timed by the pitiless mallets –

for me, no great shakes
at research, you're good enough.
Your wood waxes to dim shapes

scaffolding the mystery
of camels, ships and men
swaying on their Calvaries.

DOUGLAS LIVINGSTONE

Giovanni Jacopo Meditates

(on Aspects of Art & Love)

The Poet's or Playwright's Function
Is to embark physically

Upon the Consciousness of his Generation;
Not merely as the Conscience

Of his Time; nor solely to reflect
Disintegration, if Disintegration

Is the Shaker of his Time's stormy Seas.
But to anchor a Present,

Nail to its Mast
One Vision, one Integrity

In a Manner so memorable
It fills Part of a Past.

A Poet's or Playwright's Enthusiasms,
These. The proper Pursuit

For a Gentleman remains to master
The Art of delaying his Orgasms.

(on the Egalitarian Society)

All Men are Brothers
– So runs the Fable,
& the First of these
Were Cain and Abel.

(on an Early European Navigator)

I adjure thee, Sir Tongue: Be Firm. Be Indiscrete.
Cast off. Your Journey start from her slightest Toes.
Set Sail upon the Creases of her Feet,

Up, over her slim Ankles; perhaps at Sea
On choosing which Course or Calf: follow your Nose;
Arrive to linger on the Pool behind each Knee.

Here, you may gather Wits & Breath to sound
Your Strength for that Expanse that lies ahead:
Those Seas reach on, each with its Round & Mound.

Tack up the Backs of her slippery Thighs
– Lash yourself to the Helm: lose not your Head,
But keep it down. Round, in between her Nates rise

To pilot the Archipelago of her Spine.
Fare to her Shoulders from her Arms' lax Sweep;
You'll reach her Nape: this be your Journey's Shrine.

But if, Sir Tongue, your Exploration's seen
A Failure by her mere Murmuring in her Sleep,
As fitting Worth and worthy Fitter to our Queen:

Why, you must coax her over. Perhaps a Tease
Is here to stretch your Voyagings. So buckle to;
Return; & make Eyelids & her Mouth unfreeze.

Down over Chin & Throat to Armpits you'll be sent,
& up those Sun-Tipped Capes from whence a Country-View
Spreads below. Coast down to her soft Belly's Dent.

Here, you may pause to ease your Rig and Sails.
Cruise in widening Circles until intervenes
That Continent's sweet Harbour from the South-West Gales.

Drop Anchor in this most redolent of Coves,
& taste for yourself Nectarines, Tangerines,
Pineapples, Grapes, Avocados, Paw-Paws, Cloves.

Now you may rest. With modest Stirrings sit
Slaking & sluicing all your long Journey's Care.
Survey the Port, Sir Tongue, where best you may refit.

Remain alert for the Storm that overtakes
Seismic Tremors with unbridled Waves. Beware:
There will be Tumults when her fevered Body wakes.

DOUGLAS LIVINGSTONE

Loving

Loving you I love
drowsy substrata of
an unsullied earth,
the elements and compounds
that shaped your birth.

Holding you I hold,
nervous in their flowing,
ineluctable tides
trembling in you but surely felt
within your sides.

Knowing you I know
– o, grass as hair, skin as sun –
the latency to which there is a key:
behind your tranquil breasts
subtends a sea.

DOUGLAS LIVINGSTONE

The Genetic Blueprint in Roses, Etc.

Flowers with no future,
who mark life's joys and sorrows
lifting indelible

brief stillnesses out from time,
of greater moment than
the linked minutes in a man

are the immediacies
of your recalled tomorrows.
Within the flawed rose stands:

not law but its consequence,
not organ but impulse,
not synapse but memory,

not cells but their function,
not atoms but their temper,
not extent but intent:

a text of the rose entire.
Perfect, within each man
the willed perfection towers.

ATHOL FUGARD

Lena's[1] Song

'Ou blikkie Kondens Milk	A small tin of condensed milk
Maak die lewe soet	Sweetens life
Boesman is 'n Boesman	Bushman is a Bushman
Maar hy dra 'n Hotnot hoed.	But he wears a Hottentot's hat

Korsten had its empties
Swartkops got it bait

Lena's got her bruises
Cause Lena's a Hotnot meid.   Hottentot woman

Kleinskool got prickly pears
Missionvale's got salt
Lena's got a Boesman
So it's always Lena's fault.

Coegakop is far away
Redhouse up the river
Lena's in the mud again
Outa's sitting with her.'   Old black man

¹The heroine of *Boesman and Lena*, a play.

PERSEUS ADAMS

Revision

At best, words are frail shards
for refracting light that seethes
that storms under them.

'Teacher' my passport says I am
and many another official form. To these
captive, bright-eyed ones, 'teacher'

is what my mannerisms proclaim,
the smell of chalk-dust, the brisk air
of rather harassed resolution I bring

into their room, the scene of my daily attempts
to lead a waterfall into pipes. 'Pupils'
say their eyes, suddenly

a little wary, the row upon row
of faces, each ironing out to a mask
and the quicksilver movements they

unleash, and as swiftly, terminate
like snakes flickering to and fro
between hidden or half-hidden holes,

their minds poised less for enlightenment
than a chance to escape
the brainwashing, the forced

march of my lesson. Fellow inmates,
I hope I gain the courage to tell you
how much I learn from your diverse ways.

Your flair for evading boredom
with imagination and high panache
is a pearl cast up on the long shores

of adult duty; the way you exploit
even a slight deviation from the norm,
following it up as if it were gold

is something my colleagues and I need
if we're not to smother
along this well-drilled, much-beaten road.

And how do you manage that balancing act,
that art of spinning such inventive lies
while keeping your compos, letters

as dull as a pep-talk from the Head?
In an age of windy hyperbole, I stand too
in admiration of your ability

to sort the false from the genuine
and that gift's darker twin, your
bloodhound detection of the Achilles heel . . . .

At such times, your stinging reminder
of the cruel soil we have risen from,
that still fattens us, makes us smile

when we should know better, is perhaps
the most valuable lesson of all.
In more ways than one, I am your pupil.

Sometimes, no more
than a fumbling Pied Piper you
kindly pretend to follow

or a ham, an old ham turning it on
half dying to see your eyes shine.
The last bell goes and like thunder

you spill out to adorn the afternoon,
its benediction and morning crown.
Though words are, at best, frail shards

know these are cut from a prism
steeped in the sunlight of your being
and come with love to redress a mortal error.

PERSEUS ADAMS

Silence

When language fails us
you are the hawk that descends.

In friendship, you are
the shining paddock of memory
where the horses of the past
come and crop sweetgrass,
the grove, the green shade.
of the listening mind.

When loved, life itself becomes
a thin span, a comma
in your perfect
wordless sentence flowing on

With your silver ears and ivory hands
your slow syllables of snow unscroll
though I am more careful now.
I risk that pure
intimacy less often.

213

For in your breath, voluminous seas
crowd and bang
the structure of the known
while your heart-beat is an
echo of an echo – if something
so quiet can be said to have one.

In a cemetery your thousands of teeth
crop a space
that is huge.

You are the host
on unseen stars.

For the lonely, a grey shark
in a pool of cold,
an ice-berg on which they've
been marooned.

I have roamed your unmapped
tremendous zero
and I find friendship's best.

Your eyes speak of moss and a
relentless sun.

PERSEUS ADAMS

The Leviathans

'*The South African Museum may claim to have one of the best collections of whale skeletons in the southern hemisphere.*' – *From the official Guide Book by Dr. K. H. Barnard.*

Foliage or flesh can sheathe a blade;
never the pure winter,
the honed and scolloped cold
of a liberating truth

and because of this and the strata,
the roots of space they promote,
the thoroughfares of height.

I visit the whale-house. They hang there
ready to share in a calm, galactic drift,
their empty bodies' inexhaustible braille
yielding to the mind's fingers
the architecture of silence,
the blue-print of timelessness and weight.

And slowly, majestically, their kin appear:
Redwoods, glaciers –
zones of the earth-held sun-birds
whirling on the latest Apollo;
the homesteads of projecting care
when two friends meet and walk

moments mounting to fullness, then overflowing

Strait-laced cumulus, moonscape
whose stillness spears my poise
then heals it bloodlessly –
as you draw me deeper in
my gaunt mime prods what it will soon outwear;
bone reaches up for bone
as if death were trying to stage a ballet

I had not known steep zeros could be
so strictly omnific,
so augmenting in what they do.
Right Whale, Sperm Whale, Fin Whale,
proud behemoths all,
you teach me this over and over
but cut me with another vista:

You alive – fathoming the dew
lifting your fountain in joy
to curl the sky, a thundering hill
a dark cloud
sending back rain into the sea

Against the blaze of your presence there
how poor this is, how icily thrifty,
purged of genesis, light's veiled fever
and all that nails one
in dire loyalty to the bruising hour
and it's because of this,

a sense of so much
                  gone astray
that I'm glad finally to forgo

your draughty X-ray's incisive exposure,

this mute act of your
tumultuous
involuntary strip-show.

PERSEUS ADAMS

The Zen Garden

Author's note: In Ryoan-ji, Japan; consists entirely of sand and stones.

This strict – almost
abstract oasis
this leafless shade
                  that could be
a dream of sunlight
so redolent is its spaced
shorthand
of sea, sky – the way the egg
                  the bone
meet here in one etched flow . . . .

Or the seed-bed
of the very first
word so replete is it
                  with articulate
silence, the bare rudiments
of saying. The white sands here
signal
acute listening, the few
                  black stones
brooding, formulating . . . .

Is nevertheless
closer to a subtle

compassion seeing how
　　　　　its bread-and-water whole
leaves so much shining
incompleteness for the mind
to fill
and how its lean lines depict
　　　　　the gravid
nought we mostly walk in,

while the calm
that has to be won
filters through

SHEILA FUGARD

Threshold

Threshold –
What does it mean
To stand stripped to the body skin?
Threshold is more –
Standing aside
And in the leftward skip,
The wink of an eye
Cross over;
Like climbing stairs
Ascending all the way,
Then climbing yet another step,
A step that isn't there
Only hanging in the mind.

Rubrics of obscurity
Clearer than rhetoric stand:
Knossus is another kind of cathedral,
Notre Dame strikes the gong of history
In the great stained glass windows.

Threshold
Where meanings stand in the air:
Unquoted they cost nothing,

I cannot price that sunset,
I am no voyeur,
For the shadow my body makes
As it falls on sea sand –
Let the Winged Victory
Remain the Winged Victory,
I scorn Leonardo to his face –
My vision,
Myself walking
Truly real,
The pavement cracking
Under my feet,
The sky blossoming red
Above my head.

My mind clear
As the pool of Narcissus,
I am
My image,
A man
With the muscles of Michael Angelo,
My own smile
Simpler than hers,
The Mona Lisa.

Exit
Artists and poets.
I exist
In my own skin.

SIPHO SEPAMLA

The Will

The house, by right,
you will have to vacate
surrender the permit
and keep your peace

The burglar-proofing and the gate
will go to my elder son
so will the bicycle
and a pair of bracelets

The kitchen-scheme and utensils
will go to my little girl
so will the bathtub
and the two brooms

The bedroom suite
will go to my younger son
who is married
so will the studio couch

The peach tree uproot
it might grow in the homelands
so might it be with your stem

The Bible
you will have to share
for you will always want its Light

The cat spotted black and white
you will have to divide
for that you'll need God's guidance.

SIPHO SEPAMLA

Da Same, Da Same

I doesn't care of you black
I doesn't care of you white
I doesn't care of you India
I doesn't care of you kleeling[1]
if sometimes you Saus Afrika
you gotta big terrible terrible
somewheres in yourselves
because why
for sure you doesn't look anader man in da eye

219

I mean for sure now
all da peoples is make like God
sometimes you wanna knows how I meaning for
is simples
da God I knows for sure
He make avarybudy wit' one heart

for sure now dis heart go-go da same
dats for meaning to say
one man no diflent to anader
so now
you see a big terrible terrible stand here
how one man make anader man feel
da pain he doesn't feel hisself
for sure now dats da whole point

sometime you wanna know how I meaning for
is simples
when da nail of da t'orn² tree
scratch little bit little bit of da skin
I doesn't care of say black
I doesn't care of say white
I doesn't care of say India
I doesn't care of say kleeling
I mean for sure da skin
only one t'ing come for sure
and da one t'ing for sure is red blood
dats for sure da same da same
for avarybudy.

¹Coloured
²thorn

ADAM SMALL

from **Black, Bronze and Beautiful**

My nipples are the noses, wet like dew
of early morning or late night
of two black lambs – two playful karakul:
their supple darkness makes your manhood new

My limbs, my love, are ebony formed fine
whose coolness kindles fires in the mind
whose quiet raises in the heart a storm:
oh you, don't fear to burn, or blow, or to be mine

Come, nest your hands and lips like birds
in my bush of black hair; perch in my branches
all your open being; be truthful utterly: come
hide away in me from people, and from stones and words

Bronze is my body like anointed soil
or the most blessed bread, or wine
hallowed by wood and years in cellars deep:
a cup is my bronze body, overflowing oil . . .

Drawn from blossoms scented sweet and wild
brown honey wets my rounded lips, my love
and milk of goats the inside of my mouth
Come let me feed you: be my unweaned child . . .

To nurse you back to life, if you but will
I am good ears of corn for you – Bake bread!
I am sweet bunches of black grapes for you – Make wine!
I hold life out to you, full and delectable

COLIN STYLE

To O-lan

She was born with eyes asleep,
Twenty years before the blossom broke
They smouldered.
There are some born who never wake,
Whose breasts stay still as wood
And they are unproductive chapels to themselves.

But she has beautified love,
And as I touch her face,
I dream of the splintered stars
That lie above the barren men
Who clutter this lost world like stones.

COLIN STYLE

Rhodes's Bed

In my grandfather's house
is a bed Rhodes slept in –
one of the many sweating catafalques
scattered on his last journey.
It is covered by a plain quilt,
in an unoccupied room floored by black planks.
There are no windows
to report on the sodden, swart air.
Its twin doors, opening to the verandah,
have swollen to seal tightly without pliers and leaden nails;
its brass handles tarnished and just faintly elaborate.
The adjacent dining-room, with porous bricks,
wizened clock on mantelshelf, is his ante-room,
for on his bed lies the heap of flesh;
waistcoat, damp, screwed-up shirts
drape the bedposts and marble wash-stand.
His watch-chain dangles from the table,
ͺthe hands are hard points of assegai
ticking like splinters crushed by Cape-carts).
A receptacle full of smoking yellow fluid is half-under the bed
and the man himself, blue cheeks,
breathing like thunder as he watches the ceiling,
Empires slowly drying at the bottom of his eyes.

JEREMY TAYLOR

Ag Pleez Deddy

Ag pleez deddy wont you take us to the drav'in
All six seven of us eight nine ten
We wanna see a flik about Tarzan and the apeman   film
When the show is over you can bring us back again

Chorus: Popcorn chewing gum peanuts and bubble gum
           Icecream candyfloss and eskimo-pie,
           Ag deddy how we miss acid-drops and liquoris,
           Pepsicola gingerbeer and Canada-dry

Ag pleez deddy wont you take us to the funfair
We wanna have a ride on the bumper-cars,
We'll buy a stick of candyfloss and eat it on the octopus
Then we'll take the rocketship that goes to Mars

Chorus:

Ag pleez deddy wont you take us to the wrestling
We wanna see an ou called Ski-Hi-Lee,   chap
When he fights Willie Liebenberg there's gonna be a murder
Cos Willie's gonna donner that blerrie Yankee   thrash   bloody

Chorus:

Ag pleez deddy wont you take us off to Durban
It's only eight hours in the Chevrolet
There's spans of sea and sand and sun and fish in the acquarium   lots
That's a lekker place for a holiday   nice

Chorus:

Ag sies deddy if we can't go off to bioscope   oh drat
Or go off to Durban life's a hang of a bore,   terrible
If you wont take us to the zoo then what the heck else can we do   hell
But go on out and moera all the outjies next door   beat up   blokes

Chorus:

WOPKO JENSMA

In Memoriam Akbar Babool

you introduced me to my first goddess
        'dis towns full a bitches
     ya wanna try one?'
afterwards we saw your home
     'loaded w'mosquitoes hea
        dey nibble ya ta pieces 'tnight'
creaky floor, a gauze door,
backyard of sand
in the middle a dagga plant   cannabis
     'lets 've suppa 'n onion 'n egg

223

drive down dry bread a drop a wine'
next day the glittering town
prêgo and café com leite   steak sandwich, coffee and milk

me without cash later some day
you flogged the camera i stole
    'ya got trouble w'ya gal?
    listen boy, go home, juss go home'
a room in ho ling, a room at least
one with the broads, one with them
    'listen boy, go home an see ya dad
    dis place's not f'ya 't all'

sudden cash from nowhere and billy
we paint the town all bloody red
    'now prawns, boy, we a'square w'all
    square as da patten on a makapulan'   cloth skirt
a flat in alto mae, all of it
clean bath, polished floor, wide bed
    'ya sudden luck's gonna change
    an ya laurentina'll juss be water'   beer

for sure it happened as bad luck wanted
this time a reed hut in xipamanine
    'palish'n makov evry day   porridge and spinach
    dis reed hut, ma love, a pit walk'
sometimes akbar, sometimes billy, always i
a walk to the beach a relief, the open sea
    'ya kid gro's up, wants grub
    da kid wants ta learn letters'

yes, i remember home and drone living
cash and 8 to 5 till you are not you
    'stop dreamin, look, a'm real
    billy's sax's lost long ago'
i love my big love, my cry
the thorn bush, my life an open plain
    'akbar, 's ya, ya rotten –
    'strue, all ya said, akbar, 'strue'

sometimes now i remember you said
someone called you bloody coolie
when you asked for help
with your first heart attack
up the steps of casa elefante

224

WOPKO JENSMA

If only a Dream were not Real

for Wilko

i know my children are hungry i must get them bread
i open the door and outside it's clear day

down the street i am in the thronging crowd –
singing along with them: 'it's all been a big lie'

our heroes have sold us down the river . . . .
i enter the market and buy a basketful bread

now in the streets there's no one and no lights
i hear a saracen passing by and soldiers

talking a language i do not understand
lost in the city i've been in since a child –

in a street i know i've not been in before –
i see a watchman sitting by his brazier

once by his side i see his dull eyes stare –
a trickle of blood down his neck dried black

in front of him a newspaper almost two years old
the headline clear: 'unrest in our capital city'

somehow i arrive at our shack in the slum –
i open the door there's no one inside and here

on the table our plates covered with years of dust –
what did i live for? what am i going to die for?

GEOFFREY HARESNAPE

Sheep

for Jack Cope

A grab at the hindquarters stopped
its bustle towards freedom.
They thonged its legs
and, wasting no time,
took the clasp knife to cancel
the vein-cords tying it to life.

Its consciousness
(such as it was)
was given up without a cry.
By the wall
it lies gushing into the sand –
old Abraham and his son are doing the job.

The cared-for blade finds its route
along the midriff, forking to the thighs:
knee joints are snapped like twigs:
part of skinning is like peeling,
pushing down into the flanks with sideways hands,
the fell coming free from the white integuments.

They lift the rear legs
and, panting, hook them on wires.
The stomach bag
comes hurrying out
at the knife's whisper,
the endless sausages of the entrails also sagging and sliding.

Patient, he takes the dirigible lungs and the heart:
severs an upside-down head:
more fluids flush:
grass mush discharges
(with gurgles) from the throat hole.
He cuts off the anus – makes all neat.

They lay the innards
on the stretched-out mat of its personal skin –

honeycomb tripes, a shining liver,
the gall bladder a black round pebble set on its own,
some sprinkles of crimson – so little blood
for so much dismemberment in the cold wind.

He touches the warm flesh gently.
How old is it then?
In jaw-depths he looks for relevant pegs
still swimming in slobber.
Later, with saw and axe, it will be squared into pieces
fit for an unperturbed eye.

This two-tooth, caught fast in the tufts it fearfully nibbled,
he takes as a gift.
His resolve: no particle will go to waste:
all must be used to strengthen the life urge.
(The only formula to make some sense
of violation.)

BRUCE HEWETT

The Pygmy

Impenetrable forest
bows
before the bulldozers of knowledge
giving up ghosts
to the freshening wind.
The pygmy
discovered
like some lemur
behind leaves
or gecko
beneath a stone
hides . . . .
or like some
desperate chameleon
short of changes
tries to camouflage
his mystery
against a jet torn sky.

BRUCE HEWETT

Innocent Lamb

The lambs
go meek and gentle
tempered by pain.
The butcher
a too mortal man
amongst hooked meats
wraps the parcel
lifeless
seeing
the sacrificial lamb
smile back a blessing
through the eyes of children
wraps it heartened
with a smile.

BRUCE HEWETT

The Lost

Speechless
they walk circles
wondering
who their neighbour is.
They hesitate
fingers to their lips
fearing the kiss of death.
They scratch the backs
of their heads
where the bats of their problems lurk
where no light burns
but a flickering element
falters red as hell.
They stand at the gate
inchoate
having forgotten the syllable

that earned the gatekeeper's
reproach.
They nod to blessed words
striving to mime
all that would grant them yes.

BRUCE HEWETT

The Crocodile

The crocodile is full of spleen:

He mulls the bile of judges.

He purifies his river;
the white corpuscle
devours the red.

His law
is the law of take
and it is just.

The water
thrashes
at his moment of truth.

Time and he continue.

BRUCE HEWETT

Elephants in the Addo Mist

Amidst
great gusts of mist
that absorb
the trivial details

of smaller game
the massive truth appears.
We behold images
the appearance of elephants
on the threshold
of unapproachable
worlds of consciousness.
Elephants
whose thick skinned presence
confirms all possibility
of improbable miracles.
They trumpet
their verities
against our disbelief.
They disappear
from our astonished gaze
and wonder
spreads the Word
across the veld.

HUGH LEWIN

Touch

When I get out
I'm going to ask someone
    to touch me
    very gently please
    and slowly,
    touch me
    I want
    to learn again
    how life feels.

I've not been touched
for seven years
    for seven years
    I've been untouched
    out of touch
    and I've learnt

to know now
the meaning of
untouchable.

Untouched – not quite
I can count the things
that have touched me

One: fists
At the beginning
   fierce mad fists
   beating beating
   till I remember
   screaming
   Don't touch me
   please don't touch me.

Two: paws
The first four years of paws
   every day
   patting paws, searching
   – arms up, shoes off
   legs apart –
   prodding paws, systematic
   heavy, indifferent
   probing away
   all privacy.

I don't want fists and paws
I want
   to want to be touched
   again
   and to touch,
   I want to feel alive
   again
   I want to say
   when I get out
Here I am
please touch me.

C. J. DRIVER

A Ballad of Hunters

My great-grandfather hunted elephants,
Shot four hundred in a year,
Till one day his death turned round
And sniggered in his ear.

> *The theme's the same, the method changes –*
> *Time has planned the ending,*
> *Has turned the hunter to the hunted*
> *And bred the next from nothing.*

My great-great-uncle farmed alone,
Made next to nothing from his land,
Till at last the cancer took him,
Eating from his living hand.

> *The theme's the same, the method changes –*
> *Time has planned the ending,*
> *Has turned the farmer to the harvest*
> *And bred the next from nothing.*

Cousins and cousins in their dozens
Were killed in their mission churches
By the tribes whose heads they broke
To teach them the Christian virtues.

> *The theme's the same, the method changes –*
> *Time has planned the ending,*
> *Has turned the clergy to the converts*
> *And bred the next from nothing.*

My father's father died at Delville Wood,
Shooting Germans for his British past –
Left his wife a private's pension
And children to make it last.

> *The theme's the same, the method changes –*
> *Time has planned the ending,*
> *Has turned the sniper to the target*
> *And bred the next from nothing.*

Both my uncles fought the war,
Like lovers died a year apart –
Left some letters and a flag or two
And silence to be their art.

The theme's the same, the method changes –
Time has planned the ending,
Has turned the fighters to the dying
And bred the next from nothing.

Now I'm my subject, a sort of hunter
Stalking the blood of my family –
But hunted too by time's revenge
For all they made of my history.

The theme's the same, the method changes –
Time will plan the ending,
Will turn the hunter to the hunted
And breed the last from nothing.

OSWALD MTSHALI

The Shepherd and his Flock

The rays of the sun
are like a pair of scissors
cutting the blanket
of dawn from the sky.

The young shepherd
drives the master's sheep
from the paddock
into the veld.

His bare feet
kick the grass
and spill the dew
like diamonds
on a cutter's table.
A lamb strays away

enchanted by the marvels
of a summer morning;
the ram
rebukes the ewe,
'Woman! Woman!
Watch over the child!'

The sun wings up
on flaming petals
of a sunflower.

He perches on an antheap
to play the reed flute,
and to salute
the farmer's children
going to school,
and dreamily asks,
'O! Wise Sun above,
will you ever guide
me into school?'

OSWALD MTSHALI

The Master of the House

Master, I am a stranger to you,
but will you hear my confession?

I am a faceless man
who lives in the backyard
of your house.

I share your table
so heavily heaped with
bread, meat and fruit
it huffs like a horse
drawing a coal cart.

As the rich man's to Lazarus,
the crumbs are swept to my lap

by my Lizzie:
'Sweetie! eat and be satisfied now,
To-morrow we shall be gone.'

So nightly I run the gauntlet,
wrestle with your mastiff, Caesar,
for the bone pregnant with meat
and wash it down with Pussy's milk.

I am the nocturnal animal
that steals through the fenced lair
to meet my mate,
and flees at the break of dawn
before the hunter and the hounds
run me to ground.

OSWALD MTSHALI

An Abandoned Bundle

The morning mist
and chimney smoke
of White City Jabavu
flowed thick yellow
as pus oozing
from a gigantic sore.

It smothered our little houses
like fish caught in a net.

Scavenging dogs
draped in red bandanas of blood
fought fiercely
for a squirming bundle.

I threw a brick;
they bared fangs
flicked velvet tongues of scarlet
and scurried away,
leaving a mutilated corpse –

an infant dumped on a rubbish heap –
'Oh! Baby in the Manger
sleep well
on human dung.'

Its mother
had melted into the rays of the rising sun,
her face glittering with innocence
her heart as pure as untrampled dew.

OSWALD MTSHALI

This Kid is no Goat

Where have
All the angry young men gone?
Gone to the Island of Lament for Sharpville.
Gone overseas on scholarship,
Gone up North to milk and honeyed uhuru.
Gone to the dogs with the drink of despair.

Yesterday I met one in a bookstore:
he was foraging for food of thought
from James Baldwin, Le Roi Jones
Albert Camus, Jean-Paul Sartre.

He wore faded jeans and heavy sweater,
he saluted me with a
        'Hi! brother!'
He was educated in a country mission school
where he came out clutching a rosary
as an amulet against
        'Slegs vir Blankes – For Whites Only'.

He enrolled at Life University
whose lecture rooms were shebeens,
hospital wards and prison cells.

He graduated cum laude
with a thesis in philosophy:

'I can't be black and straight
in this crooked white world!
'If I tell the truth
I'm detestable.
'If I tell lies
I'm abominable.
'If I tell nothing
I'm unpredictable.
'If I smile to please
I'm nothing but an obsequious sambo.

'I have adopted jazz as my religion
with Duke Ellington, Count Basie,
Louis Armstrong as my High Priests.
'No more do I go to church
where the priest has left me in the lurch.
'His sermon is a withered leaf
falling from a decaying pulpit tree
to be swept away
by violent gusts of doubt and scepticism.

'My wife and kids can worship there:
they want to go to heaven when they die.
'I don't want to go to heaven when I'm dead.
'I want my heaven now,
here on earth in Houghton and Parktown;
a mansion
two cars or more
and smiling servants.
Isn't that heaven?'

OSWALD MTSHALI

Men in Chains

The train stopped
at a country station.

Through sleep curtained eyes
I peered through the frosty window,
and saw six men:

men shorn
of all human honour
like sheep after shearing,
bleating at the blistering wind,
'Go away! Cold wind! Go away!
Can't you see we are naked?'

They hobbled into the train
on bare feet,
wrists handcuffed,
ankles manacled
with steel rings like cattle at the abbatoirs
shying away from the trapdoor.

One man with a head
shaven clean as a potato
whispered to the rising sun,
a red eye wiped by a tattered
handkerchief of clouds,
'Oh! Dear Sun!
Won't you warm my heart
with hope?'
The train went on its way to nowhere.

PETER STRAUSS

The Tortoise

He sought longevity; vegetarian
He cut pale leaves of clover with bony gums
On the hill-side. Having mastered this art,
Found he could feed on invisible influences
In the atmosphere, scent-essences and ghosts.
His membraned nose sucked in the pure ice,
Greyish-blue tinted, aetherized, of mountain air.
Like a fish winter-bound
Hibernated, bloodless.

Next turned to imitate the life of stones.
Brilliant impurities in his clay
Rose streaking to the surface and were combed

To consistent sheens. On the sea's bed
Became inured to pressure, that laid rings
On him, flake pressed down upon flake.
Or in temporary release, uplifted,
Things outside this world, the seven stars,
Aurora borealis, imprinted
Blue flickering strands on his charmed loins.
Learnt to be composite, humped with embedded stones,
Petrified wood, animal skeleton, sand.

Was rock. Only, always,
At the base of his throat,
Like a bubble in purple lava
Rolling, horrible,
Without escape, his pulse.

JENI COUZYN

We Found Him Amid Stones

We found him amid stones.
Covered in soft red dust
darting from ring to ring, arms
gesticulating
skin like winter grass
bones ungoverned.
There was no pretence in him
eyes clear blue, quick and curious
two birds.
Swiftly he moved.

The settlement was all circles
Taught by the easy sun and the seasons
stone followed stone in
perfect symmetry.
Built to look out of
the sky a huge blue tent, sure curve
and swing of the mountains
its outer walls. Within, sleeping cells
granaries and mosaic ovens
curled in tight as wombs.

'Five hundred years these people
lived here without confusion
nor fought a war
nor sought a new world. Lived here
before the gathering of ships
hunting elephant, rearing cattle,
mining platinum in the echo-tone of
grassland and low bushveld,
stone-age and iron-age men with verandahs
sliding doors and precise, identical doorposts.

This little jar was for cosmetics;
here was a conical hut where the smith lived
and here, the tribal butcher who must have been
half bushman
carved up the elephant and deer
between these two stones.
At the summit here the chief lived
see how sheltered it is
and at this gate the cattle
were taken out to pasture.

They were here before the great trek
they were here through the long wars
they were here when the first seam of gold
ruptured like an artery across the land.
We have found bullets under ash . . . .'
We found him amid stones.
With his small brush and careful trowel
he was sifting grains of truth
from a tangled jungle of red earth
time and prejudice and root and thorn.

ARTHUR NORTJE

Preventive Detention

Pale teaboy juggling cups and saucers
once taught Othello to our class,
and a spindly scholar's imprisoned because
winter is in the brilliant grass.

Liberal girl among magnolias born
was set to clipping dahlias
in the prison yard, her blonde locks shorn.
Winter is in the shining grass.

Twine the tattered strands together,
loves and passions that amass.
What's discoloured in the blowing clouds
winters in the luminous grass.

ARTHUR NORTJE

Native's Letter

Habitable planets are unknown or too
far away from us to be
of consequence. To be of
value to his homeland must the wanderer
not weep by northern waters, but love
his own bitter clay
roaming through the hard cities, tough
himself as coffin nails.

Harping on the nettles of his melancholy,
keening on the blue strings of the blood,
he will delve into mythologies perhaps
call up spirits through the night,

or carry memories apocryphal
of Tshaka, Hendrik Witbooi, Adam Kok,
of the Xhosa nation's dream
as he moonlights in another country.

But he shall also have
cycles of history
outnumbering the guns of supremacy.

Now and wherever he arrives
extending feelers into foreign scenes
exploring times and lives,

equally may he stand and laugh,
explode with a paper bag of poems,
burst upon a million televisions
with a face as in a Karsh photograph,
slave voluntarily in some siberia
to earn the salt of victory.

Darksome, whoever dies
in the malaise of my dear land
remember me at swim,
the moving waters spilling through my eyes:
and let no amnesia
attack at fire hour:
for some of us must storm the castles
some define the happening.

ARTHUR NORTJE

Cosmos in London

Leaning over the wall at Trafalgar Square
we watch the spray through sun-drenched eyes,
eyes that are gay as Yeats has it:
the day suggests a photograph.
Pigeons perch on our shoulders as we pose
against the backdrop of a placid embassy,
South Africa House, a monument of granite.
The seeds of peace are eaten from our brown palms.

My friend in drama, his beady black eyes
in the Tally Ho saloon at Kentish Town:
we are exchanging golden syllables
between ensembles. I break off to applaud
a bourgeois horn-man. A fellow in a yellow
shirt shows thumbs up: men are demonstrative.
While big-eyed girls with half-pints stand
our minds echo sonorities of elsewhere.

One time he did Macbeth
loping across like a beast in Bloemfontein

(Othello being banned along with Black Beauty).
The crowd cheered, they cheered also
the witches, ghosts: that moment you could feel
illiteracy drop off them like a scab.
O come back Africa! But tears may now
extinguish even the embers under the ash.

There was a man who broke stone
next to man who whistled Bach.
The khaki thread of the music emerged
in little explosions from the wiry bodies.
Entranced by the counterpoint
the man in the helmet rubbed his jaw
with one blond hand, and with the other
pinned the blue sky up under his rifle.

Tobias should be in London. I could name
Brutus, Mandela, Lutuli – but that memory
disturbs the order of the song, and whose
tongue can stir in such a distant city?
The world informs her seasons, and she,
solid with a kind of grey security,
selects and shapes her own strong tendencies.
We are here, nameless, staring at ourselves.

It seems at times as if I am
this island's lover, and can sing her soul,
away from the stuporing wilderness where
I wanted the wind to terrify the leaves.
Peach aura of faces without recognition,
voices that blossom and die bring need for death.
The rat-toothed sea eats rock, and who escapes
a lover's quarrel will never rest his roots.

ARTHUR NORTJE

Sea-days and Summerfall

Sea-days, their loss
aches. Maturity echoes
the green swell in the hills, surf rues

the almost vanished beachprints of its mermaid.
Beyond innocence you bear
the clear tide in your firm limbs.

Sensuous sands of the dunes slide
with rough lust making flesh desirous,
but you held cool rein on your shadow.
Shore-dusk redolent of willow burnt
softly in the soul with no concern
of hourglass or stars.

Not squinting into grained winds
or stripping in the salt breeze:
your sweet skin had but been
caressed by the vitamin sun,
the slim waters fondled your
beige blossoms: O the sea-days.

Summerfall: it brought me
in search along peripheries
of mellow swells, your waves of woman, silk
fur waiting in the shy things.
You love till hurt surrenders, you
subdue me with a shy pleasure.

ARTHUR NORTJE

All Hungers Pass Away

All hungers pass away,
we lose track of their dates:
desires arise like births,
reign for a time like potentates.

I lie and listen to the rain
hours before full dawn brings
forward a further day and winter sun
here in a land where rhythm fails.

Wanly I shake off sleep,
stare in the mirror with dream-puffed eyes:

I drag my shrunken corpulence
among the tables of rich libraries.

Fat hardened in the mouth,
famous viands tasted like ash:
the mornings-after of a sweet escape
ended over bangers and mash.

I gave those pleasures up,
the sherry circuit, arms of a bland girl
Drakensberg lies swathed in gloom,
starvation stalks the farms of the Transvaal.

What consolation comes
drops away in bitterness.
Blithe footfalls pass my door
as I recover from the wasted years.

The rain abates. Face-down
I lie, thin arms folded, half-aware
of skin that tightens over pelvis.
Pathetic, this, the dark posture.

STEPHEN GRAY

Sunflower

Poor sunflower, your
neck so stretched and
drooping to your feet

can't see the mossies
can't see your own
glory reflected around

sentenced to death
dropping seed in plastic
bags, it's all over

like the hanged man
Pretoria Central
Wednesday dawn.

STEPHEN GRAY

Mayfair

O suburb of stripped cars & highrise hollyhocks
    where the greater unemployed
swat sweat that crawls like flies down fallen legs
    where cataracted chickens gawp
from turning spits in Costa's Terminus Cafe
    where housewives vie on volume
down a one-way street flushed with soap-opera
    & their potato-fat serving girls
shine the Dandy polish on their red knees

backyard archaeology turns up a shard
    plastic rattles glass coal
& the condensed milk throat of the neighbour's
    bat-eared military son
breaks all siesta on his A-minor bugle practice
    the jackpot days are over for
the Dixi Cola pensioners in the Thursday
    post-office payout queue
decay like rope around their contoured necks

the mother's clinic scrapes a formless arm with vaccine
    tetanus is in the wind
scabby wild cats track their corrugated clawy paths
    to the bins of the Limosin Hotel
& miners from Frelimo stroll in unofficial gangs
    against the menace of stick em up & defence
& trespass on the Gaza Strip where Reggie and Honey
    packing through Majestic Mansions
deny all knowledge all involvement in crime

down the plane-tree Ninth Avenue rides a blue nun
    on a cross-barred bicycle
down the brick of the Dolphin Street swimming pool
    loiter kids held up by candy floss
down the intersection bounce Clover Dairies ice cream
    sidecars & bells of appetite
down the coach-house whitewash plunge rust and creeper
    & the ritual taxi ride to church
rounds a Pentecostal Sunday curve towards heaven

246

O Mayfair & a Chinaman's chest flat as a slime-tray
    parades the verandas of concrete waggon wheels
how uplifting! – the pumpkins on roofs still
    the TRG car comes for southern flesh
& Mr Fonseca Builder unclasps his racing pigeons
    to spiral over smallness & the dumps
the fine golden sand the cyanide lagoon the synagogue
    the alcoholic pavements & knives & curlers
into undefeated clarity of the whitest air.

STEPHEN GRAY

The Tame Horses of Vrededorp

Their realm is from Piel's Sausage Wholesale
the Fresh Produce market at the cooling towers
skidding on onion skin and tar under M1
to No Animal Drawn Vehicles by Brixton
Tower residential area I tell you a slum

down the Rand they shuffle past Phineas
McIntosh children's park they used to play
centaurs in the old days out for spoils
horses and men raiding over to Langlaagte
taking off over fences and clover with our girls

past the clipped mown green and the Indian gravel
pits dropping off mielies for black bus queues
and then over Church Street Bridge and then
door to door the hawker yelling man
like five for a bob's back in commerce again

they wear horseshoes for luck blinkers bells the lot
shafts bend with them snort in their nosebags
you can hear Pegasus rising from the fumes
stirring flies he travels high on octane
stabled at sunset curried by golden grooms

no chances the tame horses trot pulling carts
back to Vrededorp sammy's in a hurry now
his whip slamming like a chariot race

at the lights it's the Mayfair cavalry
trampling ghettos enemies of the state

shame you'd think they'd let a gelding retire
on the highveld where lucerne's so high but
that sack of worms knock-kneed shrunken-withered sight
makes a last obliging haul past Piel's Wholesale
to the abattoir mark X on his forehead and Petz-D-Lite.

STEPHEN GRAY

In Praise of Archaeologists

There lies ingrown by destruction from above
humiliated under the mule's hoof the detritus
of another and another culture giants are still walled in
by mountains these days the banded sun
keeps on excoriating the achieved flower

but at Sterkfontein and Olduvai Gorge surface
at the tip of persuasive shovels the mementoes
of a prelapsarian forgotten but not gone
man evidently human under the eroding dust
trenched out again skull by skull and dated

there is only refinement after that be these fragments
that composed a crater lips like flamingoes
with breasts exactly where you need them
containers for mass production intercalated
skin on skin thrust one into the other

death by natural process by intimate ceremony
exhumed for X-ray and carbon-14 nothing
left of this one was greedy that one mean
but the general greedy mean pulverisation
of all that was superbly mobile and erect

so with the next catastrophe I hope to be
buried in a characteristic position one finger pointing
up my mouth on a sunset hymn calling for
meat and wine in the last second before the turf
frazzles me and the digger's spade chops me free.

PETER WILHELM

The President and the Dwarf

The President of the People's Republic of South Africa
was taking a leisurely evening stroll in the Gardens,
accompanied by his favourite dwarf, Tinyman. It had
been a difficult but rewarding day in Parliament.

'So, sir,' Tinyman said, 'now your word is truth.'

The President paused and frowned. 'No,' he said,
'now my word is law.'

The dwarf looked up wonderingly at his master.
'You're always so precise,' he said.

PETER WILHELM

Love Poem

Love bursts the skin of history,
The blood of the dead is the juice of the fruit.
In wind,   waves,   stone,   art,
The dramatic contours of flesh have remembrance.
The ecstasy of our time
Is every lover's ecstasy and present.
Love has this antiquity:
Your flesh and mine commemorate Eve and Adam.
Ecstasy goes to dust
In the Black Hole of entropy;
But dust will have its resurrection.
I will meet you in our children
Who will write this poem again.

MIKE KIRKWOOD

Henry Fynn[1] and the Blacksmith of the Grosvenor[2]

1
Bones sleeping in the cove – toes tight
in gullies, the sweet dreams of skulls
tucked under the sandy coverlet,
a jaw-bone braying where the swells

whiten and hiss the reef -- I sing
not these first dead, the Indiaman's
quiet clerk or termagant bosun
sitting out the sea's stiff dance;

not the remaindered mythic band
who made eight hundred miles on prayer,
the flesh of oysters, limpets and
other who lost their grip, it's feared;

not those left propped up in caves,
nor the sunburned virgins with eyes
brighter than beads, whose blood still leaves
pallor on a tribesman's features;

but you, blacksmith, who chose to stay,
and by the time the last sleeve waved
or hat lifted where the long bay
turns, had hefted, hurled and heaved

pig-iron of the ship's ballast
up the beach with a realist's hands.
On that cliff-top your forge flame faced
out the tough sea, a continent's

tougher customers, the trials
by conscience, women, work
and the casual round of wars
you made your life by. And your luck

held, which was all you hoped; months, years.
Shipwrecks of kraals, extinguished tribes,
and lost scouts behind whom all ways
went thorny with spears, came to your fire.

II

Fifty years on came Fynn, starving,
living from root to root, begging
at hovels and hide-outs from skins
already too stretched and staring

to shrink from any new horror.
This was after Chaka's impis
had been that way and back. Further
north, over his morning coffee

on the beach, alone, his two guides
sweating somewhere in the undergrowth,
Fynn had watched the army glide
incuriously by; in his throat

Chaka, the charm sounded over
and over, while they passed so close,
twenty thousand shield to shoulder,
he sat all morning in one place.

Light-headed from his month of hunger,
Fynn thought he'd found the Grosvenor gold
when iron outcrops made him stumble
in long grass growing through the forge

or where the forge had been, but soon
mastered the truth: saw with calm blows
a new day's sun driven to its noon,
ship's ballast lying straight in rows.

[1]Fynn, H. F. (1803–61), came to S.A. in 1818. After 4 years in E. Cape, went to Natal, where he negotiated trade agreements with Shaka & Dingane. Became a Zulu Chief in 1831.

[2]English East Indiaman, with cargo including gold & jewels, was wrecked in 1782 on the Coast of Pondoland. A few survivors reached the Cape; others intermarried with Blacks.

CHRISTOPHER HOPE

The Old Men are Coming from the Durban Club

After lunching agreeably but not too well,
The old men are coming from the Durban Club
Breathing easily and just nicely full.

They pass the Natal Building Society
And the Netherlands Bank
Where the tellers are giving out money.

They pass the phthisical hag who laughs
By the wall of the Protea Assurance Company
And coughs her difficult cough.

The old men's bellies show like whales
Above their waistlines, their eyes
Are oysters, their laughs are snails.

You'd never say that before dawn each sits
On a lavatory seat, expensive trousers
Around his ankles, and hawks and spits.

Long after the drinkers have left their pubs
And sat down at their desks again,
The old men are coming from the Durban Club.

CHRISTOPHER HOPE

The Last M.O.T.H.[1]

He fronts the world with the hard-earned
Assurance of one who saw the war
Stop, but not the century turn.

Don't misunderstand,
He's not brave, but he has the fierce
Dedication of the maimed.

Nor is he a violence lover,
Though his wounds are well preserved,
Their soft, red centres sugared over.

His girls once came in drifts of prints sudden
And shy to be kissed;
They had the butterfly's light, indeliberate cunning.

Alone, he cooks chips
Peering into the troubled oil; then rheumy images revive
And the sting of lips.

He orders his memory with steel persistence;
The shriek's swallowed;
The regressive flow is gone against.

Aged Spitfires sag and rust,
The grass knots
And delicately contains their too brazen thrust.

[1]Memorable Order of Tin Hats: an ex-serviceman's organization

CHRISTOPHER HOPE

Kobus Le Grange Marais

He sways on his stool in the Station Bar
    and calls for a short white wine
And knocks it back and sheds a tear and
    damns the party line,
And talks to himself and blocks his ears
    when the tired old locos shunt:
'Way back in '48,[1] we said, die koelie uit
    die land   expel the Indians
And kaffir op sy plek, we said, the poor   blacks in their place
    white wants his share
They put me in my place, all right,' said
    Kobus Le Grange Marais.

'I was all my life a railwayman, all my life
    a Boer,
And there's none unkinder than a man's
    own kind, I tell you that for sure;
I fought in the O.B.[2] till I was caught and I
    sweated my guts in a camp
For the bombs I threw and the bridges I
    blew and here's what I get for thanks;
The turning wheels took off my legs and
    I'm not going anywhere
But downhill all the way from here,' said
    Kobus Le Grange Marais.

'My pension held up far worse than my
    legs, so I went to the dominee: *pastor*
A bed in the garage will do, I said. "Man,
    where's your pride?" says he.
He wanted to pray but I turned to go when
    the police decided to raid,
They took him away in the big gray van and
    came back for the kaffir maid.
I have an idea he did a lot more than park
    his Ford in there,
Or so the Women's Federasie said,' said
    Kobus Le Grange Marais.

'O it was dop and dam and a willing girl   *brandy and water*
    when we were young and green,
But Jewish money and the easy life are the
    ruin of the Boereseun,   *Afrikaans boy*
He disappears into the ladies' bars and is
    never seen again
Where women flash their thighs at you and
    drink beside the men,
And sits with moffies and piepiejollers and   *homosexuals   male teenyboppers*
    primps his nice long hair:
You'd take him for an Englishman,' said
    Kobus Le Grange Marais.

'The meddling ghost of Reverend Philip,[3]
    he haunts us once more –
His face is pressed to the window-pane, his
    knock rattles the door;

254

From Slagtersnek[4] to Sonderwater[5] he
    smears the Boers' good name;
And God is still a rooinek God, komman-   *redneck (British)*
    dant of Koffiefontein.[6]
If what I hear about heaven is true, it's a
    racially mixed affair;
In which case, ons gaan kak da' bo,' said   *we'll shat up there*
    Kobus Le Grange Marais.

'The times are as cruel as the big steel
    wheels that carried my legs away;
Oudstryders like me are out on our necks   *veterans*
    and stink like scum on a vlei   *small shallow lake*
And white man puts the white man down,
    the volk are led astray;   *tribe*
There'll be weeping in Weenen[7] once again,
    no keeping the impis at bay;   *black armies*
And tears will stream from the stony eyes
    of Oom Paul[8] in Pretoria Square: *Uncle*
He knows we'll all be poor whites soon,'
    said Kobus Le Grange Marais.

He sways on his stool in the Station Bar and
    calls for a short white wine
And knocks it back and sheds a tear and
    damns the party line,
And talks to himself and blocks his ears
    when the tired old locos shunt:
'Way back in '48, we said, die koelie uit
    die land
And kaffir op sy plek, we said, the poor
    white wants his share:
They put me in my place, all right,' said
    Kobus Le Grange Marais.

[1] The 1948 election which brought the Nationalist Party to power.
[2] The Ossewa Brandwag, a political organization which opposed South African participation in the 1939–45 war. Many of its members were interned for the duration of the war. Some were found guilty of acts of sabotage.
[3] See page 25, note 3. For most frontiersmen, Philip was the archetype of the interfering missionary.
[4] The place of execution by the British of members of a Boer frontier rebellion. (This event took place before the arrival in S.A. of the Rev. Philip.)
[5] A military training camp during the 1939–45 war.
[6] Internment camp for political prisoners, 1940–45.
[7] The site of a massacre of Boers by Zulu during the Great Trek.
[8] President Kruger.

CHRISTOPHER HOPE

The Flight of the White South Africans

(In 1856, a young Xhosa woman, named Nongquase, preached that the day was approaching when Europeans in their country would be driven into the sea – Encyclopaedia of Southern Africa)

I

Kinshasa, we feel, is not the place to reach
At noon and leave the plane to endure inspection
By a hostile ground-hostess, observing the bleach
On her face, her cap tacked with leopard skin,
Faked, and far too tired for the erection
A good bristle requires. We make no fuss,
However, knowing why she snarls at us;
But proffer our transit cards, and march in

To stand at the urinal complaining aloud
Of filth, flies and spit, amazed that this
Is it, an Africa the white man bowed
Before, growling outside the walls of the Gents:
We fumble uncomfortably, unable to piss
Till a soldier, bursting from a booth, clodhops
Past, still buckling up, and the talking stops.
Steady yellow stains white marble in silence.

II

Perhaps, Nongquase, you have your revenge. Tell me
Why, when surf rides like skirts up a thigh, we bare
Ourselves, blind behind black glass, bellies
Up, navels gaping at the sun? We lie
Near ice-cream boys, purveyors of canvas chairs:
While they and the fishermen who stand
Off-shore, shooting seine, busily cram
Their granaries: we gasp, straining to fly:

While in the upstairs lounge, our waiting wives
Caress expensive ivory souvenirs;
By rights, white hunters' spoil; and home-made knives.
We flounder about, flying fish that fail,
Staring with the glazed eyes of seers
At our plane, hauled from the sky, lying like dead
Silver on the tarmac, feeling hooks bed
Deep in our mouths, sand heavy in our scales.

III

Our sojourn: what might dear Milne[1] have made of it
Or Crompton,[2] Farnol,[3] even the later James,[4]
Who promised homely endings, magi who lit
The lamp we wished to read by, gave us The Queen,
A Nanny we almost kissed, our English names?
We blink and are blinded by the Congo sun
Overhead, as flagrant as a raped nun.
Such light embarrasses too late. We've seen

So little in the little time spent coming
To choke on this beach of unbreathable air
Beyond the guns' safety, the good plumbing;
Prey of gulls and gaffs. We go to the wall
But Mowgli,[5] Biggles[6] and Alice[7] are not there:
Nongquase, heaven unhoods its bloodshot eye
Above a displaced people; our demise
Is near, and we'll be gutted where we fall.

[1]A. A. Milne, author of the Christopher Robin children's books.
[2]Richmal Crompton, author of the 'William' boys' books.
[3]Geoffrey Farnol, author of romantic love stories.
[4]Henry James, great American/British author.
[5]Mowgli: hero of a series of stories by Rudyard Kipling.
[6]Biggles: Aviator hero of a series of boys' books by Captain W. E. Johns.
[7]Alice: Heroine of Lewis Caroll's *Alice in Wonderland*.

MONGANE WALLY SEROTE

For Don M. - Banned

it is a dry white season
dark leaves don't last, their brief lives dry out
they dive down gently headed for the earth

not even bleeding.
it is a dry white season brother,
only the trees know the pain as they still stand erect
dry like steel, their branches dry like wire,
indeed, it is a dry white season
but seasons come to pass.

MONGANE WALLY SEROTE

The Clothes

I came home in the morning.
There on the stoep,
The shoes I knew so well
Dripped water like a window crying dew;
The shoes rested the first time
From when they were new.
Now it's forever.

I looked back,
On the washing line hung
A shirt, jacket and trousers
Soaked wet with pity,
Wrinkled and crying reddish water, perhaps also salty;
The pink shirt had a gash on the right,
And stains that told the few who know
An item of our death-live lives.

The colourless jacket still had mud
Dropping lazily from its body
To join the dry earth beneath.

The over-sized black-striped trousers,
Dangled from one hip,
Like a man from a rope 'neath his head,
Tired of hoping to hope.

MONGANE WALLY SEROTE

City Johannesburg

This way I salute you:
My hand pulses to my back trousers pocket
Or into my inner jacket pocket
For my pass, my life,
Jo'burg City.

My hand like a starved snake rears my pockets
For my thin, ever lean wallet,
While my stomach groans a friendly smile to hunger,
Jo'burg City.
My stomach also devours coppers and papers
Don't you know?
Jo'burg City, I salute you;
When I run out, or roar in a bus to you,
I leave behind me, my love,
My comic houses and people, my dongas and my ever-whirling dust,
My death,
That's so related to me as a wink to the eye.
Jo'burg City
I travel on your black and white and roboted roads,
Through your thick iron breath that you inhale
At six in the morning and exhale from five noon.
Jo'burg City
That is the time when I come to you,
When your neon flowers flaunt from your electrical wind,
That is the time when I leave you,
When your neon flowers flaunt their way through the falling darkness
On your cement trees.
And as I go back, to my love,
My dongas, my dust, my people, my death,
Where death lurks in the dark like a blade in the flesh,
I can feel your roots, anchoring your might, my feebleness
In my flesh, in my mind, in my blood,
And everything about you says it,
That, that is all you need of me.
Jo'burg City, Johannesburg,
Listen when I tell you,
There is no fun, nothing, in it,
When you leave the women and men with such frozen expressions,
Expressions that have tears like furrows of soil erosion,
Jo'burg City, you are dry like death,
Jo'burg City, Johannesburg, Jo'burg City.

JENNIFER DAVIDS

A Poem for my Mother

That isn't everything, you said
on the afternoon I brought a poem
to you hunched over the washtub
with your hands
the shrivelled
burnt grenadilla
skin of your hands
covered by foam.

And my words slid like a ball
of hard blue soap
into the tub
to be grabbed and used by you
to rub the clothes.

A poem isn't all
there is to life, you said
with your blue-ringed gaze
scanning the page
once looking over my shoulder
and back at the immediate
dirty water

and my words
being clenched
smaller and
smaller.

ROBERT GREIG

The Abortion

Too late now to recriminate.
Appalled, each consulted friends.
One said he knew a doctor who might . . . .
Love-making now didn't seem right.

Somehow they spoke less and less,
Knowing three months could be dangerous.
Rather the pain than marriage, she said,
But she still loved him, she confessed.

Told himself it had been worth it,
Solicitous as a husband, tense
As a murderer. 'It happens
If you're careless' was all her parents said.

They understood, took the cheque, gave consent.
That night he spent with a girl
He screwed on and off. She wouldn't get pregnant
He'd ensured she was on the pill.

When he called with flowers,
She was loving and pale in bed.
No need for the solemn face,
She laughed. Inside he was dead.

'Yes, a bit of blood – not painful.
Feel – my breasts are all milky.'
Swollen eyes. 'Was it a boy or a girl?'
He did not expect her to cry.

MARK SWIFT

In my Father's Room

In my father's room the telephone
held its breath or blared
in its tangle of circuits, crackling out
the static-plaint of farmers ill
on hill-top, windy acres.
　　　In the rack beside his clothing,
letters and razors, the guns reeked
in their oil; a cut-down, rebored rifle,
an inlaid shotgun, pistols, bullets, and shoes
worn down with stalking.

His instincts were pitted against bushes
which exploded into horns
and a cataract of hooves. His hair blew
with the grass, his love moved out
to strike at the limbs of the chase.
    The barrel was turned but once in hate;
    at the dark, secret twistings of his own
intestines, the gradual accretions of cancer,
and the blunting of his rifled, sniper's eye.

PASCAL GWALA

We lie under tall Gum-trees

We lie under tall gum-trees
hidden from the moonlight,
the stars and the silvery summer clouds,
in the thick shadows of tall gum-trees.

Mosquitoes hover round
and above us,
swarming from the black swamps
of a pulp factory nearby
– like jetbombers blackening the Vietnam skies.
And as we spiralled
towards awareness
they bit us.
First you.
Then me.

Now, no more a virgin,
you have tasted
the painful joy of love.

MOTŠHILE NTHODI

South African Dialogue

Morning Baas,
Baas,
Baas Kleinbaas[1] says,
I must come and tell
Baas that,
Baas Ben's Baasboy says,
Baas Ben want to see
Baas Kleinbaas if
Baas don't use
Baas Kleinbaas,
Baas.

Tell
Baas Kleinbaas that,
Baas says,
Baas Kleinbaas must tell
Baas Ben's Baasboy that,
Baas Ben's Baasboy must tell
Baas Ben that,
Baas says,
If Baas Ben want to see
Baas Kleinbaas,
Baas Ben must come and see
Baas Kleinbaas here.

Thank you
Baas.
I'll tell
Baas Kleinbaas that,
Baas says,
Baas Kleinbaas must tell
Baas Ben's Baasboy that,
Baas Ben's Baasboy must tell
Baas Ben that,
Baas says,
If Baas Ben want to see
Baas Kleinbaas,
Baas Ben must come and see
Baas Kleinbaas here,

Baas.
Goodbye Baas.

Baas Kleinbaas,
Baas says,
I must come and tell
Baas Kleinbaas that,
Baas Kleinbaas must tell
Baas Ben's Baasboy that,
Baas Ben's Baasboy must tell
Baas Ben that,
Baas says,
If Baas Ben want to see
Baas Kleinbaas,
Baas Ben must come and see
Baas Kleinbaas here,
Baas Kleinbaas.

Baasboy,
Tell Baas Ben that,
Baas Kleinbaas says,
Baas says,
If Baas Ben want to see me
(Kleinbaas),
Baas Ben must come and
See me (Kleinbaas) here.

Thank you
Baas Kleinbaas,
I'll tell
Baas Ben that,
Baas Kleinbaas says,
Baas says,
If Baas Ben want to see
Baas Kleinbaas,
Baas Ben must come and see
Baas Kleinbaas here,
Baas Kleinbaas.
Goodbye
Baas Kleinbaas.

Baas Ben,
Baas Kleinbaas says,
I must come and tell

Baas Ben that,
Baas says,
If Baas Ben want to see
Baas Kleinbaas,
Baas Ben must come and see
Baas Kleinbaas there,
Baas Ben.
Baas Ben,
Baas Be-ne . . . .
Baas Ben.
Goodbye
Baas Ben.

[1]Young Boss

CHRIS MANN

Cookhouse Station

for Jackie

If you ever pass through Cookhouse Station
make certain you see what is there,
not just the long neat platform beneath the escarpment,
and the red buckets
and the red-and-white booms,
but the beetle as well
which sings like a tireless lover
high in the gum-tree all the hot day.

And whether your stay is short,
and whether your companions
beg you to turn from the compartment window
does not matter, only make certain you see
the rags of the beggarman's coat
before you choose to sit again.

And though there might be no passengers
waiting in little heaps of luggage
when you look, make certain you see

265

the migrant workers with their blankets
as well as the smiling policeman,
the veiled widow as well as the girl
the trainee-soldiers whistle at, otherwise
you have not passed that way at all.

And if it is a midday in December
with a light so fierce
all the shapes of things quiver
and mingle, make certain you see
the shades of those who once lived there,
squatting in the cool of the blue-gum tree,
at ease in the fellowship of the afterdeath.

And if you ever pass through Cookhouse Station
make certain you greet these men well, otherwise
you have not passed that way at all.

CHRIS MANN

To – Returning Overseas

Sweetest love, do not pretend
a willingness to stay,
do not let your kindness keep
tucking the truth away;
and if you wish
to make a friend,
why, bring it to one storm of pain
and not this drizzling end.

The frogs chirp in the trees,
October is the spring,
strange languages enclose
strange worlds within their ring.
And that is what
a tourist sees.
I knew you wouldn't know me till
you'd penetrated these.

Each man retains an everywhere,
the place which hatched his spawn.
Did I think you'd wive yourself,
to someone taut and torn?
Men take weapons,
bloodshed is near,
each group spurs self-righteousness
and aches with hidden fear.

I don't say as it might seem
that leaving has no grace,
you've never hidden loyalty
to your own childhood's place.
An oak tree drinks
a distant stream.
Did I want what I preserve
to be a homesick dream?

Repeat these reasons to me till
they do what you intend.
Love never has more logic
than when it nears its end.
Then let our past
and pain distil,
and cram them to a final kiss
for one who loves you, still.

CHRIS MANN

In Praise of the Shades

Akudlozi lingay'ekhaya
No shade fails to go home – Zulu proverb

Hitching across a dusty plain last June,
down one of those deadstraight platteland[1] roads,
I met a man with rolled-up khakhi sleeves,
who told me his faults, and then his beliefs.
It's amazing, some people discuss more
with hitchhikers than even their friends.

267

His bakkie[2] rattled a lot on the ruts,
so I'm not exactly sure what he said.
Anyway, when he'd talked about his church,
and when the world had changed from mealie-stalks
to sunflowers, which still looked green and firm,
he lowered his voice, and spoke about his shades.

This meant respect I think, not secrecy.
He said he'd always asked them to guide him,
and that, even in the city, they did.
He seemed to me a gentle balanced man,
and I was sorry to stick my kitbag
onto the road again and say goodbye.

When you are alone and brooding deeply,
do all your teachers and loved ones desert you?
Stand on a road when the fence is whistling.
You say, 'It's the wind', and if the dust swirls,
'Wind again', although you never see it.
The shades work like the wind, invisibly.

And they have always been our companions,
dressed in the flesh of the children they reared,
gossiping away from the books they left,
a throng who even in the strongest light
are whispering, 'You are not what you are,
remember us, then try to understand.'

They come like pilgrims from the hazy seas
which shimmer at the borders of a dream,
not such spirits that they can't be scolded,
not such mortals that they can be profaned,
for scolding them, we honour each other,
and honouring them, we perceive ourselves.

When all I ever hear about these days
is violence, injustice, and despair,
or worse than that, humourless theories
to rescue us all from our human plight,
those moments in a bakkie[2] on a plain
make sunflowers in a waterless world.

[1]flat country
[2]van

268

CHRIS MANN

The Prospect from Botha's Hill on Good Friday

Far below,
in the grey-blue valley,
the valley of a thousand wrinkly hills,
an unseen donkey and cockerel
utter their own particular cries.

What provoked
both them and the herdboy
who somewhere deep in a dim-blue hillside
keeps floating out a line of song,
is hazier than the tiny farms.

No calm is falser
than the distance's,
and working through that braying and crowing
leaves my thought in such a shambles
of dismay at human weakness and betrayal,

I almost shut my self
against the music of that single line of song.

CHRISTOPHER TRENGOVE-JONES

May the Universe Lament?

Don't be patronising.
Mightily he,
the old grandfather, resents
our assured handling: it's shift-work
with death's crows.

Nightly, they nest
free and easy with him; at dawn –
they move when they're ready –
set out with blatant ease:
their position is secure.

It's not faith,
or hope, the mother's surrogate,
that he desires;
a terrible dimension of tenderness
greater than the entire species can provide,

a yearning for swans:
on the aqueous, glassy plain
                delicately mourning –
such a fine fire
in the bowing of their heads!

MIKE NICOL

The Refugees

We have been through it all
and cannot face the going back.

The officials at the border posts,
the miles of railway and the cicadas
loud in the bush when the train stops.
How will we get used to the soldiers
and the threat of death?

We were too long beneath
the palm trees, too content
in the warm waves for this.

When the heat brought the leguans
out on the pavements we thought
no more of them than did the natives.
We were at home there.

Yet we cannot face the going back.

Some will return. The idealists
and the old who have always been there,
have known no other way of life.

But what is there to return to?
The palm trees and the tropical sea.

The city we built, the life
we knew is no longer what it was.
One week changed everything.
We lived out those days in
locked houses, listening
to sporadic shots in distant streets.

Even the day we left, in the train
our shirts wet against the plastic
seats, there was no relief.

And here we are still uneasy. Rumours
reach us of more trouble, more deaths.

There is no relief from that.

BIOGRAPHICAL AND BIBLIOGRAPHICAL NOTES

Prepared by the National Documentation Centre for English, Grahamstown

Publications listed refer only to verse. In some cases, only a selection of titles is given.

ABRAHAMS, Lionel
Born Johannesburg, 1928. University of the Witwatersrand. Edited much of Herman Charles Bosman's work. Founded the literary magazine *Purple Renoster*, which has encouraged young South African writers. Edited *South African Writing Today* (Penguin) with Nadine Gordimer, as well as *Quarry* '76 and '77 with Walter Saunders. His poems, short stories and articles have appeared in South African periodicals and anthologies. Founder of Renoster Books, which published the work of several South African poets and at present is co-director of Bateleur Press. Received Pringle Award for creative writing, 1976.

Thresholds of Tolerance, Johannesburg: Bateleur Press, 1975.

ADAMS, Peter Robert Charles (pen-name Perseus)
Born Cape Town, 1933. University of Cape Town. Teacher of English, poet and short-story writer. In 1953 hitch-hiked through Africa to England. Served a prison sentence in Wormwood Scrubbs, for stowing away. Taught in Cape Town until 1965, when he travelled to the Far East. Lived in Hong Kong for eighteen months, and on the Greek Islands for periods in 1966, 1971 and 1972. Contributed verse to numerous South African literary periodicals and anthologies.
   Awards: The South African Poetry Prize 1963; Eastern Province Poetry Prize 1964; Festival of Rhodesia Poetry Prize 1970; 2nd prize in The John Keats Memorial Prize, London 1971.

The Land at my Door, Cape Town: Human and Rousseau, 1965.
Grass for the Unicorn, Cape Town: Juta, 1975.

BAIN, Andrew Geddes
Born Thurso, Scotland, 1797. Road-builder, geologist, explorer, soldier, writer and artist. Arrived in South Africa in 1816. In the 1820s travelled far beyond the Orange River and discovered his writing and drawing abilities on these expeditions. His travel descriptions proved popular and he became the regular correspondent of the *South African Commercial Advertiser*. Worked as a geologist, and became a road and pass-builder of note (e.g. Bain's Kloof). *Kaatje Kekkelbek; or Life among the Hottentots* was performed in Grahamstown in 1838.

BARTER, Charles
Born Sarsden, Oxfordshire, 1820. New College, Oxford; admitted as a
Fellow in 1839. After a spell in New Brunswick he came to Natal in 1850,
and became a staff member of the *Globe*. Eventually settled in Natal as a
farmer. Resigned his Fellowship of New College on his marriage in 1853.
Elective member of the Legislative Council and Resident Magistrate of
Pietermaritzburg. Died 1904.

The Dorp and the Veld, London: Ward and Lock, 1852.
Stray Memories of Natal and Zululand, Pietermaritzburg: Munro Brothers,
1897.

BERLEIN, Elizabeth (Katherine Moher, *pseud.*)
Born in Northern Ireland and was married in South Africa. Went to live
in the United States of America in the 'twenties and died there in 1935.

Remembering, Oxford: Blackwell, 1921.

BOSMAN, Herman Charles
Born Kuils River, near Cape Town, 1905. University of the Witwatersrand
and Normal College, Johannesburg. Taught in the Groot Marico district.
Served a four-and-a-half year prison sentence for culpable homicide. Short-
story writer, novelist, poet and essayist. His essays appear in South African
periodicals in the 1930s, including the literary magazine *Touleier*, which he
founded in 1930. He was a journalist in Johannesburg and Europe for
many years.

The Blue Princess, Johannesburg: the author, 1932.
Jesus, Johannesburg: Brill Bros. (Printer), 1933.
Rust, Johannesburg: African Publishing, 1932.

BOWKER, Robert Mitford
Sixth son of Miles Bowker, the settler who lived at Tharfield in the Eastern
Cape. Born in 1812 in England. Represented Somerset East as Member of
the Legislative Assembly for 40 years. Apart from his parliamentary
activities seemed to have lived a secluded life on his farm. Owing to his
light-hearted manner, his jokes and his rhymes, he was known as Robert
the Jester. A soldier during the Frontier Wars. Died at Craigie Burn in
1892.

BRANFORD, William Richard Grenville
Born Southhampton, England, 1927. University of Cape Town and St.
John's College, Cambridge. Lectured in English at the University of Natal.
Professor of Linguistics, Rhodes University, Grahamstown. Is a member

of the National Place Names Committee and editor of *Voorloper*, an interim presentation of materials for *A Dictionary of South African English*. Has published poems and articles in South African literary periodicals. Author of *Mine Boy*, an authorized stage version of Peter Abraham's novel, produced in Durban, 1955.

BRETTELL, Noel Harry
Born Lye, Worcestershire, 1908. University of Birmingham. Went to Rhodesia in 1930, and became headmaster of rural schools in remote regions. His poem 'Mantis and Moth' was placed as runner-up in the 1972 Best Poem of the Year Competition, run by the English Association of Britain. Recipient of 1972 PEN Literary Award, and the Book Centre of Rhodesia Literary Award 1973. Has had poems published in South African and Rhodesian magazines. Retired and living in the Inyanga highlands of Rhodesia.

A Rhodesian Leave, (privately published).
Bronze Frieze, Oxford University Press, 1950
Season and Pretext, Salisbury: Poetry Society of Rhodesia, 1977.

BRODRICK, Albert
Born Gosport, England, 1830. Came to South Africa in 1859. Settled in Pretoria as a merchant, was interested in mining and an ardent prospector. Versifying was his hobby; was a regular contributor to *Die Volksstem* (established 1873). In 1875 his first book of verse was published in Pretoria, the first book of its kind to be printed north of the Orange River. Died in England in 1908. In his verses he left behind an intimate picture of life in early Pretoria.

Fifty Fugitive Fancies in Verse, Pretoria, 1875
A Wanderer's Rhymes, London: Wilkinson Bros., 1893.

BROOKE, Brian
Born Aberdeenshire, 1889. Aberdeen University. Emigrated to British East Africa at 18. At 20 went tea planting in Ceylon, but soon returned to Africa, and settled in Uganda. Volunteered at the outbreak of World War I. Died of wounds in France, 1917.

Poems, London: The Bodley Head, 1918.

BRUCE, Robert Michael
Born Grahamstown, 1857. Served as volunteer in the Frontier War of 1877–78, and died of a fever contracted during the campaign.

Under the Yellow-woods, Grahamstown: T & G. Sheffield, 1878.

BRUTUS, Dennis Vincent
Born Salisbury, Rhodesia, 1924. Educated Fort Hare University College and the University of the Witwatersrand. Left South Africa in 1966 after imprisonment on Robben Island, for opposition to apartheid. Has travelled extensively since leaving South Africa, including lecture tours and sports conferences. Professor at North-Western University in Evanston, Illinois. Awarded the Mbari Prize for Poetry 1962.

Sirens, Knuckles, Boots, Ibadan, Nigeria: Mbari Publications, 1963.
Letters to Martha, London: Heinemann, 1968.
A Simple Lust, London: Heinemann, 1973.
Strains, Austin, Texas: Troubadour Press, 1975.

(Permission to include poems by Brutus has been refused by the Minister of Justice. Eds.)

BUCKTON, Alice M.
Born 1867. Educated at home at Haslemere. As a young girl she read her poems to Tennyson. Her play *Eager Heart*, one of the first imitations of the old moralities, attracted some attention, but her poetry did not. She never visited South Africa. Died 1944.

The Burden of Engela, London: Methuen, 1904.

BUTLER, Frederick Guy
Born Cradock, Cape Province, 1918. Rhodes University, Grahamstown, where he was awarded the Queen Victoria Scholarship to Oxford. After war service in the Middle East, Italy and the United Kingdom, he went up to Brasenose College, Oxford. Lectured at the University of the Witwatersrand from 1948–1950, and since 1952 has been Professor of English at Rhodes University, Grahamstown. Well-known poet, playwright and educationalist. His poetry has been published in literary journals in South Africa, Britain and the United States. Plays performed by South African National Theatre. Awarded several poetry prizes, including the C.N.A. Literary Award 1975. Founder (with Ruth Harnett) of *New Coin*, a poetry journal.

Stranger to Europe, Cape Town: Balkema, 1952.
South of the Zambezi, London: Abelard Schuman, 1966.
On First Seeing Florence, Grahamstown: New Coin, 1968.
Selected Poems, Johannesburg: Ad. Donker, 1975.
Songs and Ballads, Cape Town: David Philip, 1978.

CAMPBELL, Ignatius Royston Dunnachie (Roy)
Born Durban, 1901. One year at Merton College, Oxford. Lived in Wales while writing *The Flaming Terrapin*. Returned to South Africa, and in 1926

edited with Laurens van der Post and William Plomer the literary periodical *Voorslag* (Whiplash). Lived in France, Spain, Portugal and England at various times of his life. Served in World War II in the British Intelligence Corps in England, East Africa and the Western Desert. Awarded the Foyle Prize for Poetry for his translation of St John of the Cross in 1951, and an Hon. D. Litt. from the University of Natal in 1954. He translated widely from French, Spanish and Portuguese poets. Died in a motor accident in Portugal in 1957.

The Flaming Terrapin, London: Jonathan Cape, 1924.
The Wayzgoose, London: Jonathan Cape, 1928.
Adamastor, London: Faber, 1930.
The Georgiad, London: Boriswood, 1931.
Flowering Reeds, London: Boriswood, 1933.
Mithraic Emblems, London: Boriswood, 1936.
Flowering Rifle, London: Longmans, 1939.
Talking Bronco, London: Faber, 1946.
Poems of Roy Campbell, chosen and introduced by Uys Krige, Cape Town: Maskew Miller, 1960.

CHIDYAUSIKU, Paul
Born near Salisbury, Rhodesia, 1927. Son of the late Chief Chinamhora, he went to Kutama Mission, a secondary school run by Marist Brothers, and to Domboshawa Agricultural School. Taught agriculture for a number of years before joining the Mambo Press in Gwelo in 1960. Has travelled in Europe and in various African countries. Has written five books in Shona, published by the Oxford University Press and by Mambo Press. Edits the Shona newspaper *Moto*.

CLOTHIER, Norman Moser
Born Shrewsbury, England, 1915. Universities of Natal and Cambridge. Fought in Western Desert and Italy during World War II. Now lives in Johannesburg. Poems included in the anthology, *South African Poetry: A New Anthology*, compiled by Roy Macnab & Charles Gulston 1948.

Libyan Winter: Poems by a Corporal in the First Division, Johannesburg: Central News Agency, 1943.

CLOUTS, Sydney David
Born Cape Town, 1926. University of Cape Town and Rhodes University, Grahamstown. Research Fellow, Institute for the Study of English in Africa, 1969. Contributed widely to South African and English literary periodicals and anthologies. Awarded the Ingrid Jonker Prize 1968, and the Olive Schreiner Award 1968. Now in London.

One Life, Cape Town: Purnell, 1966.

COLVIN, Ian Duncan
Born Inverness, Scotland, 1877. Edinburgh University. Journalist, bio-
grapher and poet; wrote satiric verse and stories under the pseudonym
Rip van Winkle. Assistant editor of the *Cape Times* 1903–7. Wrote the
lengthy introduction to Sydney Mendelssohn's *Bibliography* (London
1910). Returned to Britain, with one more visit to South Africa in 1920.
Died in 1938.

The Parliament of Beasts, Cape Town: Cape Times, 1905
The Leper's Flute, London: Bird, 1920.
A Wreath of Immortelles, London: Russell, 1924.
Intercepted Letters, London: Rivers, 1913.

COPE, Robert Knox (Jack)
Born Mooi River, 1913. Durban High School. Worked as a newspaperman
in South Africa and a political correspondent in Fleet Street in London.
Spent some time farming in Natal. Travelled widely in Europe, America
and Africa. Joint founder and editor of *Contrast* in 1960. Has published
numerous novels. Winner of a number of literary awards, among them,
the C.N.A. Prize for his novel, *The Rain-maker*, 1972. Poems published in
Poetry Commonwealth, *Vandag*, *Izwe* and *Unisa English Studies*. Lives at
Onrusrivier, Cape.

Lyrics and Diatribes, Cape Town: privately printed, 1938
Marie: A South African Satire, Cape Town: Stewart, 1948.
Joint editor of *Penguin Book of South African Verse*, Harmondsworth:
  Penguin, 1968.
Editor of *Seismograph: The Best South African Writing from Contrast*.
  Cape Town: Rejger, 1970.

COUZYN, Jeni
Born Johannesburg, 1942. University of Natal. Taught for the African
Music and Drama Association in Soweto. Left South Africa in 1965 to
live in Britain, where, after a brief spell of teaching, she became a full-time
freelance poet. Has held numerous poetry readings at universities, art
festivals, and on radio and BBC Television. In 1971 she was awarded a
British Arts Council Grant for poetry. Chairman of the National Poetry
Secretariat since its inception in 1973. Married to a Canadian poet, she
now lives in Toronto, and has recently worked in the Department of Crea-
tive Writing at the University of Victoria, British Columbia.

Flying, London: Workshop Press, 1970.
Monkeys' Wedding, London: Jonathan Cape, 1972.
Christmas in Africa, London: Heinemann, 1975.

CRIPPS, Arthur Shearly
Born Tunbridge Wells, 1869. Trinity College, Oxford. Boxing Blue. Ordained 1892. To Mashonaland in 1907, where he lived among the Shona as a missionary until his death in 1952.

Titania and Other Poems, London: Mathews, 1900.
The Black Christ, Oxford: Blackwell, 1902.
Jonathan; A Song of David, Oxford: Blackwell, 1902.
Lyra Evangelista, Oxford: Blackwell, 1909.
African Verses, Oxford University Press, 1939.

CULLINAN, Patrick Roland
Born Pretoria, 1932. Magdalen College, Oxford. Has travelled in Europe and Africa. Sawmiller, farmer and publisher, living in Machadodorp, Eastern Transvaal. Founder of Bateleur Press. His poems have been published in South African periodicals. Also writes under the pseudonym Patrick Roland.

The Horizon Forty Miles Away, Machadodorp: the author, 1973.
Today is Not Different, Cape Town: David Philip, 1978.

CURREY, Ralph Nixon
Born Mafeking, 1907. Wadham College, Oxford. Senior English master, author and broadcaster. Served in the Royal Artillery in World War II. Recipient of Viceroy's Poetry Prize 1945, and the South African Poetry Prize 1959 (with Anthony Delius). His poems, short stories and critical articles have appeared in South African periodicals and anthologies.

Tiresias and Other Poems, London: Oxford University Press, 1940.
This Other Planet, London: Routledge, 1945.
Indian Landscape, London: Routledge, 1947.
The Africa We Knew, Cape Town: David Philip, 1973.

DAVIDS, Jennifer Ann
Born Cape Town, 1945. Hewat Teachers' Training College. Taught in Cape Town schools, and has also worked in a department store and a factory. From 1966 her poems have been included in South African periodicals such as *Contrast*, *New Coin* and *New Nation*. Travelled to Britain in 1969, where she taught at a school in Southwark. Returned to South Africa in 1972 and now lives in Cape Town.

Searching for Words, Cape Town: David Philip, 1974.

DE LA HARPE, Norman
Born 1901 in the Graaff-Reinet district. Farmed in the Karoo until his retirement. Edited the Merino Breeders' Journal. Has published poems in *The English Poetry Review*, and *American Lantern* and *New Coin*.

Forty Poems, published privately, 1977.

DELIUS, Anthony Roland St. Martin
Born Simonstown, 1916. Rhodes University, Grahamstown. War service in the South African Intelligence Corps. Has been a journalist since 1947, becoming Parliamentary Correspondent and leader writer on the Cape Times. English editor of *Standpunte* until 1956. Broadcaster on the BBC. Lives in London. Has contributed poetry and short stories to South African and overseas literary journals. Awarded the 1976 C.N.A. Literary Award for his novel *Border*.

The Unknown Border, Cape Town: Balkema, 1954.
The Last Division, Cape Town: Human and Rousseau, 1959.
A Corner of the World, Cape Town: Human and Rousseau, 1962.
Black South Easter, Grahamstown: New Coin, 1966.

DHLOMO, Herbert I. E.
Born 1903. American Mission Board School (Adams College). Taught in Johannesburg, contributed to newspapers and journals and eventually joined the staff of *Bantu World*. In 1937 he became Librarian-Organizer for the Carnegie Library in Germiston and was responsible for establishing library facilities for Blacks throughout the Transvaal. In the early forties he became assistant editor of the Zulu newspaper *Ilanga laseNatal*. Died in Durban in 1956.

The Girl who Killed to Save: Nongquase the Liberator, Alice: Lovedale Printing Press, 1936.
Valley of a Thousand Hills, Durban: Knox, 1941.
Chaka: A Tragedy, Johannesburg: African Dramatic & Operatic Society, 19—(?)

DRIVER, Charles Jonathan
Born Cape Town, 1939. University of Cape Town, and Trinity College, Oxford. Former President of the National Union of South African Students. Was imprisoned under the ninety-day detention law, and left South Africa in the late sixties for England. Schoolmaster, poet and novelist. Has contributed to periodicals and anthologies in South Africa and Britain. His novels are banned in this country. Now lives in Hong Kong.

DUGMORE Henry Hare
Born in Birmingham, 1810. Came to South Africa with his parents as a member of the Gardner party of settlers in 1820. Went to a Wesleyan night-school in Grahamstown and entered the Wesleyan ministry in 1834. Held various missionary posts throughout the Eastern Cape and in the circuits of Grahamstown, Salem and Queenstown. Was prominent in educational and cultural affairs. Especially gifted as a preacher, lecturer and writer. Was responsible for many Xhosa hymns and translating numerous books of the New Testament into Xhosa. Retired to Queenstown where he died in 1897.

Octogenarian musings: a legacy for my children, Queenstown: Printed by Barrable, 1896.
Verse: compiled and edited by E. H. Crouch. Birmingham: Printed by Birbeck 1920(?)

EGLINGTON, Charles Beaumont
Born Johannesburg, 1918. University of the Witwatersrand. Served in North Africa and Italy in World War II. Worked on various South African newspapers until 1962, when he became editor of *Optima*, the quarterly journal of a mining corporation. Poet, art-critic, broadcaster and translator. Contributed poems to South African literary journals and anthologies. He also translated from Afrikaans (two novels by Etienne Leroux) and Portuguese. Unpublished manuscript *A Lap Full of Seed*, 1967. Died suddenly 1970.

Under the Horizon, Cape Town: Purnell, 1977.

EYBERS, Elisabeth Françoise
Born Klerksdorp, Transvaal, 1915. In 1916 her family moved to Schweizer-Reneke where she went to school. Her parents introduced her to English literature, especially the Victorian poets, and her first verses were therefore written in English. In 1932 she went to the University of the Witwaters-rand where she became interested in Afrikaans and modern Dutch poetry and published her first volume of verse in Afrikaans in 1936. One of the most important Afrikaans poets, she has been living in Amsterdam, the Netherlands, since 1961.

FAIR, C. A. (pseudonym)
Born Kenya, 1923. London University. After teaching in England and Kenya, she came to South Africa and is now lecturing in English at Rhodes University. Has published poems in South African anthologies and magazines, including *The Penguin Book of South African Verse* and *New Coin*.

FUGARD, Athol
Born Middelburg, Cape, 1932. Port Elizabeth Technical College and University of Cape Town which he left to hitch-hike through Africa. Playwright, director and actor since 1959. Director of Serpent Players, Port Elizabeth since 1965. Founder of the Space experimental theatre in Cape Town in 1972. His plays have been produced internationally. Lives in Port Elizabeth.

FUGARD, Sheila
Born Birmingham, England, 1932. Came to South Africa at the age of five. Studied speech and drama at the University of Cape Town. Married playwright/actor Athol Fugard in 1956. Has been involved in the theatre, but more recently has turned to publishing novels and poetry. Was awarded the C.N.A. Literary Prize, 1972 and the Olive Schreiner Prize for Prose, 1973 for her first novel, *The Castaways*. Poems previously published in *New Coin, Ophir, Classic*, etc. Lives in Port Elizabeth.

Threshold, Johannesburg: Ad. Donker, 1975.

GIBBON, Perceval
Born Carmarthenshire, Wales, 1879. Poet, journalist and war correspondent. Educated in Germany. Worked for the *Natal Witness* and later joined the *Rand Daily Mail* at its inception in 1902. Travelled extensively in South, Central and East Africa. During World War I worked for the British Intelligence Department. Numerous contributions to English and American magazines established his reputation as a writer. Died 1926.

African Items, London: Elliot Stock, 1903.

GOODWIN, Harold
Born Grahamstown, 1893. Grey High School, Port Elizabeth. Travelled in Europe and Central Africa. Lived in Nyasaland (now Malawi), from 1919–53, where he practised as an accountant. Published much satirical verse in *Grocott's Mail* during latter part of his life in Grahamstown. Died in 1969.

Songs from the Settler City, Grahamstown: Modern Printing Works 1963.

GOULDSBURY, Henry Cullen
Born 1881. Son of an officer in the Indian Police. Joined the British South Africa Company in 1902, where he served first in Native Administration and then as District Officer in Northern Rhodesia. Joined King's African Rifles in 1915. Died at Tanga, East Africa, 1916.

Rhodesian Rhymes, Bulawayo: Philpott and Collins, 1909.
Songs out of Exile, London: Fisher Unwin, 1912.
From the Outposts, London: Fisher Unwin, 1914.
Shots and Splinters; War Poems, Bulawayo: Argus Printing & Company 1915.

GRAY, Stephen
Born Cape Town, 1941. Cambridge and Iowa State Universities. Senior lecturer in English at Rand Afrikaans University, Johannesburg. Was joint-editor of *Izwi* magazine. Poems published in numerous periodicals. Author of two published novels. Editor of several anthologies of South African verse and prose.

The Assassination of Shaka, text by Stephen Gray; 43 woodcuts by Cecil Skotness, Johannesburg: McGraw-Hill, 1974.
It's about Time, Cape Town: David Philip, 1974.
Editor: *A World of Their Own: Southern African Poets of the Seventies*, Johannesburg: Ad. Donker, 1976.

GREENER, Alice Mathilda
Born England 1858. Received certificate of practical efficiency in teaching and the theory, history and practice of teaching from the University of Cambridge in 1885. Came to South Africa in the 1880's and taught at the Girls' Collegiate School in Port Elizabeth during the 1880s. Corresponded with Olive Schreiner and Emily Hobhouse. Involved in political issues like Women's Enfranchisement League, and wrote articles on such topics as The Native Land Act of 1913. Returned to England where she died at Trevone, Cornwall in 1920.
Poems included in the volume *Songs of the Veld* 1902

GREIG, Robert
Born in Johannesburg, 1948. University of the Witwatersrand. Travelled in Europe and southern Africa. Worked as feature-writer and reviewer on the *Cape Times*. Won the *Pringle Award* in 1976 for book and play reviews, and the *Olive Schreiner Prize* for his volume of poetry, *Talking Bull* in 1977. Now works as drama critic for *The Star* in Johannesburg.

Talking Bull, Johannesburg: Bateleur Press, 1975.

GWALA, Mafika Pascal
Born Verulam, Natal, 1946. Matriculated at Vryheid. Has worked as a legal clerk, secondary school teacher, factory hand and publications researcher. Edited *Black Review* in 1973. Poems published in *Classic, Ophir, New Nation*, etc.

Jol'iinkomo, Johannesburg: Ad. Donker, 1977.

HAMILTON, William
Born Scotland, 1891(?). Came to South Africa from Dumfries when young. Obtained an M.A. from the old Cape University. Lecturer in Philosophy at University of Cape Town. Died fighting in Flanders in 1917.

Modern Poems, Oxford: Blackwell, 1917.

HARDY, Thomas
Born Dorset, England, 1840. King's College, London. After completing his apprenticeship became an architect. Assiduously wrote poetry which did not attract a publisher until 1898. Wrote fiction to secure a regular income. In 1896 turned his attention fully to writing of poetry. Had numerous awards and honorary degrees bestowed upon him. Died in 1928.

The Complete Poems, J. Gibson (ed.), London: Macmillan, 1976.

HARESNAPE, Geoffrey
Born in Durban, 1939. University of Cape Town. Senior lecturer in English at the University of Cape Town. Short stories and poems published in journals and anthologies in South Africa, United States of America, and Great Britain. Author of *Pauline Smith* in Twayne's World Authors Series.

Drive of the Tide, Cape Town: Maskew Miller, 1976.

HEWETT, Bruce William Dixie
Born Cape Town, 1939. Diocesan College, Cape Town. Works as a businessman in Cape Town. Poems published by *New Coin* and broadcast by the S.A.B.C.

The Man from Bridegroom, Cape Town: Children of Atlantis, 1974.
Celestial Citadel, Cape Town: published privately, 1977.

HOPE, Christopher David Tully
Born Johannesburg, 1944. Universities of Witwatersrand and Natal. Travelled in Europe and taught for a year in England. Worked for some time in Durban; now lives in England. Has had his work published in *Bolt*, *New Coin*, *Contrast* and *Purple Renoster*. Received the Pringle Award in 1973.

Whitewashes, with Mike Kirkwood. Durban: privately published, 1971.
Cape Drives, London: London Magazine Editions, 1974.

284

JENSMA, Wopko Pieter
Born Ventersdorp, Transvaal, 1939. Universities of Potchefstroom and Pretoria. Taught art at a school in Serowe, Botswana and later worked as graphic and layout artist for the Botswana Information Department in Gaberone. Returned to South Africa in 1971. Now lives in Durban. Much of his poetry has appeared in *Ophir* and *Contrast*, as well as in overseas journals.

Sing for our Execution, Johannesburg: Ophir/Ravan, 1973.
Where White is the Colour, Black is the Number, Johannesburg: Ravan, 1975.
I must show you my Clippings, Johannesburg: Ravan, 1977.

JOLOBE, James James Ranisi
Born at Indwe, Cape Province, 1902. Patterson High School and St. Matthew's College, Keiskammahoek. Taught in the Cape Province until 1926 when he enrolled at Fort Hare College to study for the ministry. From 1938–1959 taught at Lovedale, and was part-time Presbyterian minister. From 1960–1970 was priest in New Brighton, Port Elizabeth, during which time he began working on the Xhosa Dictionary Project. In 1970 became Moderator of the Presbyterian Church of Southern Africa. In 1974 received an honorary doctorate from Fort Hare University in recognition of his contribution to Xhosa literature. Died in 1976.

Umyezo (An Orchard), Johannesburg: Witwatersrand University Press, 1936.
Poems of an African, Alice: Lovedale Press, 1946.
Lovedale Xhosa Rhymes, Alice: Lovedale Press, 1946.

KING, Jill
Born King William's Town, Eastern Cape, 1922. Educated in Pretoria and at Rhodes University. Published short stories in South African and overseas periodicals. Poems first published in *New Coin*. Lives in Cape Town.

KIPLING, Joseph Rudyard
Born Bombay, 1865. United Service College, Westward Ho. In 1882 became a reporter on the Civil and Military Gazette at Lahore. First visited the Cape in 1891; second journey 1898. From 1900–8 the family visited South Africa every year. Appointed associate editor of *The Friend* in Bloemfontein in 1900 when it was taken over by the military as a newspaper for the British forces during the Second Anglo-Boer War. Awarded the Nobel Prize for Literature in 1907. Died in London in 1936.

The Five Nations, London: Methuen, 1903.
South Africa: A Poem, New York: Doubleday, 1906.
Twenty Poems, London: Methuen, 1918.

KIRKWOOD, Robert Michael
Born St Vincent, West Indies, 1943. University of Natal. Lectured in English, University of Natal, Durban. Has contributed to numerous South African periodicals. Editor of *Bolt* and joint founder of *Staffrider*.

Whitewashes, with Christopher Hope. Durban: published privately 1971.
Between Islands, Johannesburg: Bateleur Press, 1975.

KOLLER, Tess Audrey Lloyd (pen-name)
Born Springfontein, Orange Free State, 1928. Studied law at the University of the Orange Free State in Bloemfontein. Practised as a lawyer in Barberton, Eastern Transvaal until she married. Now lives in Bloemfontein. Received the Pringle Award of the English Academy of Southern Africa for her poems published in *New Coin*.

KUNENE, Mazisi
Born Durban, 1932. University of Natal. Won the 'Bantu Literary Competition' in 1956. In 1959 went to the School of Oriental and African Studies in London to work on a dissertation on Zulu poetry. He writes plays and poems in Zulu and then makes his own English versions. He has published articles and poems in *The New African*, *Présence Africaine* and *Transatlantic Review*. Now at the University of California at Los Angeles.

Zulu Poems, New York: African Publishing Corporation, 1970.

LANG, Andrew
Born Selkirk, Scotland, 1844. Universities of St Andrews, Glasgow, and Oxford. Married and settled down to a life of letters and journalism in London. Collaborated with Rider Haggard in *The World's Desire*, 1891. Received honorary doctorates from St Andrew's University 1885, and Oxford 1904.

Poetical works of Andrew Lang, Mrs Lang (ed.), London: Longmans, 1923.

LEIPOLDT, Christian Frederick Louis
Born Worcester Cape, 1888. Grew up in Clanwilliam; taught by his father. Worked as a journalist before travelling to England to study medicine. On his return became medical inspector of schools in the Transvaal. Later established a practice as paediatrician in Cape Town. Wrote for various newspapers and in 1926 became part-time lecturer in medicine at University of Cape Town. Received the Hertzog Prize for poetry 1934, and a D.Litt. from the University of the Witwatersrand. Wrote primarily in Afrikaans. Used the pseudonym *Pheidippides* when writing in English.

The Ballad of Dick King & Other Poems, Cape Town: Stewart, 1949.

LEVINSON, Bernard
Born Johannesburg, 1926. Spent his childhood in Chicago. Served on the
hospital ship *Amra* in the Middle East during World War II. Qualified as a
doctor at the University of the Witwatersrand in 1951, and specialized in
psychiatry. Poems have been published in *New Coin, Jewish Affairs, Ophir,
Purple Renoster*, etc. Practises in Johannesburg.

From Breakfast to Madness, Johannesburg: Ravan, 1974.

LEWIN, Hugh
Born in the Eastern Transvaal, 1939. Rhodes University, Grahamstown.
Worked as journalist for *Post* and *Drum* in Johannesburg. Left for London
after serving a seven-year prison sentence for sabotage activities. His poems
have appeared in *Sechaba* and *Lotus*. Works as information officer of the
International Defence and Aid Fund, London.

LIVINGSTONE, Douglas James
Born Kuala Lumpur, Malaya, 1932. Educated in Natal and Rhodesia.
Employed as bacteriologist in Natal. Poems published in numerous
British, American, Rhodesian and South African journals. Awarded first
prize, Guiness Poetry Award, Cheltenham, England 1965, and Cholmon-
deley Award for Poetry 1970.

The Skull in the Mud, London: Outposts Pamphlet Series, 1960.
Sjambok and Other Poems from Africa, London: OUP, 1964.
Poems, with Thomas Kinsella and Anne Sexton, London: OUP, 1968.
Eyes Closed against the Sun, London: OUP, 1970.
The Sea my Winding Sheet and Other Poems, Durban: Theatre Workshop
   Co., 1971.
Rosary of Bone, Jack Cope (ed.), Cape Town: David Philip, 1975.
The Anvil's Undertone, Johannesburg: Ad. Donker, 1978.

MACLENNAN, Donald Alasdair Calum
Born London, 1929. Witwatersrand and Edinburgh Unviersities. Travelled
extensively in Europe, Canada, U.S.A. and Africa. Senior lecturer in
English at Rhodes University, Grahamstown. Poet, playwright and short-
story writer.

Life Songs, Johannesburg: Bateleur Press, 1977.

MACNAB, Roy Martin
Born Durban, 1923. Jesus College, Oxford. Served in the Royal Navy in
World War II. Became a journalist in Durban and later entered the
Diplomatic Service. Held various posts in Europe, 1955–67. Poems pub-

lished in *Contrast, New Coin, Standpunte*, etc., as well as in numerous anthologies. Has edited a number of anthologies. Now lives in London.

Testament of a South African, London: Fortune Press, 1947.
The Man of Grass and Other Poems, London: St Catherine Press, 1960.

MACNAMARA, Michael Raymond Harley
Born Bloemfontein, 1925. University of South Africa. Served in the Radar Division of the South African army in World War II. Has travelled in the Middle East, Britain and Europe. Over a hundred of his poems have been published in South African and overseas literary journals. Professor of Philosophy at the University of South Africa.

The Falls Run Back, Johannesburg: Ophir/Ravan, 1976.

MADGE, Charles Henry
Born Johannesburg, 1912. Magdalene College, Cambridge. Professor of Sociology, University of Birmingham, 1950–70. Co-founder of Mass Observation, 1937.

The Disappearing Castle, London: Faber & Faber, 1937.
The Father Found, London: Faber & Faber, 1941.
Poets in South Africa, (ed.) Cape Town: Maskew Miller, 1958.

MANN, Christopher Zithulele
Born Port Elizabeth, 1948. University of the Witwatersrand. While Rhodes Scholar at Oxford, won the Newdigate Prize for poetry. Subsequently took a degree in African Studies at the School of Oriental and African Studies, London. Taught in Swaziland. Lectures in English at Rhodes University. Has broadcast poems on SABC, BBC and Swaziland Broadcasting Service.

First Poems, Johannesburg: Bateleur Press, 1977.

MARAIS, Eugène
Born in Pretoria, 1871. Matriculated at Paarl in 1897. Bought the newspaper, *Land en Volk* in 1892 and used it to champion the cause of Afrikaans in the Transvaal. His earliest poems were written in English and published in the *Paarl District Advertiser* in 1885. Wrote intermittently in English all his life. In 1896 went to London to study law and acquired an elementary knowledge of medicine. Returned to Pretoria at the end of the Second Anglo-Boer War. In 1905 sold his newspaper. After practising at the bar in Pretoria for a time, he moved to a farm in the Waterberg district. His studies of the behaviour of termites and baboons pioneered much modern biological thinking. He died near Pretoria in 1936.

MILLARD, Geoffrey Charles
Born Lüderitz, South-West Africa, 1931. Natal and Rhodes Universities. Taught English at Fort Hare University College, and at the University of Botswana, Lesotho and Swaziland. Studied drama for some time. Now teaches in England. Poems published in *New Coin* and included in the *Penguin Book of South African Verse*.

MILLER, Ruth
Born Uitenhage, Cape Province, 1919. Taught English at St Mary's Convent, Johannesburg, until the end of 1965. Poems published in journals in South Africa, Britain and the United States and included in the anthology, *War Poems of the United Nations* (1943). First book of verse, *Floating Island*, won the Ingrid Jonker Prize for Poetry in 1966. Died in 1969.

Floating Island, Cape Town: Human & Rousseau, 1965.
Selected Poems, London: Chatto and Windus, 1968.

MOODIE, Duncan Campbell Francis
Born Cape Town, 1838. Historian and poet. Had left South Africa for Australia by 1858 and lived for a time in Adelaide where he owned and edited a newspaper. Here he wrote a book on the Zulu wars. He returned to Natal in the early 1880s. Edited a volume on the life of John Dunn, the pioneer game hunter. Furthered his historical writing by publishing a revised, extended edition of his Zulu history. Died 1891.

Southern Songs, Pietermaritzburg: Adams, 1887.

MTSHALI, Oswald Mbuyiseni
Born 1940, Vryheid, Natal, where he matriculated. At 18 went to Johannesburg and in 1967 began submitting poetry for publication. His poems have appeared in various anthologies and poetry magazines including *The Classic*, *New Coin*, *Ophir*, *The Purple Renoster*, and various local newspapers, and have been broadcast by the SABC. Won the Olive Schreiner prize for English literature 1975. Is at present studying in America.

Sounds of a Cowhide Drum, Johannesburg: Renoster, 1971.

NAUDÉ, Adèle
Born Pretoria, 1910. University of Cape Town. Has travelled widely in Europe, the Middle East and the U.S.A. Has been editor of various women's journals, a freelance journalist, and has done a great deal of scriptwriting and broadcasting for the SABC.

Pity the Spring, Cape Town: Balkema, 1953.
No Longer at Ease, Cape Town: Balkema, 1956.
Only a Setting Forth, Cape Town: Human & Rousseau, 1965.
Time and Memory, Cape Town: Maskew Miller, 1974.

NICOL, Mike
Born in Cape Town, 1951. University of the Witwatersrand. Works as a journalist on *The Star*, Johannesburg. Poems have appeared in *New Coin*, *Izwi*, *Contrast* and *London Magazine*.

Among the Souvenirs, Johannesburg: Ravan, 1978.

NORTJE, Arthur
Born Oudtshoorn, 1942. University College of the Western Cape. Taught for a year before being awarded a scholarship to Jesus College, Oxford. After teaching in Canada for 2 years, returned to Jesus College. Won the Mbari Prize for poetry 1962. His work was first published in *Black Orpheus* (Ibadan). His poems were published in the revised, enlarged edition of *Modern Poetry from Africa* (Penguin), *African Arts/Arts D' Afrique*, and the *Anglo-Welsh Review* and various little magazines. Died suddenly in 1973.

Lonely Against the Light, Grahamstown: New Coin, 1973.
Dead Roots, London: Heinemann, 1973.

NTHODI, Motšhile wa –
Born in Lady Selborn Township near Pretoria in 1948. Went to school in Pretoria. Has exhibited his graphic art widely in South Africa and has work in private collections in the U.S.A., Germany, France and Austalia. Has had poems published in *Quarry '76*. At present studying Fine Art on a scholarship in Paris.

From the Calabash: poems and woodcuts, Johannesburg: Ravan, 1978.

PATER, Elias (pseudonym) Jacob Horace Friedman
Born Cape Town, 1916. Obtained his medical degree at the University of Cape Town in 1938 and served with the South African Medical Corps from 1940–46. Went to England to study for the priesthood in 1946 and joined the Order of the Carmelites in 1948. Ordained a priest to the Roman Catholic Church in 1953 and became a member of the Stella Maris Monastery in Haifa in 1954. Received the Olive Schreiner prize for English Poetry 1971.

In Praise of Night, Cape Town: Purnell, 1969.

PATON, Alan
Born Pietermaritzburg, 1903, University of Natal. Taught in Natal schools
for eleven years; in 1935 was appointed principal of Diepkloof Reforma-
tory near Johannesburg; resigned in 1948 to devote time to writing. Honor-
ary degrees from several universities including Harvard, Yale, Edinburgh
and Rhodes. Elected National Chairman of the South African Liberal
Party in 1956, a position which he held until 1968 at the demise of the party.
He has written two novels, a collection of short stories, several books on
contemporary South Africa, its politics and problems, as well as bio-
graphical and autobiographical works. Won the CNA Literary Award in
1973.

Knocking on the Door, Cape Town: David Philip, 1975.

PLOMER, William Charles Franklyn
Born Pietersburg, Northern Transvaal, 1903. St John's College, Johannes-
burg and Rugby College, Britain. After farming in the Eastern Cape
Province and trading in Zululand, he worked with Roy Campbell to pro-
duce the literary magazine *Voorslag* (Whiplash) in Natal, 1926. Later lived
in Japan and Greece, then settled in the U.K. where he worked as literary
adviser to a London publisher. Was awarded the Queen's Gold Medal for
Poetry in 1963. Died in 1973.

Collected Poems, London: Jonathan Cape, 1960.
Taste and Remember, London: Jonathan Cape, 1966.
Celebrations, London: Jonathan Cape, 1972.

PRINCE, Frank Templeton
Born Kimberley, 1912. Balliol College, Oxford; Graduate College, Prince-
ton. Intelligence Corps 1940–46. Was Professor of English at the University
of Southampton from 1958–75 and is at present Professor of English in
Jamaica.

Poems, London: Faber, 1938.
Soldiers Bathing, London: Fortune, 1954.
The Doors of Stone, London: Hart-Davis, 1963.
Memoirs in Oxford, London: Fulcrum Press, 1970.
Afterword on Rupert Brooke: A Long Poem, London: Menard, 1976.

PRINGLE, Thomas
Born Scotland, 1789. Edinburgh University. Acquainted with Scott and
subsequently Coleridge. Emigrated to South Africa with British Settlers in
1820. After two years on the frontier he was appointed as Government
Librarian, Cape Town. With his friend Fairbairn, established the *South
African Journal* (1824). Their stand against the Governor, Lord Charles

Somerset, who wished to suppress the journal, established the concept of press freedom in South Africa. After a further visit to the frontier, he returned to England in 1826, where he was appointed Secretary to the Anti-Slavery Society. Died 1834.

Afar in the Desert: and Other South African Poems, London: Longman, 1881.
The Autumnal Exeursion, or Sketches in Teviotdale; with Other Poems, Edinburgh: Constable, 1819.
African Sketches, London: Moxon, 1834.
Ephemerides; or Occasional Poems, Written in Scotland and South Africa, London: Smith, Elder, 1828.
The Poetical Works of Thomas Pringle, with a Sketch of his Life, London: Moxon, 1838.
Poems Illustrative of South Africa; African Sketches, Cape Town: Struik, 1970.

ROSS, Alan
Born Calcutta, India, 1922. St John's College, Oxford. Poet, author of travel and children's books. Served in the Navy in World War II. On the staff of the British Council from 1947–50. Cricket correspondent for a London newspaper 1950–71. Recipient of the Rockefeller Atlantic Award for Literature 1949. Since 1961 has been editor of the *London Magazine*.

African Negatives, London: Spottiswoode, 1962.

RUNCIE, John
Was attached to the staff of the *Cape Times* for several years.

Songs by the Stoep, Thomson, 1905.
Idylls by Two Oceans, Cape Town, 1910.

SCHREINER, Olive
Born Wittebergen Mission Station, Cape Province, 1855. Had little formal education, but was governess to various families on Cape farms. Went to England in 1881, where her novel *The Story of an African Farm* was eventually published under the pseudonym Ralph Iron. In 1889 returned to South Africa and in 1894 married Samuel Cronwright, a Cradock farmer. She was a pacifist, passionately involved in the 'women question', and a champion for the causes of the Boer and Black peoples of South Africa. She published much on these questions. Died 1920, Cape Town.

SELWYN, William
Born, Ledbury, England, circa 1834. As a young boy he came to South Africa with his uncle Captain (Later Major) Charles Jasper Selwyn, and

lived for a time in Grahamstown, where he was educated. He was appointed as a schoolmaster in Bathurst and later lived in Port Elizabeth where he became a prominent member of the community, serving on numerous committees, and on the boards of various institutions. Died in Port Elizabeth at the age of 58.

SEPAMLA, Sidney Sipho
Born 1932, Krugersdorp. A trained teacher, he has worked on the stage and as a personnel officer. His writings include poems, essays, short stories and plays which have appeared in various South African literary journals, as well as the anthology *Quarry 76*. Was editor of *S'ketch* and is at present editor of *New Classic*.

Hurry up to it, Johannesburg: Ad. Donker, 1975.
The Blues is you in me, Johannesburg: Ad. Donker, 1976.

SEROTE, Mongane Wally
Born Sophiatown, Johannesburg, 1944. Writer. Poems in *Ophir*, *New Coin*, *Classic*, *Playboy*, *Purple Renoster*, and read over the SABC. He was detained under the Terrorism Act in June 1969, and released 9 months later without being charged. Won the Ingrid Jonker Prize for Poetry in English in 1975.

Yakhal'inkomo, Johannesburg: Renoster Books, 1972.
Tsetlo, Johannesburg: Ad. Donker, 1974.
No Baby must Weep, Johannesburg: Ad. Donker, 1975.

SINCLAIR, Francis Duncan
Born Inverness, Scotland, 1921, and came to South Africa when he was on service with the R.A.F. Returned later to settle. Lectured in English at the University of South Africa, Pretoria. He was occupied on a book of essays on Afrikaans poets when he died in 1961.

The Nine Altars, Cape Town: Unie-Volkspers, 1945.
The Cold Veld, Cape Town: Rustica, 1946.
The Island: A Metamorphosis, Maseru: Mazenod Institute, 1951.

SLATER, Francis Carey
Born near Alice, Cape Province, 1876. Lovedale Training College. From 1899 to his retirement he served in banks in various towns in the Eastern Cape. Died 1958.

Footpaths through the Veld, London: Blackwood, 1905.
From Mimosa Land, London: Blackwood, 1910.

The Karroo, London: Blackwood, 1924.
Editor: *A Centenary Book of South African Verse*, London: Longmans, 1925.
Drought, London: Benn, 1929.
Dark Folk, London: Blackwood, 1935.
Collected Poems, London: Blackwood, 1957.

SMALL, Adam
Born Wellington, Cape Province, 1936. University of Cape Town. Became a lecturer in philosophy at the University College of the Western Cape. Much of his verse is written in the 'Cape Coloured' argot. He is also an Afrikaans playwright and essayist. Became member of the English Academy of Southern Africa in 1975. In 1973 took up a post at the University of the Witwatersrand in Johannesburg and is now working for a publisher in Cape Town.

Black Bronze and Beautiful: Quatrains, Johannesburg: Ad. Donker, 1975.

STRAUSS, Peter Erik
Born Pietermaritzburg, 1941. University of Natal and University of Cambridge. Has travelled in Europe, and spent several years in England and Germany. Lecturer in English at the University of Natal. Leading critic and co-editor of the literary journal *Donga*. His poetry has been published in South African periodicals *Theoria* and *Thalia* (University of Natal journal), as well as Cambridge journals *Delta* and *Griffin*.

Photographs of Bushmen, Johannesburg: Bateleur Press, 1974.

STYLE, Colin Thomas Elliot
Born 1937 in Salisbury, Rhodesia. Rhodes University. Market research manager for TV. Poetry in various magazines and anthologies as well as broadcast on SABC, RBC, and Rhodesian TV. Edited *Chirimo*, a 'journal of the humanities', with his wife, and co-produced the long-playing record *Rhodesian Poets*.

Baobab Street, Johannesburg: Bateleur Press, 1977.

SWIFT, Mark
Born Cathcart, 1946. East London Technical College, where he studied art. Has been writing poetry since the age of ten, and has published poems in most South African literary magazines. He is a member of the editorial staff of the Standard Encyclopaedia of Southern Africa. He has also published prose, criticism and children's verse, and has exhibited graphics.

Works in Cape Town as a newspaper sub-editor. Recipient of the Ingrid Jonker Poetry Prize 1974–1975.

Treading Water, Cape Town: David Philip, 1974.

TAYLOR, Jeremy
Born Newbury, Berkshire, 1939. Trinity College, Oxford. Came to South Africa in 1962 and taught at St Martin's, Rosettenville. In 1963 the show, *Wait a Minim*, became a hit. He wrote the satirical songs, among them *Ag Pleez Deddy*. Taylor visited South Africa again briefly in 1966 before returning to England where he taught at Eton College. He lives in England and appears in shows and cabarets.

TRENGOVE-JONES, Christopher
Born Cape Town 1950. University of Natal. Taught English at the Grosvenor Boys' High School, Durban. His poetry was published in *Contrast* and *New Coin*. Died tragically after a motor-cycle accident in 1973.

TYFIELD, Thelma
Born 1906. University of Cape Town. Headmistress of the Good Hope Seminary Girls' High School 1943–61. Taught English for many years. Her poems were published in numerous South African periodicals, including *Contrast*, *Standpunte* and *New Coin*. Compiled two anthologies of English poetry, and is the author of an English grammar book, which was widely used in schools. Died 1968.

Time Prized, Cape Town: Purnell, 1972.

WALLACE, Richard Horatio Edgar
Born London, 1875. After negligible schooling, became successively a newsboy, bootmaker, cabin boy, milkman, labourer, printer and finally soldier. In 1896 was sent by the army to South Africa and began to write articles for South African newspapers. Later he saw action in the South African War as an official war correspondent. After a brief sojourn in England, he returned to South Africa for a short while and was the first editor of the *Rand Daily Mail* 1902–03. He wrote 23 plays, 957 short stories and 173 crime novels, translated into 25 languages.

War ! and Other Poems, Cape Town: Eastern Press, 1899.
Writ in Barracks, London: Methuen, 1900.

WELSH, Anne
Born Johannesburg, 1922. University of the Witwatersrand and Somerville College, Oxford. Sometime lecturer in Economics, University of the Wit-

watersrand. Poems in various anthologies and periodicals including *A Book of South African Verse*, *New Coin* and *Contrast*. Now lives in Oxford.

Uneven World: Poems, London: Hand & Flower Press, 1958.
Set in Brightness, Cape Town: Purnell, 1968.

WILHELM, Peter
Born Johannesburg, 1943. A trained teacher, his profession is journalism. Has published poetry, critical articles and fiction in a variety of magazines. Was involved in the establishment of the Artists' and Writers' Guild of South Africa. Joint receiver of the Mofolo/Plomer prize for his unpublished novel, *An Island of Grass* (1977).

White Flowers, Johannesburg: Bateleur Press, 1977.

WILSON-MOORE, C. and A.P.
Brothers who worked on the mines in Kimberley and Barberton.

Diggers' Doggerel, Cape Town: Argus, 1890.

WRIGHT, David John Murray
Born Johannesburg, 1920. Left South Africa 1934. Northampton School for the Deaf and Oriel College, Oxford. Has travelled throughout Africa and Europe. Has contributed to several South African and overseas anthologies and literary journals, including *A Book of South African Verse* and *New Coin*. Won the Atlantic Award in Literature, 1950; Guiness Poetry Award, 1958, 1960; Gregory Fellowship in Poetry, University of Leeds, 1965–67. Now lives in Cumbria.

A South African Album, Cape Town: David Philip, 1976.
To the Gods the Shades: New and Collected Poems, London: Carcanet Press, 1976.

ACKNOWLEDGEMENTS

The editors and publisher gratefully acknowledge permission to reproduce copyright poems in this book.

Lionel Abrahams: from *Bateleur Poets*. Reprinted by permission of the author.

Perseus Adams: from *Grass for the Unicorn*. Reprinted by permission of the author and Juta and Company Limited.

A. G. Bain: from *Van Riebeeck Publications No 30*. Reprinted by permission of the Van Riebeeck Society, South African Library (Cape Town).

H. C. Bosman: from *The Earth is Waiting*. Reprinted by permission of Mrs. H. R. Lake and Human and Rousseau Limited.

R. M. Bowker : from the autograph album of Helen Gardener 1835. Reprinted by permission of Mrs. Marion R. Currie.

William Branford: reprinted by permission of the author.

Noel Brettell: from *Season and Pretext*. Reprinted by permission of the author and Dr. Olive Robertson.

A. M. Buckton: from *The Burden of Engela*. Reprinted by permission of Methuen and Company Limited.

Guy Butler: 'Stranger to Europe' and 'Sweetwater' from *Collected Poems*, 'The Divine Underground' and 'Home Thoughts' from *Selected Poems* reprinted by permission of Ad. Donker (Publisher) 'Body Grows Old, Heart Stays Young' and 'Epitaph for a Poet' from *Songs and Ballads* reprinted by permission of David Philip (Publisher).

Roy Campbell: lines from 'The Wayzgoose' and lines from 'The Flaming Terrapin,' reprinted by permission of the executors of the Roy Campbell Estate and Jonathan Cape Limited. 'Luis de Cameos' from *Talking Bronco* reprinted by permission of Faber and Faber Limited. 'Poetry and Rugby' by Roy Campbell published by the Bodley Head. All other poems from *Adamastor* are reprinted by permission of Curtis Brown Limited.

Paul Chidyausiku: from *African Voices* 1973. Reprinted by permission of the author.

Norman Clothier: from *South African Poetry*. Reprinted by permission of the author.

Sydney Clouts: 'The Sea and the Eagle' from *The Penguin Book of South African Verse* reprinted by permission of the author. All other poems from *One Life* reprinted by permission of the author and Purnell and Sons.

Ian Colvin: from *The Parliament of Beasts*. Reprinted by permission of *The Cape Times* Limited. (S.A. Associated Newspapers).

Jack Cope: from *Marie*. Reprinted by permission of the author.

Jeni Couzyn: from *Seven South African Poets*. Reprinted by permission of the author.

A. S. Cripps : from *Africa: Verses*. Reprinted by permission of Oxford University Press.

Patrick Cullinan: 'The Billiard Room' from *A World of Their Own*, 'The Evangelists in Africa' and 'Monsieur François le Vaillant Recalls his Travels to the Interior Parts of Africa 1780–85' from *Today is not different*, all reprinted by permission of the author.

R. N. Currey: from *The Africa We Knew*. Reprinted by permission of David Philip (Publisher).

Jennifer Davids: from *Searching for Words*. Reprinted by permission of David Philip (Publisher).

Norman de la Harpe: from *Forty Poems*. Reprinted by permission of the author.

Antony Delius: 'The Gamblers', 'The Deaf-and-Dumb School' and 'Emerald Dove' from *A Corner of the World*, 'Distance' from *The Penguin Book of South African Verse*, 'These Million English' and 'The Ethnic Anthem' from *The Last Division*, 'Makana' from *Black South Easter* all reprinted by permission of the author.

H. I. E. Dhlomo: from *The Valley of a Thousand Hills*. Reprinted by permission of Knox Printing Company Limited.

C. J. Driver: from *Seven South African Poets*. Reprinted by permission of the author.

H. H. Dugmore: from *Verses of H. H. Dugmore*. Reprinted by permission of the Methodist Publishing House and Book Depot.

Charles Eglington: 'Old Prospector' and 'Rocks' from *Under the Horizon*. Reprinted by permission of Purnell and Sons. 'Cheetah' and 'Meeting' from *A Book of South African Verse* reprinted by permission of Oxford University Press.

Elisabeth Eybers: from *Afrikaans Poems with English Translations*. Reprinted by permission of DALRO (Dramatiese, Artistieke en Letterkundige Regte Organisasie (Edms) Beperk).

C. A. Fair: 'Grasmere' from *New Nation Sept. 1968*, 'Kangra Paintings' from *New Coin Vol. 2 1966* and 'To Mack' (previously unpublished). Reprinted by permission of the author.

Pamela May Förs: From *New Coin Vol. 2 1966*. Reprinted by permission of *New Coin*.

Athol Fugard: from 'Boesman and Lena'. Reprinted by permission of the author.

Sheila Fugard : from *Threshold 1975*. Reprinted by permission of Ad. Donker (Publisher).

H. Goodwin: from *Songs of the Settler City*. Reprinted by permission of Miss. P. A. Goodwin.

Stephen Gray: 'Sunflower', 'In Praise of Archaeologists' and 'The Tame Horses of Vrededorp' from *It's about Time* and 'Mayfair' from *Hottentot Venus* reprinted by permission of the author and David Philip (Publisher).

Poems; 'The Sleep of my Lions', 'Gentling a Wildcat', 'A Flower for the Night', and 'Splinter of the True Cross' from *Eyes Closed Against the Sun* reprinted by permission of the author and Oxford University Press: 'Mpondo's Smithy, Transkei' and 'Dust' from *The Anvil's Undertone* reprinted by permission of the author and Ad. Donker (Publisher).

Don Maclennan : from *Bateleur Poets.* Reprinted by permission of the author and Bateleur Press.

Roy Macnab : from *The Man of Grass and other Poems.* Reprinted by permission of the author.

Michael Macnamara: from *The Falls Run Back.* Reprinted by permission of the author and Ravan Press Limited.

Charles Madge: from *The Disappearing Castle.* Reprinted by permission of Faber and Faber Limited.

Chris Mann: from *First Poems.* Reprinted by permission of the author and Bateleur Press.

Eugène Marais: from *Eugène Marais.* Reprinted by permission of N. W. Swets and Zeitlinger.

G. C. Millard: 'Dream'. Reprinted by permission of the author.

Ruth Miller: 'Blue Mantled Mary' from *Selected Poems* reprinted by permission of Hogarth Press; 'Honey' from *A Book of South African Verse'.* All other poems from *Floating Island* reprinted by permission of L. Abrahams on behalf of Mrs Pat Campbell.

D. C. F. Moodie: from *The Poetry of South Africa.* Reprinted by permission of Juta and Company Limited.

Oswald Mtshali: from *Sounds of a Cowhide Drum.* Reprinted by permission of the author and Oxford University Press.

Adèle Naudé : from *No Longer at Ease.* Reprinted by permission of the author.

Mike Nicol: from *Among the Souvenirs.* Reprinted by permission of the author.

Arthur Nortje : 'Preventive Detention', 'Native's Letter', 'Cosmos in London' and 'All Hungers Pass Away' from *Dead Roots* reprinted by permission of Heinemann Educational Books Limited. 'Sea Days and Summerfall' from *Lonely Against the Light, New Coin* reprinted by permission of Mrs. C. Potgieter.

Michael Nthodi: from *Quarry 1976.* Reprinted by permission of the author.

Elias Pater : from *In Praise of Night.* Reprinted by permission of the author and Purnell and Sons.

Alan Paton : from *Knocking on the Door.* Reprinted by permission of David Philip (Publisher).

William Plomer: 'The Devil Dancers' from *Visiting the Caves* and 'A Transvaal Morning' from *Collected Poems* reprinted by permission of The Estate of William Plomer and Jonathan Cape Limited; 'Johannesburg', 'The Scorpion' and 'The Boer War' from *The Five-*

Fold Screen, 'The Explorer' and 'The Pioneers' from *Notes for Poems* reprinted by permission of the Estate of William Plomer and Hogarth Press.

F. T. Prince : from *Collected Poems*. Reprinted by permission of the author.

Thomas Pringle: from *Poems Illustrative of South Africa*. Reprinted by permission of Struik Publishers.

Alan Ross: from *Poems 1942-67*. Reprinted by permission of the author.

J. Runcie: from *American Song Trails*. Reprinted by permission of Hodder and Stoughton Educational Publishers.

Olive Schreiner: from *Life of Olive Schreiner*. Reprinted by permission of Mr. P. C. Raine.

William Selwyn: from *The Poetry of South Africa 1887*. Reprinted by permission of Juta and Company Limited.

Sipho Sepamla: from *The Blues is You in Me*. Reprinted by permission of the author.

S. D. Sinclair: from *Lovers and Hermits*. Reprinted by permission of the Sinclair Estate.

Wally Serote : from *Yakhal 'inkomo*. Reprinted by permission of Ad. Donker (Publisher).

F. C. Slater: from *Selected Verse*. Reprinted by permission of Mr. R. C. Slater.

Peter Strauss: from *Photographs of a Bushman*. Reprinted by permission of the author and Bateleur Press.

Colin Style: 'Rhodes's Bed' by Colin Style was first published in the Sewanee Review 85 (spring 1977). Copyright 1977 by the University of the South. Reprinted by permission of the editor. 'O-Lan' from *Poetry in Rhodesia – 75 years* is reprinted by permission of the author.

Mark Swift: from *A World of Their Own*. Reprinted by permission of the author and Ad. Donker (publisher).

Jeremy Taylor : 'Ag Pleez Deddy' from the *Wait a Minim Show*. Used by kind permission of Music Publishing Company of Africa, (Pty.) Limited, P.O. Box 6216, Johannesburg.

Christopher Trengove-Jones : from *New Coin Vol. 10 1974*. Reprinted by permission of Miss G. Leigh.

T. Tyfield : from *Time Prized*. Reprinted by permission of Purnell and Sons

Edgar Wallace : from *Writ in Barracks*. Reprinted by permission of Methuen and Sons.

Anne Welsh: from *Set in Brightness*. Reprinted by permission of Purnell and Sons.

P. Wilhelm: from *Bateleur Poets*. Reprinted by permission of Bateleur Press.

C. and A. P. Wilson-Moore: from *Diggers' Doggerel*. Reprinted by permission of *The Argus* Printing and Publishing Company Limited.

AUTHOR INDEX

INDEX OF TITLES AND FIRST LINES

Titles in *italic* type; first lines in roman.

305